Acknowledgments

T he Money Mastery philosophy is a work of the ages. Its ideas, principles and methods are the accumulated time-value endeavors of the financially secure from ancient to modern times. It is precisely for this reason that this book cannot be considered the work of just a few, and to recognize all who have contributed to it would be impossible — it is truly the labor of many. However, the authors wish to acknowledge those individuals who have been instrumental in the creation of the Money Mastery concept and who have inspired and enlightened us as we have sought to bring the power of its ideas to you, the reader.

We must first acknowledge George S. Clason's ageless masterpiece, *The Richest Man in Babylon* as the wonderful philosophical basis for the Money Mastery Principles. The essence of paying oneself, dealing forthrightly with debt, and seeking financial mentors is what this book is built upon.

To Larry Adamson, our friend and partner, we express sincere thanks for his technical expertise and inspiration. He has helped create a total financial management system that aids people in taking control of every area of their financial life, thus allowing them to make the most of the money they already have and to find additional wealth they never dreamed possible.

We wish to acknowledge Suzanne Kimball Rekow, the managing editor of this book, for her expert writing skills and creative direction in the composition and overall tone of the work. This book would not have been possible without her capable management of the project from start to finish and her understanding of the greater purpose and impact of the Money

Mastery Principles in people's lives. Suzanne has immersed herself in those principles and lives the work. This book could not have been written without her.

We express appreciation to Gary Weinberg, CEO of National Seminars, whose life's work has been to educate hundreds of thousands of people about how to have better and more effective lives, and who has encouraged us to bring the Money Mastery concept to the general public.

To Financial Health Educators' formative partners, Glen Lowry and Lyle Shamo, we give thanks for their long pursuit of a satisfactory means to convey their spending and debt management ideas. We will always be grateful for their friendship.

We acknowledge Jim Christensen and Clint Coombs, the authors of *Rich on Any Income*, who have contributed to the Money Mastery program with class and dignity. Their sincere help and support in the development and presentation of the tracking systems are greatly appreciated. We will always be thankful for their inspiration.

We especially wish to thank the thousands of clients and seminar participants who have personally validated the principles and concepts presented in this book. Almost every strategy found within has come from observing these participants' financial lives. Without our clients, these strategies would be mere thoughts — from their experience, we have seen the absolute legitimacy and inspiration of the Money Mastery Principles and Tax Strategies taught herein.

Not the least of those to be acknowledged are our family and friends who have contributed to, made suggestions for, and lived the Money Mastery and Tax Strategies systems and tested them extensively. Their patience and love have been empowering.

Finally, we express our thanks to you, the reader, for taking the time to seek out this book. You are our purpose.

Alan Williams
Peter Jeppson
Sandy Botkin

Contents

Why You Should Read This Book

W hy do you work? Is it for the money? Do you hope to afford a nicer car, a bigger house, or college tuition for the kids? Do you work simply so you can acquire more "stuff?" These may be your conscious motivations for working, but if you really ponder the question, no doubt you'll discover that deep inside you're actually working to buy yourself more time. If quality of life matters to you (and it probably does!) very likely your long-term goal is to provide yourself and family with enough cash surplus and financial resources to allow you more time to spend in meaningful pursuits with those you love.

Most of the people we work with at Money Mastery, whatever their circumstances — whether they're overspending, in debt, trying to retire, or worrying about their stock portfolio — are full of fear about what's happening to them financially. They are fixated on today and how much money they're making (or not making) rather than looking towards the future with confidence that they will have all the time and resources they need to reach their full potential and make their deepest desires a reality. We teach our clients that this fixation stems more from a lack of understanding about the emotions they feel about money than from how little or how much money they make.

Counter to what most people have learned over the years,
money is emotional, not mathematical.

Without a clear understanding of these emotions, people's perception of what money can and cannot do for them is skewed. It locks them into a perpetual cycle of fear, worry, and frustration and forces them to live only for today, unable to achieve the security that proper money management creates over time.

Most of the people we coach come to us knowing that whatever they have been doing financially is not working, but they can't figure out why. They feel that they should know how to manage their money, especially given the fact that they have read numerous books and articles on personal finance. They ask themselves why they don't have more money saved after following the strict and oft-repeated rhetoric of popular financial "experts" to invest in the stock market and squirrel away money in 401(k)s year after year. Attempts to get out of debt have proved futile and even though many of them have applied the pat advice of the news media in efforts to manage their money, they are still in deep and agonizing financial pain. Much of that pain spills over into their personal relationships and mars their hopes for the future. What we have observed over years of mentoring thousands of individuals and families is that most people are trying the best they can to manage their money with only a small fraction of the knowledge they need to do so successfully. With a plethora of information all about them, they are perplexed by their inability to make prudent financial decisions.

Although North Americans are living in the wealthiest society on the face of the earth and in a time with the most resources and opportunities, most don't have a clue about how to truly manage and maximize those resources. They are ill-prepared to face the complexities of today's financial markets, and instead follow opinion leaders and financial "gurus" who know little themselves about how to teach people the way to fix these problems (but act as if they do).

What about you? Are you living in the dark financially, never looking ahead because you're so mired down in the present? Have you tried following the advice of the financial advisors of our time about how best to manage your money in today's economy and yet still feel that you're not "seeing the big picture?" Do you wonder why you're no better off today financially than you were five years ago?

How would you feel if you could step into the light and stop being fearful and frustrated? Wouldn't it be wonderful if your money were working for you to create the abundance of time and peace of mind you're really craving? What if you could actually get in control of your finances so you could have the resources to not only purchase that which you both need and want, but the time to pursue your life's most cherished dreams and aspirations? What if you had enough time and money to develop worthwhile employment for yourself and others, to have the freedom to spend time in warm associations with family and friends and in service to others, and to experience the ultimate thrill of having adequate funds to be able to give generously to those in need?

This book presents the secrets for making such dreams a reality. It is unlike any other book you'll ever read about money and its management. Counter to other books and programs that spew out a mishmash of partial information in the wrong order and without context, this book deals with *every* aspect of personal finance — the way you spend, pay off debt, save for retirement, AND pay taxes — and how each aspect is emotionally interrelated and *must work together in harmony with the others*. It teaches that your financial life is like a puzzle and that an abundance of time, wealth, and resources are only possible when all the pieces fit.

Most best-selling titles on personal finance are full of financial theories and feel-good philosophies that sound nice on paper but are hard to apply personally. What most sources give people are bits and pieces of a larger puzzle that when placed on the "table of life" make absolutely no practical sense to the typical consumer because there's been no instruction on how to properly sort through those pieces, how to assess exactly what those pieces mean, and how they must fit together in a logical and orderly fashion.

It is not enough, then, to know that you need to make sense of the financial pieces you hold in your hand — until you are shown how, those pieces are not likely to fit together. Rather than endorsing popular people or trends, this book provides a hands-on, practical means of applying immediately the ideas taught within it using 10 time-proven principles of solid financial management, providing a complete approach for making all the pieces of your puzzle fit. Through this book you will see how your emotions affect the way you deal with each of these pieces, thus affecting your ability to successfully manage them.

This book will teach you how to:

- Gain immediate control of your spending and help you find at least 1 percent of your gross annual income you are using inefficiently through poor spending habits.

- Live within your means and still have fun doing it.

- Get out of all debt, including your 30-year mortgage, in nine years or less.

- Save up to 10 percent of your gross monthly income.

- Double, and in some cases, even triple your retirement income.

- Legally and ethically cut your tax burden by as much as half.

- Improve your relationship with your partner so you can stop arguing about money.

As you read this book, you will meet others who have learned how to put all the pieces together and have successfully dealt with their emotions so that they could stop working simply for things and begin creating more time to pursue that which really mattered to them. You will also read about the authors' own personal struggles to make sense of the puzzle — you will see that if we can do it, so can you.

In our seminars and coaching sessions, we ask people to assess how well their financial puzzle is coming together by responding to the following searching questions. Take a moment to rate yourself to see what pieces of the puzzle you're missing and what areas need improvement, then total your points at the end of the assessment to see how well you score (100 points possible):

1. **How often do you argue with your spouse about money?**

Never:	10 points	Monthly:	4 points
Seldom:	8 points	Often:	0 points

2. **How often do you worry about having adequate money for your needs?**

Never:	10 points	Monthly:	4 points
Seldom:	8 points	Often:	0 points

3. **Do you have a monthly spending plan where you track how much you spend, save, and earn?**

10 points:	I have a plan, track everything I spend every day, and compare what I've spent with available income to be sure I am staying on track.
6 points:	I keep track of the big things.
2 points:	I try to see what I've spent when I balance my checkbook.
0 points:	I spend without thinking about where the money goes.

4. **How much of your gross income are you saving monthly?**

Save 10%:	10 points	Save 1%:	4 points
Save 6%:	8 points	I have little or no savings:	2 points
Save 3%:	6 points	I spend more than I make:	0 points

5. **Are you adequately prepared for the future?**

10 points:	I have at least six month's liquid emergency reserves and adequate life, health, and disability insurance.
8 points:	I have adequate insurance and three month's savings.
4 points:	I have adequate insurance but no savings.
2 points:	I have a savings account somewhere.
0 points:	I'm not sure about my financial future.

6. **What percentage of your income goes toward paying debt?**

I have no debt:	10 points	Less than 40%:	4 points
Less than 20%:	8 points	Less than 50%:	2 points
Less than 30%:	6 points	Over 30%:	0 points

7. **Do you know the rules of the financial games you are playing and the risks associated with changes to those rules?**

      10 points: I have read my credit card contracts, insurance policies, and other important papers in the past year.

      5 points: I am somewhat familiar with the terms of the financial contracts I have entered into.

      0 points: I have never read my contracts or policies.

8. **Do you have a plan for retirement?**

      10 points: I have chosen a retirement date, know how much I need to retire, and have a written plan in place to reach that goal.

      8 points: I have discussed retirement and am working on a plan.

      6 points: I make consistent deposits into retirement savings.

      4 points: I make occasional deposits into retirement savings.

      0 points: I have not thought about retirement.

9. **Do you understand how taxes can affect your finances?**

      10 points: I understand tax law, keep good records, understand the difference between tax-free and tax-deferred investments, and pay no more taxes than are required by law.

      8 points: I understand some tax law and keep fairly accurate records.

      4 points: I have considered investing in tax-free and tax-deferred retirement programs.

      0 points: I let my accountant take care of my taxes.

10. **Do you know what you are worth financially?**

      10 points: I could draft a personal income statement, balance sheet, and show my personal net worth.

      5 points: I have recorded assets and have a basic idea what I'm worth.

      0 points: I do not know my financial net worth.

How did you do? Many of our clients are startled to find that they score no more than 50 points on this assessment, and begin to see that many of their financial puzzle pieces are missing in areas they had no idea were even a problem. When we ask them to make observations about those flawed areas, we often hear comments about the frequency of arguments with their partner about money, that they can't remember exactly what they spent money on even one or two days previous, that they have more than $15,000 in credit card debt, and because of that debt they don't see how they can be expected to save anything.

What about your score and your feelings about the areas in which you scored poorly? If this assessment indicated for you, as it does for so many of our clients, that your debt-load is high, that you overspend, that you're not saving enough for the future, and that you overpay your taxes, perhaps now is the time to stop and ask yourself why. What might you be doing wrong and how committed are you to continue reading this book so you can change your life for the better?

Let's meet a couple whose struggle with finances caused them to stop and ask what they were doing wrong and how they could overcome their problems.

Mark and Joyce: Out of Control

Case History

Mark and Joyce* came to Money Mastery for help at the height of an emotional power struggle over their family finances. Both were in their mid-thirties, raising two children in southern Idaho and struggling to deal with their financial situation. Their "discussions" on money had evolved into arguments and were becoming more frequent. Mark was a pharmaceutical rep working a fairly new territory in Idaho and Oregon. He felt that he made more than enough money to support the family. Yet both Mark and Joyce knew they were out of control and couldn't understand why.

At the height of their financial struggles, Mark and Joyce had accumulated $15,982 in consumer debt alone. This figure did not include their mortgage. When it was combined with their consumer debt and all the interest, their total debt load came to a whopping $306,000. They had accumulated debt on two credit cards and were only making the minimum monthly payment. Although they had an after-tax monthly income of more than $3,000, Mark and Joyce always spent more money than they made. To compound the problem, each insisted on using their own system for paying bills and managing their finances. Neither shared this system with the other. Any communication about finances came in the form of emotional outbreaks, finger-pointing, and failure to take personal responsibility.

"I began to hate driving to my parents' house on Sundays," says Joyce. "During that 45-minute drive it was either stark silence or constant arguing over our finances. I began to wonder if we would ever be friends again, like we had been when we first got married."

"I had just about given up," recalls Mark. "I hated the confrontation. I worked hard for every bit of money I earned, but we never could seem to make it. I made as much money, if not more, than my neighbors and I just couldn't understand why we never had enough at the end of the month. We couldn't talk about it either with any sort of mutual understanding, and I eventually just wanted to avoid the whole situation and pretend it wasn't there."

*Names have been changed to protect privacy.

Sound familiar? Mark and Joyce's situation is typical of many households across the U.S. and Canada today. Their struggle wasn't about how much money they made. It wasn't even about their excessive debt. It wasn't based on the numbers, but rather on a lack of understanding about the emotions behind their spending and borrowing habits and how those habits were interlinked and adversely affecting each other.

Many people are doing their best to manage their finances, but based on our experience, 93 percent of them are struggling. It's ironic that in an age of relative prosperity and unbelievable opportunity, a majority of people are suffering financially due to overspending and excessive debt. An additional few, while not burdened with debt, worry constantly that their savings and investments will not be secure, that they will experience a loss in income due to reduced interest rates on their savings programs, and that taxes will ultimately devour most of their assets. We believe that these worries stem from trusting in the advice of today's popular financial "experts" while at the same time lacking understanding about how various forces at work in the world can affect emotional perceptions about money, and consequently the ability to control finances. Many people are victims in today's economy, because even though they are aware of these forces, they are not fully conscious of how deeply these powers are influencing their lives. Let's take a closer look at them.

Consumerism: Caving in to Relentless Media Hype

Studies show that the average consumer is now being exposed to over 3,000 marketing messages per day[1] and that just since 1995, advertising pitches have jumped from 1.52 billion annually to 4.29 billion.[2]

In today's sophisticated and highly technological world, we are constantly bombarded by emotional media messages suggesting that in order to be successful we must capitalize our lives to the fullest by adopting a particular standard of living. These media forces urge us to embrace extravagant lifestyles regardless of whether we can afford to or not. Billboards, magazines, television, the Internet, and other media subtly insist that to be successful and to reach our full potential, we must do everything we can to accentuate our situation, take advantage of every opportunity that comes across our path, and keep up with everyone else around us lest we be left behind. We must wear the right labels, prevent the most facial wrinkles, and drive the hippest car. We are victims of today's product-oriented society that screams for attention and demands that we buy. Many of us have caved into the emotional media hype, becoming so accustomed to spending and borrowing in order to answer Consumerism's siren call that we never question whether something should be purchased — we only ask ourselves if there will be enough money to make the minimum monthly payment. Even if there aren't enough funds to cover a monthly payment, many individuals will make a purchase anyway. We call this reckless spending the "Disease of Consumerism."

Countless individuals across the U.S. and Canada have become infected with this disease yet don't realize how sick they are. You may be one of them and not understand the gravity of the situation because you are doing what's expected of you — you're living, spending, borrowing, and existing much like everyone else around you. "I don't see that I'm doing anything out of the ordinary," you may find yourself thinking, "what's the big deal? Everyone else is doing it!" The big deal is that just because your peers, family, neighbors, politicians, and fellow citizens may be doing it doesn't mean it's what you ought to be doing — just because they may be infected doesn't mean you need to join them in their illness.

If you are a victim of the Disease of Consumerism, you cannot entirely blame the way others around you are living or today's supercharged media hype for your illness. While media messages are often prevalent, passionate, and persuasive they are not accompanied by a taskmaster with a whip. You have the choice whether to listen to these messages or not. Ask yourself: Am I caving into peer pressure and media hype or am I driven to consume by a taskmaster of my own creation — one born of guilt, greed, pride, materialism, and expectation?

The materialism and expectation that plague today's generation stem partially from a lack of respect towards money, a respect that's been lost as a whole from our society since the ending of the Great Depression. The generation who suffered through the Depression carried a real fear of not having the basic necessities of life since most people of that era went many years without being able to provide adequately for themselves or their families. The Depression taught people a profound respect for money and its power over life. It also taught them the value of self-reliance, the importance of self-denial, and the danger of overindulgence. Unfortunately, as America came out of that great economic trial into the most prosperous time in all of history, it did not teach subsequent generations to fear and respect money as it ought. Instead post-Depression parents wanted to spare future generations the feelings of scarcity and fear they had experienced as young adults during the massive economic disaster of the 1930s, so they taught their children to hold their hands out in expectation. Because of this we now live in a time of great self-indulgence and very little financial self-control.

*Today's generation, instead of fearing that it will not have **anything**, fears that it will not have **everything**.*

Another issue that compounds the Consumerism problem is the increased complexity of the financial system within which we live. While it's true that people are more inclined today to spend than their parents or grandparents would have been 60 or 70 years ago, their parents and grandparents also had a much simpler financial system within which to work and much less available money to spend. Today, we must function within a highly sophisticated financial world about which we have been taught very little. In addition, we have access to easy credit that allows us to buy virtually anything we want, introducing a slew of new problems with which our parents and grandparents never had to deal. This financial ignorance and easy credit, combined with a sense of entitlement that has been instilled in society since the ending of the Great Depression, is crippling and enslaving today's generation.

Did you know that 25 to 50 percent of all consumer purchases in the U.S. are unplanned and unneeded? And here's another terrifying statistic: the average American will retire with just $60,000 at age 65 — that's after making more than $2 million during his or her lifetime![3] As a nation, we now have a negative personal savings rate of just under 0 percent of disposable income, compared with about 11 percent in 1984.[4] In fact, that rate is the lowest since the stock market crashed in 1929.[5] That's why more than two-thirds of all Americans who have reached retirement age today are not sufficiently prepared to retire,[6] and why many older Americans are going back to work after age 65. The AARP (American Association of Retired Persons) reports that 68 percent of workers between age 50 and 70 plan to work in retirement or never retire at all.[7]

A lack of respect for money, combined with the absence of a system for successfully handling the complexity of the fiscal games we are all forced to play in today's consumeristic and monetarily sophisticated society largely account for our financial unhappiness. So many of us do not yet see how the force of Consumerism is eating away at our lives. What about you? Are you spending money simply because in today's economy it's become so easy to get the credit needed to make your wanted purchases? Do you spend money in order to keep up with everyone else around you and as a way to meet childhood-instilled expectations? Do you spend to make yourself feel that you are maximizing your life to its fullest potential? If you are, then you're spending money based on the naive assumption that there will always be more cash to offset the consequences of your spending decisions whether that cash exists or not. Perhaps it's time to take a hard look at how Consumerism might be affecting you.

Indebtedness: Becoming a Slave to Lenders and Easy Credit

Another force at work in many people's lives — Indebtedness — goes hand-in-hand with Consumerism. Unless its power to control you is completely understood you will fall victim to credit card companies, lending institutions, and other entities that wait with bated breath to put to work for them the compound interest they collect from you. Most people take debt for granted in today's world of easy credit and assume that debt is a "normal" way of life. "After all," they reason, "if I don't have the money to purchase something, I can always just borrow it."

Unfortunately, people don't realize that when the initial loan amount is combined with compound interest (which is interest on top of interest) they can end up paying three times the amount they actually borrow!

Credit card companies and other credit issuers are keenly aware of this fact. These entities know that compound interest is the way to make big money. That's why they send out more than five billion offers for new credit cards each year (which equates to nearly 50 per household) — even to those with bad credit .[8]

After being seduced into spending through emotional media messages, those sick with the Disease of Consumerism seem driven to further compound the problem by adding an interest payment to their load. Even though personal income has increased by 5 percent in the U.S. over the past five years, personal debt has increased by 10 percent.[9] And average credit card debt for people with at least one card now stands at just under $10,000, which is triple what it was in 1990![10] Is it any wonder that the majority of Americans cannot keep most of the money they make?

This type of debt enslavement is like taking one step forward and two steps back. It's impossible to get ahead so long as you fail to understand the power that credit issuers can have over you if you let them. As John Cummuta, author of *Transforming Debt Into Wealth*, notes: "We are seduced into using credit by the illusion of prosperity and the short-term pleasure. We don't think about the long-term pain, or the fact that buying on credit means we will pay far more for something than it's actually worth."[11] The ease with which most people can get credit today, along with the inability to fully and completely comprehend the enslaving power of the compound interest that comes with that credit is what keeps people chained to the credit-issuing institutions that control them. Without a system for getting out from underneath this enslavement, people remain in debt much longer than is necessary, living in homes and driving cars that they don't actually own but are simply "renting" from the credit issuer. Are you being deceived by the false notion that you actually have ownership in the items you purchase on credit and that debt is a normal and expected part of life? Do you believe that there's no other way to live other than as a slave to those with money to lend? If so, maybe it's time to free yourself!

Excessive Taxation: Getting Sheared by the Tax Systems

A third force at work today that can have a powerful affect on your emotions and lifestyle is Excessive Taxation. Over-taxation is one of the most subtly destructive forces at work in your life but it's unlikely you realize just how much it is affecting your long-term financial well being. That's somewhat due to the fact that most financial gurus repeat rhetoric about getting out of debt and investing in retirement savings, but rarely discuss the pickling effect taxes have on overall financial health. Unfortunately, those individuals who do realize the full impact taxes can have on them often feel powerless to control it.

> *Did you know that taxes have become the largest expense*
> *for most people, exceeding what they pay for food,*
> *clothing, housing, and transportation combined?!*

Most Americans believe a myriad of tax myths that keep them perpetually yoked to a relentless tax machine that marches forward with precision and intimidation to seize what it believes will be necessary for its survival.

What are some of the myths you may be embracing that keep you under the control of this powerful force? One of the most pernicious myths is the assumption that a huge tax burden is inevitable and inescapable. Less than 100 years ago, the average taxpayer forked over only $60 annually in taxes?[12] Through the continual expansion of government, however, more taxes are extracted from you each year in order to sustain growth, only adding to the belief that there's nothing that can be done to reduce such a burden. Under recent tax laws, the government is limiting the amount of employee deductions that can be taken and raising Social Security taxes. The result: both spouses feel compelled to work in order to keep the family going. Even then, with tax laws such as they are, a two-income household rarely brings the desired financial relief it seeks.

In fact, when the average federal income tax bill of 39.2 percent is added to all the other "add-on" taxes such as FICA, state income tax, sales tax, property tax, and so forth, the average American ends up paying between 42 and 55 percent of their earned income to the government.[13]

With that kind of money being paid by seemingly unquestioning tax-payers, is it any wonder that the IRS and other government entities are unsympathetic and relentless in their efforts to ensure that the cash continues to roll in? While many grumble over the high cost of taxes, few seem to question what they can do about it, assuming they must pay such ridiculous sums of money. All of this makes most people feel like sheep being led silently and helplessly into a pen for shearing.

The truth of the matter is, you don't have to be a sheep.

The government gets away with taking far more money from you than is required by law simply because you don't know any better. One way Uncle Sam ensures that the money continues to roll in is by keeping you in the dark about what it can actually exact from you. It is up to you to come out of the dark and get informed about how to change this unacceptable situation.

Another tax myth that keeps you chained to excessive taxes and which goes hand-in-hand with the previous myth is the idea that a large and complex government is necessary. Through an attitude of "entitlement" many people are unknowingly subjecting themselves to larger and larger tax burdens. Post-Depression generations have held their hands out in expectation, demanding more services and greater benefits from government than at any other time in the history of the United States. Walter Williams, a professor of economics at George Mason University, explains:

> *Americans from all walks of life, whether they realized it or not....have decided that government should care for the poor, the disadvantaged, the elderly, failing businesses, college students, and many other "deserving" segments of our society. It's nice to do those things, but we have to recognize that government has no resources of its own. Congressmen and senators are not spending their own money for these programs. Furthermore, there is no Tooth Fairy or Santa Claus who gives them the resources. The only way the government can give one American one dollar is to confiscate it first...from another American.[14]*

"But," you may be thinking, "I don't have my hand out looking for government assistance. I'm the poor sucker who pays the taxes for all those other people who expect the government to take care of them." What you may not realize, however, is that it isn't just those on welfare who have their hands outstretched in anticipation to receive government benefits. You do not have to receive a welfare check to get federal "assistance" in some form or another. This "assistance" ranges from small things like reduced entry fees into federally controlled national parks, to larger benefits such as subsidized education and federally funded health care. If you are in favor of such entitlements, that's fine, but remember: someone has to pay for them, and that someone is you.

Many people today want to receive government benefits without considering how much they will cost. The greater number of benefits we are willing to receive, the larger government grows and the greater the tax burden we must expect to pay. Is it possible that the mentality that leads some to buy the cell phone in the mall, even when they have no real way of paying for it, is the same mentality that leads some to accept more government programs, even though they will not be able to afford the taxes required to support these programs?

While the idea that a large tax bill is inevitable is a hazardous one, the most dangerous tax myth of all is one that never gets any attention and isn't discussed at roundtables in Washington. It is one of the worst wealth killers today and is only seven words long. These seven words make more money for the IRS and steal more of your wealth than almost anything else — and the funny thing is, you'll never hear them mentioned in other books on personal finance or by today's popular financial experts. These seven words are:

My accountant takes care of my taxes.

We equate this myth to the equally absurd notion that a doctor takes care of your health. To believe such a notion assumes that you can eat all the fattening foods you want, rarely exercise, and then once a year have a doctor give you the equivalent of a plumbing job to clean out your clogged arteries. The idea is ridiculous and the idea that your accountant can magically clean up your tax life is equally preposterous.

If you don't know the rules for good "tax health," you can't expect your accountant to save you thousands of dollars in taxes at the end of each year. If you believe that your accountant takes care of your taxes, you will pay more to the government than even it requires! Only you can keep your tax bill fully under control. Unless you understand the importance of taking personal responsibility for your own taxes and learn how to take advantage of the good tax laws that are available to you, you will always pay more than is required by law. Excessive taxation is only excessive because you lack the knowledge to fix the problem. Without a system for eliminating unnecessary taxation you will be forever subject to a powerful force to which you have unknowingly yoked yourself. In fact, the subject of taxation is so important and so misunderstood that we have devoted the entire second part of this book to tax planning and tax-return bullet-proofing strategies.

The Time/Value of Money

These three forces — Consumerism, Indebtedness, and Excessive Taxation — are largely taken for granted by most people, and their casual attitude towards such powers leads to victimization. They know there must be something wrong with their impulsive spending habits, but they have not yet linked those habits to their financial ignorance and inability to tune out the media hype that urges them to consume, at any cost. These same people long to have more money for retirement, for their children's education, for vacations, and yet they realize they're not saving anything. Unfortunately they have not yet seen the correlation between their enslavement to credit issuers and their inability to save for the future. These people feel overwhelmed by the amount of taxes extracted from their paycheck each month, and by the way that estate taxes eat into their savings and investment nest eggs, but have not yet connected big government shearing with their own ignorance about the way the tax system really works. These people see tremendous financial opportunity in the world but lack the knowledge and skills necessary to control these powerful forces and harness the wealth and prosperity all around them.

Without a big picture view of how these forces can affect you over time, you may be forever trapped in the moment, failing to understand what's called the "Time/Value of Money." If you're living paycheck to paycheck, the daily struggle to survive inhibits your ability to see the true value that money can have over time — the kind of return it can bring over the course of several years. If you choose to remain in debt, you will not be able to see how the *time* it takes to pay off compound interest is affecting the long-term *value* of your money. The money that you could be using wisely to give a return over time is instead being paid to creditors, completely stripping your money of any value it could bring to you. If you continue to pay excessive taxes you are, in a similar fashion, failing to see the Time/Value of Money because you don't realize the *value* that your money will bring you over *time* if you pay your taxes correctly.

If Consumerism, Indebtedness and Excessive Taxation are weighing you down, it's probably hard for you to understand the exponential value that money can have if given a little time to grow. The Time/Value of Money can only be explained to a point, and then it must be experienced in order to fully comprehend it. Many of the people we work with are so caught up in the worry and frustration of the moment that they can't see what's waiting for them in the future. Others think they already have all the answers about money management — financial planners and accountants, for instance. They come to us for help already possessing an intellectual and mathematical knowledge about how to deal with money. Yet they are thousands of dollars in debt because they do not fully comprehend the power of these forces, the emotional impact they can have on lives when they are taken for granted, and how a casual attitude affects the value of their money over time. Are you one of them?

Are you limited by the things you don't know you don't know because you're wrapped up in the daily struggle for survival?

OR

Are you blinded by your own brilliance in thinking that you already know everything you need to know about money and its management?

It's been said that if all the money in the world were pooled together and then divided equally among each man, woman, and child, each person would have over $1 million. However, in less than 10 years, the majority of people would misuse that money so that they would end up with the same amount they started with. Amazing as this sounds, such loss of wealth is a direct consequence of the emotional mindset and attitudes about money that most of us struggle with today.

A Message of Hope

The intent of this book is to inspire and motivate you to see that there is a logical and systematic way to solve financial problems. The first step is to help you see the negative habits you may be engaging in so you can be aware of your own situation, whatever it is. We have seen countless people improve their lives the minute they became aware of their own behavior. The next step is to help you learn the system for eliminating any negative behavior and accentuating the positive habits you may already have.

Mark and Joyce are just one couple who have been helped by the Money Mastery system you will learn in this book. Let's go back to their story to see how this system and the principles it teaches totally changed their lives.

When they first came to Money Mastery, Mark and Joyce were thousands of dollars in debt and constantly fighting about money. Once they were made aware of how Consumerism and Indebtedness were eating away at them, they made a conscious decision to stop unnecessary and impulsive spending by implementing a spending plan and tracking system and by applying debt power down techniques that we will explain in greater detail in coming chapters. Instead of paying off their house in 29 years, if they stick to their current plan they will eliminate their mortgage and become completely debt-free in just over eight years. This quick debt elimination is saving them close to $124,000 in interest alone. By investing that saved interest, they will accumulate over $1 million at retirement. With their understanding of how to avoid Excessive Taxation, they are also protecting that retirement money. And best of all, they're doing all this without any additional out-of-pocket expense. If you're thinking this kind of success is only possible through slick financial wheeling and dealing, think again. Because Mark and Joyce now understand their emotions surrounding money and are approaching money with the respect it deserves and with a systematic plan for fitting all the pieces of their financial puzzle together, retiring with more than a million dollars is totally possible for them.

It can be totally possible for you, too.

How can you make it happen? First you must learn how to limit the power of Consumerism, Indebtedness, and Excessive Taxation. To do this, you must be aware of just how much they influence you and your emotions. Next, you must understand the importance of having a system that will help you deal with each of these forces. Putting this system in place, as we noted earlier, is much like putting the pieces of a puzzle together, or to use another analogy, is like baking a cake — you must follow a proper recipe if you expect to get the results you want.

First, you must have all the proper "ingredients" if you expect the "cake" to turn out just right. That means you must be aware of what it takes to become financially successful before you even begin creating that success. We will give you those ingredients within the pages of this book.

Second, you must have the correct amount of these ingredients — too much or too little of one particular thing can spoil the result. We'll explain how much of which "ingredients" to include.

Third, you must add the ingredients in the right order. A cake will not turn out right if you try to add the egg after the cake is baked. The same holds true for personal financial success — you must do what is expedient first, then add more "ingredients" later. We can show you how to do "first things first."

Many experienced folks have attempted to share the recipe for financial happiness, but unfortunately most of these "experts" do not include everything necessary to help you. Some provide all the ingredients but don't tell you in which order to "bake" them. Others know the order, but don't tell you how much of one particular ingredient to include. Contrary to what we're taught, the best information on how to bake the perfect "financial cake" or piece together a complete "financial puzzle" is not found on Wall Street. It isn't locked behind the doors of bankers or financial counselors. It isn't available in schools.

*The secret to successful money management is understanding first that money is **emotional**, and second that because it is emotional it requires a **system** for carefully controlling it.*

In these pages we will begin to explain the powerful secrets behind this system of true money mastery. You will learn the meaning of the Time/Value of Money and how financial security can release you from being nickled and dimed to death by tedious daily financial concerns. Isn't it about time that you stopped living in fear of tomorrow because you don't have control over today? The moment has come to start on the road to creating all the time and resources you need to make all your dreams come true.

We invite you to stay with us as we explain how you can stop being a victim and instead become victorious over your circumstances. We will give you the tools you need to get your emotions and your money under control. Meet other struggling couples like Mark and Joyce, and see how these people overcame their own ignorance and inability to deal with the emotions surrounding their money. Read how they learned to take the emotion out of their financial decisions and how this totally changed their lives.

Make a commitment to change your own.

Decide now to remove yourself from the cycle of failure that has kept you in a pattern of unhappiness. Read as if you know nothing about money — read as if all those "expert" voices around you know nothing about money. Ask yourself what you want to get out of reading this book. Whatever your goals, you can make them happen, one step at a time. All it takes is a personal commitment to change.

To help you get enthused about making that commitment, we invite you to consider one of the most powerful arguments for committing yourself to change that has ever been recorded:

> *Until one is committed there is hesitancy, the chance to draw back, always ineffectiveness. Concerning all acts of initiative (and creation), there is one elementary truth, the ignorance of which kills countless ideas and splendid plans: that the moment one definitely commits oneself, then providence moves too.*
>
> *All sorts of things occur to help one that would never otherwise have occurred. A whole stream of events issue from the decision, raising in one's favor all manner of unforeseen incidents and meetings and material assistance, which no man could have dreamt would have come his way.*
>
> *I have learned a deep respect for one of Goethe's couplets: "Whatever you can do, or dream you can, begin. Boldness has genius, power, and magic in it."*
>
> — W. H. Murray
> (the first man to photograph the top of Mt. Everest)

Our Promise

If you stay with the book, "definitely committing" yourself as Murray puts it, you'll learn a system of financial success and happiness that will open you to all the following possibilities:

- Learn immediately how to live within your income and have fun doing it!
- Find an extra $312 every month, on average, you are using inefficiently.
- Understand how to get out of ALL debt, including your mortgage, in nine years or less.
- Learn how to begin saving at least 1 percent of your gross annual income and work your way up to 10 percent or more.
- Understand how to forecast the dollars you will need for retirement and how to double — even triple — your retirement income.
- Learn how to legally and ethically reduce taxes by as much as 50 percent.
- Understand how to prioritize money so you can have anything you want as well as everything you need.
- Stop arguing with your partner about finances.

Best of all, you can learn how to do all this, and more, without any additional money from your pocket and without any additional risk.

Now, let's get started!

PART I

THE MONEY MASTERY PRINCIPLES

CHAPTER 1

Spending Is Emotional

W e began this book with a bold statement: money is more about emotions than it is about math. With that in mind, let's begin examining
the ways that emotions affect your money by taking a look at the first
Money Mastery Principle.

Principle 1: Spending is Emotional

Think back to the last time you spent money. Perhaps it was yesterday,
or even a few hours ago. Maybe you can't remember the last thing that you
bought. If so, think hard until you can pinpoint the last thing for which you
spent money.

Ask yourself the reason for making that spending decision. Did you
buy something necessary like groceries or medication? Was the item something you needed or just wanted at that moment? Did you worry about having enough money to pay for the item? Did the purchase cost more than
you thought it should or did you even worry about the price? Will this
spending decision have a big effect on whether you'll be able to purchase
other things later? Did spending the money make you feel guilty or did it
give you pleasure?

Now, try to recall a particular incident where spending money had a
strong emotional impact on your life or the lives of your family members.
What made that incident so emotional?

> *One of the most important questions you can ask is:*
> *"How does spending money make me feel?"*

Through years of counseling thousands of people, we have heard countless reasons why people spend money. Many of those reasons have more to do with a person's circumstances, his or her feelings about those circumstances, and what he or she decides to do about them rather than whether there is (or is not) enough money to spend. Let's take a closer look at what we consider the three most significant reasons for spending money.

Impulsiveness

As noted in the Introduction, we live in a world full of emotional media messages. These messages often play upon people's deepest psychological needs, pointing out all that a person may lack in his or her life. Responding to this supposed lack, many individuals spend money impulsively, without thinking, as a way to meet unfulfilled desires. Without the proper respect for money, our current society has become notorious for impulsive, reckless spending. According to Richard A. Feinberg, professor of Retail Management and director of the Center for Customer-driven Quality at Purdue University, up to 50 percent of all consumer purchases are made on impulse.[1]

Here are some of the responses we've heard from people who spend money on impulse:

"Spending money fills an emotional void in my life...I just feel like I can't get what I really desire, so I acquire material things to fill myself up."

"I like to give my children what they want because it gives me joy. Sometimes I feel like it's the only thing I can really do right for them."

"Having the money I want to spend, when I want to spend it, makes me feel important. I know my dad never could feel that way and I always felt sorry for him."

"I can't say no to my children...they pester me until I give in and get them what they want. They're just plain stronger than I am."

The Haywood* family are a perfect example of how emotions can trigger impulsive spending. They had a habit of going to All A Dollar, a bargain chain store that sells every bit of stock for $1 or less. The store's low prices made the trips seem so innocent, and purchasing small items like candy or inexpensive toys for the children gave the Haywoods pleasure without making them feel guilty. But once the family started to keep track of how much they were spending at All A Dollar, they were shocked to find it was over $300 per month. Low prices combined with their impulsive desire to please their children cost the Haywoods some serious cash they would rather have spent elsewhere.

*Names have been changed to protect privacy.

Most people are trapped in an impulsive mentality that prevents them from keeping much of the money they make for any length of time. Remember the Time/Value of Money we discussed in the Introduction? Impulsive spending completely eliminates the possibility of increasing the value of money over time. Did you know that 85 percent of all Americans who win lotteries spend every penny of their winnings on consumable goods rather than putting that money away for the future or investing it in high-yield programs?[2] Based on this statistic, it's plain that the majority of individuals do not understand the profound power of the Time/Value of Money and are destroying their future because of it. Are impulsive emotions affecting the way you spend?

Economic Hardship

Experiencing a financial disaster is another matter that can greatly affect feelings about money and how it should be spent. Have you ever lost a job and had to come home to your spouse with the bad news? What kind of an emotional impact did that have on you and the way you spent money as a family? After the trauma of losing a job, or some other economic hardship such as illness or divorce, we often hear responses like these about the way spending money makes people feel:

"I just hate not having enough money for the things I want. I get so depressed just thinking about it."

"Spending money makes me feel guilty, like I don't deserve the thing I bought, or that it will come back to haunt me later."

"My divorce has wiped me out financially. I have nothing left after I pay child support and alimony for anything I might want to get myself."

Doug was a young father of three when he experienced the economic trauma of divorce. Within 12 months of the divorce, he began paying over $900 a month for alimony and child support. Having recently graduated with a degree in graphic design, Doug wasn't advanced enough in his career to make the kind of money he needed to support his three children and an ex-wife. He was forced to move in with his parents and sell his car. Even then, he barely made enough to meet his financial obligations. The only thing he indulged in was music, buying a CD or two every once in a while. Doing so made him feel extremely guilty because he worried that indulging himself would somehow affect the happiness of his children. Doug's economic hardship was an emotional situation that had a huge impact on the way spending money made him feel.

When we are forced into a bad financial situation due to some kind of economic disaster, spending money can be a highly emotional issue capable of producing deep personal unhappiness.

Daily Financial Obligations

The struggle for daily survival can also affect why and how we spend money. Even those who are frugal and don't spend impulsively have heavy debt loads and excessive taxes and are impacted emotionally by the sheer effort of just making ends meet from day to day. We have counseled thousands of clients who have felt burdened and depressed by this daily struggle:

"I feel angry that I have to fight just to pay taxes and my debts....It leaves me nothing left over to spend on myself or kids."

"We were just audited recently and I felt so intimidated by the IRS. Taxes are the first thing that comes out of my paycheck and it just makes me sick that I still feel like the government controls my life."

"We were so poor growing up. I promised myself I would never make my kids wear hand-me-downs but we don't have enough money after all of our other expenses are paid for me to really give my kids what I dream of."

"I can't believe that I have to work almost six months out of the year just to pay my taxes. It really upsets me just thinking about it."

The Martinellis* are a good illustration of how this daily struggle to survive can greatly affect the emotional well being of a family. Don and Keisha Martinelli were struggling to make ends meet on the East Coast with its high cost of living. The couple had three boys under the age of seven and were concerned about financing their children's college education. Don was working 14-hour days as a controller for a corporation in Manhattan, but even with the long hours, they weren't able to find enough money to build a savings program for their sons' future education. In an attempt to earn extra money, they had invested in a business opportunity that never took off because they didn't have the time to put into it, forcing them into further debt and farther away from the boys' educational funding. This daily struggle simply to survive was draining the Martinelli family and killing the fun times they wanted to have with their boys because they never dared spend money to take them anywhere or go on any vacations.

* Names have been changed to protect privacy.

Emotional Events Affect Money

Impulse purchasing, economic hardship, and daily financial obligations are just some of the things that affect the way people spend money. Because of these emotional events, whether we end up with anything to show for all our hard work has less to do with the math behind the money, i.e., how much we make, but rather with how well we understand that these emotional events can affect our money over time.

Many people mistakenly assume that if they only had a job where they "made the big bucks," they wouldn't have to deal with these emotional issues. They think that more money would eliminate the problems that their impulse spending causes, or that more money would alleviate the burdens of economic hardship and the daily struggle to survive. But more money doesn't usually solve the problem. "In our seminars on money management," says Jim Christensen, co-author of *Rich on Any Income*, "we often quote a George Gallup survey which highlights four groups of workers (farmers, factory workers, business executives, and doctors). These four groups were asked if they felt they needed more income to make ends meet, and if so, how much. Every income group, from $30,000 to more than $200,000 annually, responded that they needed about 10 percent more income to work things out."[3] From this survey we can see that financial happiness has nothing to do with making a large income. Individuals making more than $200,000 a year are just as likely to be financially stressed as those who make a modest income. That stress is not caused because people don't bring home enough pay, but because they do not understand their own emotional reasons for spending money or have become a victim of financially draining events due to poor planning.

When our clients are tempted to blame their salary for their financial problems, we like to point out the following:

It matters not how much you make,
only how well you manage your money that counts.

Now let's meet a couple who were unable to manage their finances because they did not understand the emotional reasons for their spending.

Doug & Sally Hamilton: Victims of the Disease of Consumerism

Case History

Doug and Sally Hamilton* had married young. They made a modest living in a rural community in the Southwest, Doug working at a parts supply house for a trucking company and Sally working in a dental office. They had three children. Both Doug and Sally had grown up without a lot of material security, and both wanted to provide their children with the things they never had as kids. This led to over-indulgence of their children, giving them virtually everything they wanted even if the family couldn't afford it. The Hamiltons had inherited some land from Doug's father and when they were first married had built a modest home on that land without going into debt. But due to poor spending habits, they had been forced to borrow money against the house and had a mortgage hanging over their heads.

They were also alienating other members of their family because Doug's parents continually bailed the Hamiltons out of financial problems. Every month they spent $500 over what they brought home and were close to $16,000 in consumer debt.

At the height of their financial distress, the Hamiltons came to Money Mastery for help. Their coach, Peter, began working with them to figure out exactly how they were spending their money. As he sat at their kitchen table, finalizing an overall picture of their spending habits and counseling them on how they would need to start cutting back, the Hamilton's 16-year-old daughter came home asking for money.

"We had just finished talking to Peter about the huge financial mess we found ourselves in when Katie* came home," says Sally. "She wanted $5 to go with her friends to McDonald's. Dinner for that night was cooking on the stove. I had a roast and vegetables waiting to serve my family after we finished our session with Peter but Katie wanted extra money to go out with her friends. Doug and I looked at Peter and then at Katie, and all I could say was 'We can't afford it Katie.'

"She looked at me like I was crazy," says Sally, "and started arguing with us and coaxing and claiming that $5 was not going to break us. She said she couldn't understand why we were making such a big deal out of her asking for money. 'C'mon Mom, be serious, it's only $5.' What she didn't know was that Doug and I had just been made to realize that we literally didn't have $5 to give her because of the way we had mismanaged our finances throughout our entire marriage. I continued to explain that dinner was already prepared and that she couldn't go to McDonald's, but she wouldn't stop arguing. Doug tried to reason with her, but she wouldn't listen. Finally, she said 'Mom, you've never told me no before!' and slammed the door in a huff. After she left, I turned to Doug and Peter and said in astonishment 'Gosh Peter, that's our problem...we just can't say no, can we?'"

*Names have been changed to protect privacy.

We introduced you to Doug and Sally because we want you to think about how their situation applies to you. Are you like the Hamiltons, even in a small way? They were totally unaware of the impact that reckless spending was having on their lives over the course of their marriage. How about you?

When you are unaware of the long-term consequences of your spending decisions you are pulled in a variety of emotional directions, spending money for all the wrong reasons.

When you spend money, even for seemingly inconsequential things, you are at a crucial moment in time that will affect the rest of your life. If you make the decision to spend money for something now, you will not have that money later. You must decide if the purchase has more value to you now than the money would have later if left alone to work for you over time. Spending money emotionally eventually forces you into a survival mode rather than a planning mode. Usually this reckless spending causes you to burn up more than you make and ultimately limits what you can do for yourself and others in the future.

Giving Back: The Law that Helps Control Money Emotions

Let's take a moment to explain an important law about money that can help overcome these emotional spending problems. The more you think about money, clutching it to yourself to make sure you have enough to spend on your every want or worried that you won't have enough to pay the bills, the less money you attract to yourself.

We have noticed that the more needy and anxious people become over money, and the tighter their grip on it, the more they repel wealth and prosperity and the less they actually attract to themselves.

How can you attract rather than repel the money you need to feel secure financially? One of the best ways is to be willing to give some of your money away. Giving money to a church, charity, or to those in need, even when you feel least able to do so, will automatically attract more money to you. Giving money back to others causes money to naturally flow toward you.

Many individuals are already aware of this law and are living it by paying "tithing" to their church (usually 10 percent of their monthly income). If you are not associated with any church congregation or religion, you can still live this law by deciding on a realistic, yet meaningful amount, and donating it to a charity or other organization devoted to causes that you support. Doing so will change your focus from one of cheapness and hoarding to one of generosity and abundance. It will help curb your need to spend impulsively, help calm your fears about economic hardship that may come your way, and will flood you with feelings of abundance that will make dealing with the daily financial struggles of life much easier.

Giving to a church, charity, or other worthy cause will open you to all that is meant to be yours. Giving away makes you more open to receive. We have personally experienced the power of this law in our own lives and watched it make a difference in countless others.

When you live this law, coupling it with a realistic definition of your own needs and desires, and learn how to meet those needs appropriately, you can then create surplus to help others. That surplus is the absolute emotional thrill — ultimately more meaningful than the brief excitement that comes from impulse spending, and certainly more joyful than terrible feelings of fear and guilt that come from spending more than you have.

Get In Control — You Can Do It!

Understanding that spending is emotional is the first step toward financial control and the key to true contentment and happiness, regardless of your income. The remaining nine Money Mastery Principles are based on understanding this first (and most important) idea. Having come this far with us already, you're obviously making an effort to better understand (and manage) your own emotional approach to money. And that means you're beginning to take control — taking control is tremendously rewarding and we encourage you to continue!

To see just how rewarding this experience can be, let's go back to Doug and Sally Hamilton. As they worked with Peter, the Hamiltons began to understand how emotions were affecting their spending. They realized that they had a problem telling their children no. They understood that they were spending money to make themselves feel better in the short-term, thus jeopardizing their long-term financial security. They began making changes by denying their children when it was necessary. This was not easy to do in the beginning. The children were not accustomed to their parents' new behavior and resisted it. But in a short time, they began to accept their parents' new way of doing things. When the Hamilton's daughter had an opportunity to go to Europe for a high school academic event, instead of stressing out about how they would send her, Doug and Sally encouraged her to get a job and earn the money to go herself. Once she realized her parents were not going to hand her the money, she got a job and earned her own way. Later she commented to her parents that she had actually enjoyed the satisfaction of making her own money for the trip and had appreciated her experience in Europe much more than if Doug and Sally had just given her the money.

Today the Hamiltons have stopped overspending and have actually begun saving an extra $300 each month. They have begun to look at every expenditure as an emotional decision, determining whether the object of their spending is something that fits their financial priorities or not.

We encourage you to think deeply about the first Money Mastery Principle by looking at how emotion affects your purchasing decisions. Take the challenge to complete the following short assignment before going on to Chapter 2. It will help you go farther in your commitment to make important changes in your life. Go ahead! Take the challenge! You're worth it!

✓ CHALLENGE #1:
How Do Your Emotions Affect Spending?

1. Pinpoint the last time dealing with money became a dramatic experience that deeply impacted you. It could be the last time you made a major purchase like a car, or sent a child off to college — or the last time you examined your paycheck and realized how much you're paying in Social Security and federal income taxes. *Note: The experience may or may not be negative; it simply needs to be significant.*

a. Write at least three emotions you felt during that event.

_____

_____

_____

b. What was your attitude toward spending money at the time the event took place? Were you affected by Consumerism and/or economic hardship?

_____

_____

_____

c. Who or what was responsible for the way the event turned out? How much did your monthly take-home pay affect the outcome?

_____

_____

_____

2. Determine a realistic yet meaningful amount of money to donate to your church, favorite charity, or other cause on a monthly basis. Record the feelings that you have when doing this, paying close attention to how this

gift helped you control your emotions surrounding money and whether it created more feelings of abundance and security:

_____

_____

_____

_____

_____

_____

CHAPTER 2

Track Your Money
to Control It

W e hope you have given some thought to the first Money Mastery Principle: Spending is Emotional. At the end of Chapter 1 we asked you to identify some of the feelings you had during a significant event in your life that involved money. This exercise should have helped you determine how emotions affect the way you spend money. Understanding why you spend will help you become more aware of how and where you spend. This leads to the second Money Mastery Principle.

Principle 2: When You Track Your Money, You Control It

Have you ever taken your car for a tune-up and received a test result form similar to the one on page 44? The value of this kind of analysis is that it allows you to visualize exactly how your money was spent in getting your car tuned up. Without it, the only thing you may know at the time you pay the mechanic is that $175, for example, seems like too much. Or you may not even consider what the $175 was worth to you at all without something to verify the value of that investment.

Having a clear picture of exactly where you spend your money is extremely important in today's consumer-driven society. The constant barrage of emotional media messages often lures us into spending more money than we have. That's why it is more crucial than ever that you learn the value of keeping track of where and how you spend your income.

ENGINE PERFORMANCE ANALYSIS

| BEFORE | | | | | | | | AFTER |

VISUAL INSPECTION / SECONDARY IGNITION

	OK	SERVICE		OK	SERVICE		OK	SERVICE
Air Filter			Throttle Body			CAP/Rotor KV		
Breather Element			Carburetor			Coil/Pack/Output		
Cold Air Intake			Choke/Pull-Off			Ignition Wires		
TAC Motor			Canister/Purge			Idle KV		
Heat Riser Tube			Dist. Cap/Rotor			Snap KV		
PVC Valve			Mech./VAC Adv.					
Fuel Filter			Ignition Wires			**CYLINDER PERFORMANCE**		
Fuel Pump			Rocker Cover				OK	SERVICE
Fuel Lines			Batt./Hold Down			Firing Order		
Radiator/Cap			Cables/Ends					
Antifreeze Electrol			VAC Hoses			Cylinder Output		
Radiator Hoses			Oil Level					
Heater Bypass Hoses			Missing Parts			Carb. Balance		
Clamps			Systems Inop					
Belts			A/C Duct. Temp			**TIMING CONTROL SYSTEM**		
Fan Clutch			Hood Struts				OK	SERVICE

COMPUTER CONTROL

TROUBLE CODE	CODE DESCRIPTION		Basic Timing		
			Mechanical Adv.		
			Total Advance		

STARTING / CHARGING / FUEL DELIVERY SYSTEM

	OK	SERVICE		IDLE	SPECS			TEST
Cranking Vacuum				CO			CO	
Cranking Current				HC			HC	
Cranking Voltage			300 amps Max	CO2			CO2	
Battery Capacity			9.6 volts Min.	02			02	
Charging Current			12.2 volts Min.	NOX			NOX	
Diode Pattern				Vacuum			Vacuum	
Regulator Voltage			14.2 Average	Acc. Pump			Acc. Pump	
				Fast Idle			Fast Idle	

PRIMARY IGNITION

	OK	SERVICE	SPECIFICATIONS	CRUISE	SPECS		CRUISE	TEST
Dwell/Timing Variation				CO			CO	
Primary Pattern				HC			HC	
				O2			O2	

COMMENTS:

Analysis by:

When you fail to do so, you can easily consume every penny you earn, on impulse and without any real awareness.

Tom and Shannon are a perfect example of this. Shannon liked music and was a member of a club that offered discounts on CDs purchased through its mail order catalog. Shannon bought multiple CDs in order to take advantage of what she thought were cost savings. Tom enjoyed computers and thought nothing of buying himself new video games to play on his PC. Neither Tom nor Shannon tracked these expenditures and were frequently overdrawn in their checking account because of them. Shannon decided to take money from their savings account to cover the bounced checks she had written, but she didn't tell Tom. In turn, Tom decided he would dip into their savings to bail himself out of his overdraft fees but didn't know Shannon had already used all their savings to cover her problems. Because they didn't keep track of how they were both spending money, Tom and Shannon had not only overdrawn their checking account, but had devoured all their savings as well.

As we mentioned in the Introduction, many people fall victim to impulse spending, which promotes a false sense of emotional well being in spite of the inevitable feelings of guilt that almost always follow.

Upbringing can profoundly influence spending behavior. Individuals whose parents granted every childhood desire often grow up to be adults who expect that they can continue to have everything they want, regardless of expense. People who felt deprived as children often grow up to be parents who overindulge their own kids.

Even with the knowledge that the money supply is not endless, some people continue to spend as though their decisions will have no consequences. It is not until a person learns to track his money that he begins to see that all spending decisions have repercussions. Remember the Haywoods who enjoyed frequenting All A Dollar? Once they began keeping track of how much they were actually spending at the bargain store, they were shocked to discover they were wasting $300 each month.

Consider the following advice from George Clason's *The Richest Man in Babylon:*

"Learn to live on 90 percent of your income."

In today's consumer-driven society, is it feasible to live on 90 percent rather than spending 100 percent of what you earn so that you can have a surplus for the future? It is, even for those who have become accustomed to devouring every penny they earn and living on borrowed credit. We have seen countless individuals do it, but they first learned to forecast how they wanted to spend their money and then tracked their spending according to that plan so they could contain that spending where necessary.

Multibillion dollar sports associations know the value of tracking. The NBA, the NFL, and other clubs keep very close track of each athlete's playing statistics so that when it comes time to trade or negotiate contracts, they will know the value of each player. They also keep track of these statistics for the purpose of making them known to the public to heighten awareness. This awareness creates interest, which in turn creates profits.

A system of tracking is vital to any big corporation that wants to stay in business. Consider the example of a California-based computer hard-drive manufacturer that was notorious for not keeping track of its inventory. The company constantly had problems filling orders and usually took an average of three weeks to find parts in order to ship products to its customers. The company's distributor got tired of waiting such long periods and went to a competing supplier. The business lost $120,000 and the distributor never came back. How big was this company's actual loss? In reality, its damages were much greater than $120,000 because it lost a valuable distributor who took his business to the competition.

And what about the IRS? Collecting taxes is a nasty business, and without a system for amassing those funds, the government knows it wouldn't stand a chance. That's why taxes are taken directly out of payroll so that no one cheats the system.

Without your own tracking system, you could be cheating yourself out of valuable money — and run a higher risk of being cheated by others.

The Difference Between Budgeting and Tracking (Why Budgets Just Don't Work)

Almost everyone has been taught that the way to control spending is to write out a budget (which determines a set amount that can be spent based on how much money comes in each paycheck), and then stick to that budget. But most people hate the idea of budgeting because it makes them feel restricted. Budgeting doesn't account for the fact that most individuals will not be strict enough with their money to limit their spending to ONLY the amount they take home each month. For that reason, budgets are generally doomed to failure even before they are implemented.

There's a better way to control spending and is the reason why the average self-made millionaire only spends 87 percent of his or her income, thereby saving 13 percent each year.[1] The secret to these millionaires saving 13 percent is that they have a system for handling spending that doesn't force them to stay within a certain budget. Instead, as Money Mastery teaches, these wealthy people spend money using a three-pronged approach:

Prong 1: First, they plan (or forecast) how they want and need to spend money within prescribed categories; they determine these spending categories based on how they have spent money in the past.

Prong 2: Second, they track how they actually spend their money within these categories.

Prong 3: Third, they compare their tracked spending with their original plan to see what's actually left over based on their income; then they adjust their spending priorities so that they can balance their income with their spending.

Using this three-pronged tracking approach allows them to "prove their priorities" to themselves as their needs and wants change, helps them remain in control when unforeseen problems occur, and, best of all, allows them to spend while still watching their bank accounts grow.

This spending approach is much different than traditional "budgeting" methods because it doesn't force you to focus on what you can't have. Instead, creating a spending plan, tracking your spending according to that plan, and then comparing that spending with available income gives you the freedom to spend in the areas of your life to which you have given the highest priority. It then helps you track how that spending will affect your daily needs, emotional wants, and long-term financial security. Rather than showing you what you have done after the fact — when it may be too late (as budgeting does) — tracking lets you see how your spending is affecting your financial situation concurrent with that spending.

By their very nature, budgets are static. They fail to account for life "coming at you" and for the need to be flexible in the way that you spend.

Planning and tracking allow you to alter your spending as needed and make different choices going forward so you can remain in control, while still giving you the freedom to spend money in areas that you deem important. A budget dictates what areas to cut, but tracking indicates the most meaningful areas for you and your family in which you want to spend. Budgets are depressing and difficult to force oneself to do, but planning, tracking, and comparing are uplifting and encouraging when they are done with specific goals and dreams for the future in mind. Budgeting is argumentative, while planning and tracking help a person make a decision in advance of the moment, leaving little room for impulsive behavior or arguments with spouse or self.

Spending according to a plan and then tracking that spending can be both pleasurable and rewarding when you know where and when you need and want to spend. You will be able to predict how much money you will need to retire, how much you will need in case of emergencies, and how much you can spend for fun. It also helps you focus on the positive aspects of your financial life and can help you feel confident about the future.

"But," you may find yourself thinking, "I've never kept track of my money this way before, and I'm concerned that it might be rather tedious." We have found over the years that most people want to get on the road to financial control but initially feel a little concerned about how hard it will be to make a plan and then track all of their spending according to that plan. They are also concerned about whether they want to take the time to do it — so they play emotional games with themselves.

Game #1: Avoid balancing the checkbook each month. Many of our clients have expressed to us that they simply don't want to know how far out of control they are or how bad things have actually become. Fear and guilt are often the reasons for this stubbornness. In fact, one of our clients was so overwhelmed by the thought of balancing her checkbook that she simply opened a new account every six months.

Game #2: Blame employers or others, and/or think there is not enough income. Many people trick themselves into thinking that their overspending and debt load should be blamed on their jobs and/or their employers.

These people convince themselves that true financial happiness can only be found in a larger salary. They assure themselves that pastures are greener elsewhere, and incur further expenses when they change jobs, uproot their families, and move across country.

Remember, it matters not how much you make,
only how well you manage your money that counts.

Even major league athletes who have not yet learned to track their spending think they don't make enough to support themselves. The Associated Press, reporting on the National Basketball Association's 1998 labor strike, quoted Jazz player Greg Foster as saying, "It hurts missing a paycheck — especially for a guy like me," who was scheduled to make more than $500,000 in 1998. After missing close to 30 games due to the strike, Foster and other NBA players felt they just couldn't make ends meet. "I mean, I'm not Patrick Ewing or one of those guys who gets the big bucks. I need every penny," said Foster.[2]

Game #3: Claim that you never dreamed anything could go wrong when emergencies hit. This is the ultimate gaming strategy, which transfers every bit of personal responsibility onto a "natural disaster" that you couldn't possibly foresee. We counsel with hundreds of clients who have no idea where the money goes each month, and yet cannot see the correlation between this lack of tracking and the total devastation that a basic emergency can bring to their family. One of our clients mysteriously lost her hard contact lenses, which would have cost her approximately $350 to replace. However, because she did not want to feel restricted, she had not tracked her money and therefore could not find the extra funds to purchase new lenses. This small amount of money put her into a state of total financial and emotional panic.

At the outset, tracking your money and how it's spent may appear tedious and time-consuming. But we know from years of helping people gain control of their finances that it's actually wonderfully rewarding.

Let's meet a couple who learned about those rewards.

Stan & Arlene Harbrecht: "We're Already Tight....We Won't Find Any More Money"

Case History

Stan and Arlene Harbrecht* were from Tennessee. Stan was a truck driver, making a modest income of about $24,000 per year. Arlene was a schoolteacher. Together the Harbrechts made enough money to meet their basic needs and to put their daughter through college. But Stan was concerned because their daughter was in real need of some money for on-campus housing, which required an additional $110 a month to cover the expense. The Harbrechts had come to Money Mastery for some basic coaching but Stan was only mildly interested. As their coach explained Principle 2, Stan said, "I know how tight we are with our money. I can't believe that you think tracking our spending is going to help us find the extra cash for our daughter. That's baloney!"

Their coach promised the Harbrechts that they would be able to find the extra money they needed and then told them that on average, Money Mastery clients find 1 percent of their annual income each month that they are wasting on unneeded items. That means that a person making $30,000 annually will easily find $300 per month extra if they will learn to track their expenditures. Because Stan was making $24,000 a year, his coach knew he could easily find the $110 he needed for his daughter.

Stan and Arlene agreed to give it a try and his coach committed Stan specifically to this challenge. She asked him to send her a copy of his expenses once a month so she could review his progress. Stan sent in his first month's spending, but it was only partially filled out, so his coach challenged him on it. "I just think this is really boring and time-consuming, and frankly, I don't want to do it," said Stan. The coach then reminded him of his need to come up with an additional $110 for his daughter's college expenses and Stan reaffirmed that he desperately wanted to keep her in college. His coach promised him again that if he would keep track of his spending faithfully, he would find the money he needed. At this point Stan replied, "Well, what if I don't find the money?" The coach promised the Harbrechts that if, by tracking their expenses, they couldn't find an additional $110 in wasted money, that Money Mastery would make up the difference. Surprised, Stan said, "You've got a deal!"

Once Stan had given the coach his full attention, she explained to him again that he would need to keep track of his spending very carefully every day. He agreed. It was only two days later when Stan called the Money Mastery offices. He was excited about a discovery he had made. He had pulled into a 7-Eleven store for his daily visit to buy a Big Gulp and some snacks while he talked with other truckers. He paid $0.84 for his 32-ounce drink, and as he had promised, recorded the expense. He had been keeping track all day of his spending and when he totaled his expenditures, they came to $11. Stan quickly realized that it was $11 of miscellaneous money that he didn't need to spend. He was clearly shocked at the amount, and realized that he had been needlessly spending that kind of money for years. He said "I can tell you right now, I know I am going to find that extra money I need for my daughter." As he meticulously kept track of his spending the Harbrechts found that Stan had spent $78 that month just on Big Gulps alone! As he proceeded over the next two months to carefully track his money, he found well over $180 a month that was being wasted on Big Gulps, Twinkies, and other junk food. Containing this unnecessary spending kept the Harbrecht's daughter in school.

*Names have been changed to protect privacy.

Many people are like Stan Harbrecht, objecting to a system of tracking. What are your reasons for resistance?

Tracking Takes Too Much Time

Over the years, we have found that in the absence of a spending plan and tracking system, people end up quadrupling the amount of time spent on taking care of finances! According to Douglas LaBier in his book *Modern Madness*, the focus on money at the expense of personal fulfillment drove 60 percent of his study subjects to suffer from depression, anxiety, and other problems.[3] Our experience shows that when you have a spending plan and system of tracking you will spend one-fifth of your time worrying about personal finances.

We have also found that when people don't keep track of their money, they think they are actually saving time. "I don't want to waste the time on all that. I trust the bank, and I think I have a pretty good feel for what I spend anyway. I just don't feel that it's necessary."

Meet Tony and Angie, a couple that didn't think tracking was necessary until they were introduced to Principle 2. While examining their financial records they found that they had paid $1,850 in bounced check charges during the previous year. Big shock! It made them both sick. They thought they had bounced a "few" checks but had no idea they had both been so careless with their money. When they took the time to track their money, they became immediately aware of how their reckless spending was costing them thousands of dollars in annual bank fees. With this new emotional awareness they were motivated to make changes by spending cash only. Today Tony and Angie are easily saving $900 per month.

With a good system, tracking your spending can actually take as little as seven seconds for each transaction. If you compared how much you are paid on an hourly basis against that seven seconds of time, you might find that tracking your spending will actually be the most money you have ever paid yourself in the shortest amount of time because of all the things you will discover about your spending habits, your emotional needs, and your actual monetary losses.

When you take the time to track your money, those monetary losses may become so appalling that you will be compelled to make some serious changes. For instance, after taking a close look at their financial situations, some families have begun to realize that having both spouses work outside the home is actually costing the family money, since taxation contributes to the loss of most of the income of a two-income household. This is illustrated in Jane Bryant Quinn's *Woman's Day* article "How to Live On One Salary."[4] Quinn noted that the husband of the family in the article was earning $40,000 per year, and his wife, Lori,* wasn't working. Every month the family was short on funds, so this prompted Lori to get an administrative job for $15,000 per year. When Quinn examined the economics of getting this extra income for the family, the results were startling!

Lori had to pay federal and state taxes on her new income. Since they filed jointly, the family's combined income was what established their tax bracket. She paid $4,500 in new taxes, most of which was non-deductible for federal and state income tax. Lori had Social Security withheld from her paycheck at the rate of 7.65 percent, which amounted to an additional non-deductible amount of $1,148 being extracted from her salary. She also had to commute to work 10 miles round trip, resulting in non-deductible commuting costs (in 1995) of $696.

Lori also had child care expenses, which gave a partial tax credit, but Quinn figured that the amount spent over and beyond the tax credit was $4,250 per year. Lori also ate out each day with colleagues, spending an average of $5 per day, five days a week. This resulted in a non-deductible expense of $1,250 a year. Now that Lori had a job she had to have better clothing and purchase more dry cleaning. Quinn assumed that Lori's increased expenses here were an extra $1,000 per year, non-deductible, of course. Finally, with both spouses working, Lori wasn't in the mood to cook. Thus, there were more convenience foods and more eating out. This resulted in increased food costs of a non-deductible minimum of $1,000 per year.

Add it all up and Lori's take-home pay was a paltry $1,156 a year, for which she had to put up with the commute and the boss and the corporate hassles. Her children also suffered by spending the majority of their day without either one of their parents. Families that begin to track often find that working for that extra money doesn't always bring desired results, especially in the face of today's tax laws. Without taking a close look at what really happens to our money once we earn it, we may be doing our families more harm than good.

What else can happen when we don't take the time to make a spending plan and to track our spending according to that plan? When there are overdrafts in our checking account, for example, or when tax day rolls around, or when a spur-of-the-moment chance to travel comes up, we realize we don't have the money to do what's necessary — and talk ourselves into fixing the problem later. In the meantime, we use credit cards to bail ourselves out, compounding the problem and certainly adding to the time it will take to actually resolve it. As we have already stated, the amount of time it takes to track your spending is minimal and brings great rewards.

Tracking your money creates awareness, which helps lead you to the emotional reason you spend money in the first place.

Make the time to create a spending plan and begin tracking today! Learn the secrets behind your own emotional spending by taking the challenge.

Tracking My Money Takes the Joy Out of Spending

We hear a few people object to tracking because they feel it makes them a slave to their money, taking the spontaneity out of buying something. This "month-to-month" mentality, although very easy-going now, leads to lots of stress later when there's no money for retirement, children's college education, or vacations. A spend-now-worry-later attitude has forced many older Americans back into the work place after retirement. And in an article by Tony Pugh of the *Mercury News*, a study by the Consumer Foundation of America and Primerica found that "one-quarter of Americans believe their best chance to build wealth for retirement is by playing the lottery, not by patiently saving and investing."[5] Decide today that tracking, rather than taking the joy out of spending, will lead to long-term happiness.

I'm Already Tight with My Money — Tracking it Isn't Going to Help Me Find Anything Else

Many people are already living frugally, trying to make ends meet by not buying expensive cars or going on fancy vacations. They may even avoid eating out or purchasing the latest fashions. But just like Stan Harbrecht, they are probably wasting more money than they know. That's because most people usually only keep track of the big expenses. Without a simple system for tracking all of your money, all of the time, you may not have as good a feel for what's going on with your finances as you think. Big Gulps add up, even if they only cost $0.84 cents each.

A good spending plan and tracking system are like a rudder on a boat. They help steer you in the direction you want to go, not in the direction that mindless spending will take you. A good spending plan and tracking system help you predict the outcome and eliminate the "spend as you go" and "month-to-month" attitudes that make it impossible to understand and benefit from the Time/Value of Money. We cannot emphasize enough the power that tracking your spending and then comparing that spending to your income will bring into your life.

Tracking according to a spending plan and then comparing that spending to your income builds a powerful level of awareness that leads to emotional control.

Adopting a system of planning, tracking, and comparing will bring huge rewards, both financially and emotionally. Learn to love keeping track of your money. We want to help by giving you a challenge and making you aware of some of the tools that can help you set up a system of complete and total tracking.

✓CHALLENGE #2:
Forecast, Track, and Compare All Your Expenditures

1. Forecast your spending by creating a Spending Plan. One of the most important ways to get control of your money is to forecast your spending. To help you get started, we have included a blank Money Mastery Spending Planner worksheet on page 58. We have also included a sample Spending Planner for Mark and Joyce on page 57. We use this Spending Planner to help our clients see how they have spent their money over the previous 12 months, and then use it to help them forecast their spending on paper.

Step 1: On the blank Spending Planner, write in your gross monthly income, then subtract from that how much you pay in Social Security tax, federal income tax, state tax, Medicare, etc. What's left is your net spendable monthly income. This is the amount of money that you fully control. As shown on Mark and Joyce's worksheet, they have a total of $3,139 they can spend each month.

Step 2: Create categories of spending such as groceries, car payments, entertainment, etc. To do so, we recommend reviewing your last 12 months of expenses to determine these categories and how much you have spent in the past. A good way to do this is to review all your credit card statements, bank statements, check registers, cancelled checks, and receipts. Doing this will be a very eye-opening experience and you might find yourself asking, "Why did I do that? That was a waste of money." This process will be an emotional experience that we can assure you will alter your future spending decisions. It will also teach you how to reprioritize your spending so that you can stop the waste.

Step 3: Once you have determined how you have spent money over the last 12 months, total the expenses for each category and then divide each by 12. This will give you the average amount of money you have spent per month in each category. With these averages in place, you can now use them to estimate what will be needed in each category for the next 12 months. You may decide that you spent way too much money on eating out last year, for example, and will cut the amount you will allow in this category for the next 12 months.

Step 4: Once you have planned the amount of money you want and/or need to spend in each category for the next 12 months, total those figures. Compare this total with your net spendable monthly income. These two figures must match as shown in the example for Mark and Joyce, where their total monthly income figure of $3,139 matches with the total amount of money they have planned to spend each month. If you find that your monthly expenses exceed your total spendable monthly income, then you are overspending. You will need to adjust your plan so that you can balance your available income with your spending. The total should equal $0. Remember, forecasting, tracking, and comparing have two purposes:

1) to help you see exactly how and where you spend money, and
2) to help you see if you are spending more money than you actually bring home.

Step 5: Track all your income and expenditures for one week, including cash. This includes every cup of coffee, every package of gum, and every can of soda. To do so, we recommend using a check register or some other tracking diary (refer to Appendix A for information on these items) to write down all expenses, even those things you purchased for which you did not write a check or use a debit card.

Plan to be shocked by how this exercise makes you feel. You may even find, like Stan Harbrecht, that you are wasting more money than you ever thought possible. Don't wait any longer to become more aware of what's really going on in your financial life. Get started today!

Mark & Joyce
Spending Planner

A. SPENDABLE MONTHLY INCOME:

	Current	Projected
Gross Monthly Income	3,550	3,650
Less Taxes (Income & FICA)	497	511
Total Spendable Monthly Income	3,053	3,139

B. SPENDING CATEGORY EXPENSES:

Spending Category	Last 12 Months Totals	Last 12 Mo. Avg Per Mo.	Next 12 Mo. Avg Per Mo.	Fixed Expense	Variable Expense	Amount to Spend	His $	Her $
Auto - Gas & Repair	1,500	125	130	0	130	130	70	60
Charitable Contributions	600	50	50	0	50	50	0	50
Cleaning & Laundry	144	12	12	0	12	12	0	12
Clothing	1,320	110	110	0	110	110	30	80
Debt Payment	20,880	1,740	1,740	1,740	0	1,740	1,685	55
Eating Out	480	40	40	0	40	40	20	20
Family Activities	300	25	25	0	25	25	0	25
Gifts	420	35	35	0	35	35	0	35
Groceries	4,800	400	400	0	400	400	0	400
Home Maintenance	300	25	25	0	25	25	25	0
Insurance	1,140	95	95	95	0	95	95	0
Medical, Dental	300	25	25	0	25	25	25	0
Miscellaneous	300	25	25	0	25	25	10	15
Property Tax - Car, Home	600	50	50	50	0	50	50	0
Recreation/Entertainment	600	50	50	0	50	50	25	25
Savings	960	80	150	0	150	150	150	0
Utilities	1,392	116	127	0	127	127	127	0
Vacations, Trips	600	50	50	0	50	50	0	50
Total Expenses	36,636	3,053	3,139	1,885	1,254	3,139	2,312	827

Spending Planner

A. SPENDABLE MONTHLY INCOME:

	Current	Projected
Gross Monthly Income	_____	_____
Less Taxes (Income & FICA)	_____	_____
Total Spendable Monthly Income	_____	_____

B. SPENDING CATEGORY EXPENSES:

Spending Category	Last 12 Months Totals	Last 12 Mo. Avg Per Mo.	Next 12 Mo. Avg Per Mo.	Fixed Expense	Variable Expense	Amount to Spend	His $	Her $
Auto - Gas & Repair	___	___	___	___	___	___	___	___
Charitable Contributions	___	___	___	___	___	___	___	___
Cleaning & Laundry	___	___	___	___	___	___	___	___
Clothing	___	___	___	___	___	___	___	___
Debt Payment	___	___	___	___	___	___	___	___
Eating Out	___	___	___	___	___	___	___	___
Family Activities	___	___	___	___	___	___	___	___
Gifts	___	___	___	___	___	___	___	___
Groceries	___	___	___	___	___	___	___	___
Home Maintenance	___	___	___	___	___	___	___	___
Insurance	___	___	___	___	___	___	___	___
Medical, Dental	___	___	___	___	___	___	___	___
Miscellaneous	___	___	___	___	___	___	___	___
Property Tax - Car, Home	___	___	___	___	___	___	___	___
Recreation/Entertainment	___	___	___	___	___	___	___	___
~~Savings~~	___	___	___	___	___	___	___	___
Utilities	___	___	___	___	___	___	___	___
Vacations, Trips	___	___	___	___	___	___	___	___
Long-Term	___	___	___	___	___	___	___	___
Emergency	___	___	___	___	___	___	___	___
Emotional	___	___	___	___	___	___	___	___
Total Expenses	___	___	___	___	___	___	___	___

CHAPTER 3

No Such Thing
as "Savings"

A wareness. It's a powerful state of mind that will allow you to anticipate and avoid unwise financial behavior, and after taking our challenge in Chapter 2 you may have discovered that, like Stan and Arlene
Harbrecht, perhaps you have been wasting money on unneeded items. Did
you spot any spending patterns of which you were unaware? Were you
shocked by some of the things you learned about yourself and the way you
treat money? Creating a spending plan and then tracking spending according to that plan is always a very emotional experience because it makes us
immediately aware of whether we are spending according to our available
income or spending more than we actually have. What we have found over
the years is that as people become more aware of the way they spend
money, they will change the way they think about money. Changing the
way you think and spend is the next step to financial happiness and the
secret behind the third Money Mastery Principle.

Principle 3: Saving is Actually "Delayed Spending"

What does this mean exactly? At Money Mastery we teach that there
is actually no such thing as "savings," and that all money is to be spent.
What matters most is when and how you spend it. Allocating money to savings is actually "spending" money by putting it aside to use at a later date
for necessary needs and wants. Because your money is going to be entire-

ly used up at some point, it is important to understand the concept of "delayed spending" so that you can be sure all of it will be spent in a way that will bring you and your loved ones the most satisfaction.

You can begin to look at savings as "delayed spending" by tracking your money as we have already encouraged you to do. This will get your spending under control, which in turn will lead you to find more money. This is good. But it is not the end result! Now your focus must be turned to the future and what you are going to do with the newfound money. Usually what people do once they see that controlled spending brings in a surplus of funds is to consume that extra money the minute they get it. This is wrong. What they should do is put this money away for "future spending" so it will be available later when it is needed. Unfortunately, most people do not understand the importance of this concept. Instead they are seduced into believing the notion perpetuated by a consumer-oriented society that they can have everything they want right now and everything they need and want later. The actual truth is that if we want to spend all our money on consumable goods and high interest credit card purchases now, then we cannot assume we will have much of anything we will want in the future, including a financially secure retirement. At some point, we all have to make a choice: We can either prioritize the way we spend our money so that we will be prepared for upcoming events, or we can recklessly spend every extra penny and have nothing for the future. Bear in mind...

> *You can have anything you want,*
> *you just can't have everything you want.*

People who understand this concept know how to prioritize their spending so that they will be able to have the things they want and need right now, as well as what they will need and want later. This often requires them to sacrifice in one area of spending so that they can have what is necessary in another area. For example, a man may feel that taking his wife and children out to eat twice a week is an important family activity. It's perfectly fine for this man to use his money this way if he wishes, but he must also realize that he may have to cut down on groceries and entertainment, if he wants to have extra money available to "spend" for the future.

Perhaps eating out isn't as important to you as buying a new outfit every month. Naturally, the choice is up to you. However, the key is that you must make a choice because it's impossible to have everything. As simple as this might sound, we are amazed by the number of people who somehow believe that they can buy a new outfit every month, for example, and eat out all the time when they have no way of paying for both. This kind of behavior not only keeps people in a cycle of perpetual overspending, but it also eliminates all possibility of seeing money grow in value over time. It prevents people from creating a cash surplus and all the advantages that come with that surplus, including the opportunity to make even more money. In our work with clients in all different kinds of financial circumstances, one of the most significant problems we encounter is the lack of understanding about the power of a cash surplus. A surplus of money lets you experience the power of the "multiplier effect," which means that even a little bit of surplus will multiply quickly in your hand. The opposite is also true: the more you spend and are behind financially, the more behind you're likely to become.

A 2005 article in the *Wall Street Journal* entitled "Why It's Good to Be Rich" by Jonathan Clements illustrates this point: "People don't really appreciate just how advantageous it is to get their finances under control and accumulate a decent dollop of wealth."[1] The article goes on to outline 25 financial benefits that people with fat wallets are able to enjoy and the ways in which those benefits create additional wealth. Here are some of those benefits:

- You can pay off your credit card balance each month, avoiding high interest costs.
- You will always have enough money to take advantage of tax-favored accounts like 401(k) plans, Roth IRAs, and so forth.
- Your fat investment portfolio helps you feel rich so you don't need to prove your wealth by purchasing new cars and designer clothing on credit.
- Your accounts are big enough that you won't get hit with annoying bank fees, annual IRA fees, and account-maintenance fees like those with smaller balances must pay.

- Your high FICO score and superb credit history ensure that you can always get a loan and qualify for no-fee credit cards.
- You can drop life insurance because you'll have so much money that your spouse and kids won't need it; you can invest the premiums in cash-producing ventures instead.
- You won't have to buy long-term care insurance, saving thousands of dollars in premiums for something you may not even need; if you do end up going to a nursing home, you can pay your own care facility or home-healthcare costs instead.
- You can sleep better at night because you don't have to worry about how you're going to pay the bills or whether your investments will see you through retirement.
- Your financial prudence provides a good example for your children, so they grow up to be financially independent and less likely to need bailing out from you.
- You won't ever be forced to sell your home and move into an apartment after you retire, or worse, in with your kids.
- You can avoid playing silly financial games such as buying lottery tickets in hopes of "getting rich quick."
- You always have the cash on hand to seize lucrative financial opportunities, whenever they present themselves.
- You have enough money to travel the world or engage in philanthropic ventures that will provide you with priceless experiences you would never have been able to have otherwise.

If you want to get to the point where you can create a cash surplus that will bring all these benefits (and many more) into your life, now is the time to decide what is important and what is not, and then spend money according to those desires and not according to the false notion that you don't have to make a choice at all.

To help you make those decisions, we asked you in Chapter 2 to create spending categories for such things as groceries, entertainment, and house payments. With these spending categories in place you can now see exactly where you spend money, what your priorities are, and what you truly value. To have the things you want right now (like the new outfit) and still be able to have what you need in the future (comfortable retirement), you may have to prioritize your spending by cutting down in some categories. Doing so will help you use your money more wisely, which in turn will lead you to find surplus funds. The next step is to prioritize the spending of these funds by creating additional categories that will be used for "delayed" or "future" spending. Most people call these categories "savings accounts," but these savings categories should be viewed no differently than any other category in which you allocate funds for the month. You must learn to "spend" money each month for savings just as you would spend money for groceries. Remember...

Saving is actually "delayed spending."

To help you learn how to create these "delayed spending" categories, take a look at the pie chart below.

Notice that it is divided into three categories: Emergency, Emotional, and Long-term (Investments). Each section of the chart represents a percentage of money that you should be "spending" for emergencies, emotional needs, and long-term retirement. We have learned that at the very least, a person should save 10 percent of his gross income throughout his life in order to create a moneymaking machine that will generate the income he will need as he grows older.

Even though the ultimate goal is saving at least 10 percent of your monthly income, if you are not already doing that, we suggest beginning with just 1 percent. We have found that anybody can save 1 percent. Some of our clients do not believe this initially, but as they track their money and learn to control it, every single client finds at least 1 percent they are wasting which can be "spent" into saving categories.

For example, if a person makes a monthly income of $4,200, then saving 1 percent would require finding $42 each month that can be spent into savings. Is it likely that a person will find $42 they have been wasting? Absolutely! We guarantee that if you aren't already saving some percentage of your monthly income, that by tracking your spending you can find at least 1 percent that you've been using unwisely elsewhere. Once you have found that 1 percent, commit a portion of it to the three savings categories we outlined in the pie chart using the 60/20/20 rule: 20 percent for emergencies, 20 percent for emotional needs, and 60 percent for long-term investments.

Following is an example of how to spend that 1 percent using the 60/20/20 Rule.

Let's suppose that Hayden and Rose have a combined gross monthly income of $6,000. After tracking their spending, they find an extra $60 a month (or 1 percent of their gross monthly income) that they can use for delayed spending. Using Principle 3, we suggest that Hayden and Rose do the following:

Emergency Spending: Deposit $12 per month (which is 20 percent of $60) into a low-risk, fully accessible fund such as a money market account, money market fund, utility stocks, etc. Work to build up this fund until it will cover three to six months' worth of expenses.

Emotional Spending: Deposit $12 per month (which is 20 percent of $60) into any type of accessible savings or investment account.

Long-term Investments: Deposit $36 per month (which is 60 percent of $60) into any long-term retirement account like a 401(k), Roth IRA, etc.

As Hayden and Rose see their money grow in each of these savings categories, their confidence will increase and their ability to manage and control their finances will be enhanced. This will help them realize that it is easy to begin saving 2 percent, then 3, and ultimately 10 percent or more.

With time, and as you implement the Money Mastery Principles you are learning in this book, it will be completely possible for you to save at least 10 percent every month.

Now that we have established the importance of setting aside a certain percentage of income for future or "delayed" spending, let's examine the significance of each of the Emotional, Emergency, and Long-Term categories.

Emotional Spending

We have already discussed at length that money is more about emotions than it is about math, so it goes without saying that we will often spend money for purely emotional reasons. This, in and of itself, is not a bad thing. It is simply something we should plan for, especially in today's product-oriented society where we are often enticed to make impulse purchases. We have found over the years in working with our clients that people spend money whether they have it or not. Saving money for emotional spending takes into consideration that there are many times we need to spend money for reasons that go beyond the categories we have assigned for basic daily survival. Tracking your money will help you balance your spending to your income, but it will not be enough when an emotional event occurs. You must put aside even more money into an "emotional spending account" so that you will be prepared when these events arise. Remember, you can have anything you want, you just can't have everything you want — and that means you must prioritize your spending so that you can fulfill your emotional needs without jeopardizing the future.

What are some of the emotional needs for which you should be saving? Typically these include such things as family vacations or new recreational vehicles. Some people use their emotional spending money to purchase clothing for a special occasion, to buy novelty decor for their home, or to treat a family member with a surprise gift or getaway. Whatever the money is used for, it is important that it be spent on something fun, and not for routine, daily sustenance. If you are married, emotional money should be spent on your family and not someone outside the household.

Have you ever had these kind of conversations with yourself?

"I work hard for my money and I owe myself these new clothes!"

"Why shouldn't I splurge to buy all these beautiful flowers for my garden? It's the one thing that brings me pleasure."

"I never buy myself anything. I'm always spending money on the kids. I want this new DVD player and I'm getting it now."

Wouldn't it be wonderful if you could meet your emotional needs when these kinds of desires pop up by dipping into your emotional spending account? Wouldn't it make you feel sensational to spend money for these wants when you've actually put it aside expressly for that purpose? Preparing for the need to spend money for purely emotional reasons eliminates reckless spending of the money that has been set aside for daily survival or for long-term investments. It helps curb debt, and it brings wonderful psychological rewards into your life and the lives of your family members. For those who don't overspend but constantly deprive themselves and their family members of those things that would help build lasting family memories and close emotional ties to loved ones, Emotional Spending can be a lifesaver. It gives people exhausted by the daily struggle for survival a chance to play, relax, and enjoy themselves a little bit when they would not otherwise feel justified in doing so.

The only time it is not appropriate to spend money for emotional wants is when you have not allocated funds for that purpose. Otherwise, it is totally acceptable to spend money for the sheer purpose of providing pleasure to you and your family members. Doing so will give you a sense of peace and satisfaction and eliminate the guilt feelings that come from spending money on emotional impulse purchases when you have not planned adequately for them.

Now let's meet a family that learned the value of saving money for emotional needs and see how they were rewarded for their self discipline.

Barb & Russell Bellfrey: Learning to Spend "Emotional" Money

Case History

Barb and Russell Bellfrey* had been deeply in debt for many years. Even though they were both working full-time jobs, they never had enough money to make ends meet. In addition, their family, which included four children, had never been on a vacation together because the Bellfreys knew they could not afford it. They came to Money Mastery desperate for a way to get their debt under control, but also looking for ways to relieve the emotional strain and put fun back into their family life. As they were taught Principle 3, Russell had a hard time accepting that they would ever be able to find even a little extra money they could put away for emotional needs. With their debt load such as it was, saving even a little money for this purpose seemed impossible to him. But as the Bellfreys began tracking their money, Barb and Russell discovered $100 a month that they had been wasting on unnecessary items that they could now spend into their emergency, emotional, and long-term categories. Barb began putting away 20 percent of that $100 (or $20 a month) into an emotional spending account. With time, as they got their spending and debt even more under control, the Bellfreys began depositing $60 a month into their emotional account. Little by little, the cash began to build up and Barb and Russell started to get pretty excited with the results. They finally reached a point where they could do something for the family of which they had always dreamed: fly to California, rent a house on the beach, and do nothing but play in the sand and sun for a whole week.

Barb and Russell decided to secretly prepare for the trip without the knowledge of their children. They packed each child's suitcase and hid the bags in the trunk of their car. They then told their children that they were going to the airport to pick up an aunt who visited them regularly. When they arrived at the airport, instead of parking the car they pulled up to the unloading zone, and the children began to ask questions. Barb and Russell then told their kids they were all going on a vacation by the sea and spend a full week body surfing and playing in the sand. The children couldn't believe it, so Barb reached for one of her girls' suitcases and pulled out the child's clothes. "Are these your clothes?" she teased. Her little daughter said yes. Barb then handed the suitcase over to the skycap and led the children onto the plane. The family spent a wonderful week on the beach and has since spent other wonderful vacations together because they learned how to save money each month for family outings. The pictures and memories they have of these activities have strengthened their family over the years. All of this was possible because the Bellfrey's realized the importance of Emotional Spending and prepared for it.

*Names have been changed to protect privacy.

Learn how and when to spend emotionally because the need to use money for reasons other than for daily survival is certain to arise.

Emergency Spending

As we all know, life can be unpredictable. We are bound to have problems that come at us out of the blue including illness, accidents, job layoffs, car repairs, worn-out appliances, bad investments, divorce, and even death. You've probably experienced at least one of these economic hardships over the course of your life. The key to dealing with these problems is to be prepared with money to meet these emergencies when they arise. If you don't plan for emergencies, you can get blindsided by them, and that's when the real stress begins! It isn't enough then to simply balance your spending to your income, which will naturally occur when you track your money. You must also learn to balance your spending and provide even more money for these surprises, just as you must for emotional needs.

Joseph and Gentry Meckling: Living on the Edge

Case History

The Mecklings* were a family that liked to play. Joseph Meckling made a good living and had grown accustomed to providing his wife and children with expensive gifts. The Mecklings felt fairly secure with their current lifestyle because they had all the necessary life and medical insurance, paid their taxes on time, and kept up with their mortgage. However, they spent all their surplus money on watercrafts and extra cars. Joseph also liked to take his wife, Gentry, on exotic vacations every year, even though they would usually go further into debt for at least four months to pay for the trips. The Mecklings felt like they had life pretty much under control, despite their extravagant tastes, until Gentry became ill with cancer. Within two months her medical expenses had exceeded $30,000. Even though the Meckling's out-of-pocket expense for Gentry's initial surgery and subsequent treatments was only $3,000, this sum actually blew them apart financially. This was because the family was not aware of their real financial situation, and had been living closer to the edge than they thought, just barely making ends meet.

"All I could think was how could I come up with $3,000" said Joseph. "These medical bills were so totally unexpected....I mean, how could we have known anything like this would happen to us? We felt like we were living life pretty much like everyone else around us. All our neighbors were doing the same things. I couldn't really see how we could have prepared for anything like this."

Although Gentry's prognosis was very good, and most of her medical treatment had been completed, the family was totally stressed out. At a time when Gentry needed to be concentrating on getting well, she and Joseph were actually considering bankruptcy because they had not saved even $3,000 to cover the medical costs she had incurred over the previous four months and were now behind in their other loan payments. What's more, it had not occurred to the family that they could resolve their financial concerns immediately if they were to sell one of their two motorboats.

*Names have been changed to protect privacy.

There's no doubt that Joseph and Gentry found it easy to spend money. Their problem was that they had not "spent" that money in the right place, allocating some of it for emergency needs. As we mentioned in Chapter 2, claiming that you never dreamed anything could go wrong is the ultimate game people play with themselves to avoid taking responsibility when they have not tracked their spending and planned for the emergency and emotional events that are sure to occur.

Financially secure individuals understand the power of preparing for emergency situations by living within their means and putting money away for a rainy day. In Tony Cook's article "Secrets from *The Millionaire Next Door*," which appeared in *Money* magazine and *The Reader's Digest*, Cook reports on the bestselling book *The Millionaire Next Door* by Thomas J.

Stanley and William D. Danko. Cook notes that in order to learn what today's millionaires have in common and how they accumulated wealth, Stanley and Danko sent questionnaires to affluent Americans. They found that "About two-thirds of those millionaires aren't trust-fund babies; eight out of ten accumulated their riches themselves. Most are extremely frugal. Although their average net worth is $3.7 million, they generally live so modestly that even their neighbors don't have a clue about their wealth."[2]

Unlike these millionaires, the Mecklings certainly weren't living frugally and were very intent on maintaining the same lifestyle as their neighbors, so when things went wrong the family was devastated. The Mecklings made $72,000 a year, which means that after 40 years of work $2.4 million will have passed through their hands. With that in mind, we have to ask why $3,000 should hurt so much? If they had actually declared bankruptcy they would have cheated their creditors simply because they wanted extra boats, jet skis, and other toys. Would declaring bankruptcy be fair in this case? Would it be honest?

In order to be well-prepared when emergencies occur, you must look at Emergency savings as a form of self-insurance. When you purchase insurance for an auto or home, for example, its purpose is to prevent financial hardship in case of a car accident, or some kind of damage or loss to property. Contributing to Emergency savings is like taking a self-insurance policy out on you and your loved ones to prevent financial difficulty in case of job layoff, illness, or other unforeseeable troubles. You can avoid all kinds of economic hardship by paying "premiums" into this "self-insurance" by depositing 20 percent of your savings to an Emergency category, accumulating at least three to six months of spendable income and ideally saving one year's worth of net earnings. To further build up this Emergency savings, you may also want to examine your existing insurance policies to see if raising the deductibles can decrease premium costs. These saved premiums can then be added to your Emergency savings to increase the amount available to you in case of trouble. When we ask our clients if they would make a claim on their auto insurance if the damages to their car in an accident were close to or a couple of hundreds dollars more than their deductible, they usually respond with, "No, I wouldn't make a claim since I don't want my insurance rates to rise." We like to point out then that if they would simply take care of the damages themselves, why not raise their deductible in order to lower premiums and put the saved costs into their Emergency funds? When our clients see how easily they can increase the amount of Emergency money available to them by simply raising their insurance deductibles, they are empowered to examine all of their insurance policies to see where they might be throwing money away that could be used to pay into their own Emergency "self-insurance."

Long-term Spending (Or Investing in Your Future)

Another event that is sure to happen in most of our lives is that we will get old. Our bodies will begin to wear out and our ability to work and earn money will slowly diminish. We will need money in the future in order to be prepared for this event. The solution to this problem, as we have noted about Emergency and Emotional spending, is not just to balance our spending to our income today, but to set aside more money in order to have what we will need as we get older.

One of the ways to assure that this extra money is available is to do as George Clason admonishes in his book *The Richest Man in Babylon*:

"Learn to live on 90 percent of your income."

The best way to live on 90 percent is to make a spending plan and then track your money according to that plan, as we have already advised. Once you get your spending under control through tracking, you will find that you have more money to "spend" into a long-term savings program.

Unfortunately, what we often find is that many of our young clients do not really think that living on 90 percent of their income is even necessary, especially when they can't envision old-age ever happening to them. They survive from day to day, knowing they do not have enough money for the future, yet feeling no urgency to do anything about it. Instead of fearing what the future might hold, they are more fearful of the present — they worry unceasingly that they will not be able to have the newest technological gadget or the latest car. Our society is so caught up with present-day consumption that it refuses to see the danger lurking in the future. We have observed many people refuse to make changes because to them nothing matters but "right now." A 2004 study conducted by the Vanguard Group supports this idea. Out of 1,000 investors who participated in the study, 62 percent of survey respondents said they weren't saving enough. A *Wall Street Journal* article reporting on the study noted that of the 62 percent who said they weren't saving enough "the problem apparently wasn't lack of a specific goal, but rather the inability to change current behavior."[3] With that kind of attitude it should not be surprising that national statistics predict that by the year 2015, 77 million Americans will be over the age of 50,[4] and only about one-third of those people will be financially secure enough to retire.[5] That may be because like many people today, the Baby Boomer generation has lived by the "spend as you go" philosophy and has taught it to their children.

Consequently, very few are prepared because they believed in the false notion propagated by media hype that they could have everything they wanted in their younger years and still be able to retire comfortably. Most of these people do not want to face the fact that they are getting older and that Social Security income will not be enough (if it is available at all). In a world that screams at us that we deserve to have everything, living on 90 percent and saving 10 percent seems utterly inconceivable.

This attitude is illustrated in a recent *USA Today* article, which reported that Americans have been spending more than they've earned, resulting in the first negative personal-savings rate since the Great Depression. The report went on to say, "Although Wall Street [boomed] during the 1990s, economic statistics suggest that only a small slice of society has benefited from the run-up in stock prices. According to a study by New York University economist Edward Wolff, the average net worth of the richest one percent of families was $9.7 million in 1997, while the bottom 40 percent averaged just $3,000."[6]

Bill & Betty Wright: Unprepared for Retirement

Bill & Betty Wright* were some of the first wave of Baby Boomers to reach retirement age, but they did not worry about putting money away for the future when they were younger. Suddenly, at age 55, it seemed neither one of them were prepared

Case History

for what was ahead of them. In relatively poor health, the couple lived on a combined disability income and only had $30,000 in the bank. In fear of their future, the Wrights came to Money Mastery, realizing they barely had enough money to pay rent on their modest apartment in a Southern California suburb.

The Wrights were taught to track their spending, and as they did, determined that the best way to save money would be to manage an apartment complex where they could earn free rent. This arrangement did wonders for their self-esteem and made it possible for them to meet their future financial challenges with confidence. However, the Wrights could have had even more financial freedom, allowing them to travel and retire in comfort if they had taken more seriously the need to plan for the future when they still had the time during their younger years.

*Names have been changed to protect privacy.

No matter how old or young you are at this moment, spending money into a Long-term Investment program is extremely important. Doing so will eliminate the fear and dread of getting older and will help you feel confident and more empowered. Because you will need more money for this spending category than either of the other two, it is important to allocate at least 60 percent of available savings funds into this category.

Delayed Spending (or Saving) Is Not Just for the Rich

Although the arguments are sound for saving emotional, emergency, and long-term funds, many individuals still resist "spending" into these categories because they labor under the idea that the only people who can save are those with lots of extra cash lying around. They often think, "I can't possibly put any money away when I struggle just to pay the bills!" Are you one of these people? If so, we encourage you to change your way of thinking. In *The Richest Man in Babylon*, George Clason teaches a wonderful way to begin that change by making the following part of your thought process:

"A part of all you earn is yours to keep."

Think of that statement often. Turn it over and over in your head until you can begin to believe it. It is false to assume that just because you have a lot of financial obligations that banks, credit card companies, and other lenders are entitled to every penny of your income. If you feel like you can't find even one additional penny to "spend" into any of the three savings categories, don't give up. There is hope! As we have already affirmed, when you track your money you will find at least 1 percent of your income that you can begin saving. Remember the Harbrechts in Chapter 2? They didn't think they could find even one additional penny, but through tracking realized they were wasting as much as $180 per month on junk food! By keeping track of your spending you will easily find an extra 1 percent per month that you could be setting aside for "delayed spending." We guarantee it and challenge you to begin looking for that money today if you haven't already found it.

If you are a person that has become infected with the Disease of Consumerism, believing that you are entitled to have everything you want whenever you want it, it may be a bit difficult at first for you to find that 1 percent. You may still be spending more than 100 percent of your net income, making it next to impossible to keep a part of what you earn since you are forced to give up that money in compound debt interest. But don't give up.

It doesn't matter at first that you may be only saving 1 percent. What is important is that you start the process. And as you follow the principles set forth in subsequent chapters of this book, you will learn how to find even more money that you can save.

To help you get on that road, we invite you to take the following challenge:

✓CHALLENGE #3:
Find 1 Percent of Your Income to Allocate
to the Three Savings Categories

1. Carefully review how you have tracked your money; be sure to look at all of your spending categories.
2. Determine, based on your monthly income, the amount of money you will need to equal 1 percent.
3. Deposit 20 percent to an Emergency fund, and 20 percent to an Emotional fund. Sixty percent should be set aside every month (regardless of how small it may be right now) to eventually invest in a high-yielding certificate of deposit, a tax-free municipal bond, an IRA account, or other long-term saving program.
4. If possible, set up a system for having funds automatically transferred from your checking account into these savings accounts (but be sure the bank doesn't charge for this service).

As you begin this challenge, we hope you will find encouragement in the following empowering statement by A.F. Bannerman:

> *Your savings, believe it or not, affect the way you stand, the way you walk, the tone of your voice — in short, your physical well-being and self confidence. A man without savings is always running. He must take the first job offered. He sits nervously on life's chairs because any small emergency throws him into the hands of others.*

> *Without savings, a man is often fearful of the present and the future. Being in a constant state of fear is a horrible place in which to live. A man with savings can walk tall. He may appraise opportunities in a relaxed way, have time for judicious estimates and intelligent decisions. He need not be rushed by life's problems or economic necessity.*

A man with savings can afford to resign from his work, if his principles so dictate. A man who can afford to change his work is much more valuable. He can afford to give his company the benefits of his most candid judgments.

A man always concerned about the immediate necessities, such as food, rent, school, and medical needs, cannot afford to think in long range career goals.

A man with savings can afford the wonderful privilege of being generous in family or other emergencies. Emergencies become opportunities for service; they help shape personality and develop character.

Schools do not teach thrift. Schools do not teach work habits. However, a man with savings can teach his children by example how to have a more successful and worry-free life.

The ability to save has nothing to do with the size of a man's income. Many high-income people spend it all, and are forever on a treadmill, always working — never able to rest. Many years ago, the dean of American bankers, J.P. Morgan, advised a young broker: "Take waste out of your spending, and you'll drive the haste out of your life."

If you don't need money for college, a home, or retirement, then save for your self-confidence and you can take a level stare from the eyes of any man, whether he be friend or stranger. Start paying yourself regularly, because the state of your savings does have a lot to do with how tall you stand and how relaxed you walk.

CHAPTER 4

Power Down Your Debt

S tand taller.

It's something we challenged you to do in the last chapter by taking our invitation to apply Principle 3. We're confident that by now your new spending and saving habits are helping you feel quite a bit better about your finances. In Chapter 3, we noted that as people become more aware of the way they spend money through tracking, they are inclined to want to use that money more appropriately by putting it away to be consumed at a later date for emergency, emotional, and retirement needs. As you learn to "spend" part of your money into funds that will cover these needs rather than using it all on consumable goods, you will be able to stand taller and experience a feeling of tremendous freedom and control. Continuing on the road to financial freedom requires that tracking and proper spending be coupled with the next Money Mastery Principle.

Principle 4: Power Down Your Debt, and Power Up Your Fortune

It goes without saying that eliminating personal debt is one of the most important keys to mastering your money. Even if you have no credit card debt, you should continue reading this chapter as we will discuss how debt that requires you to pay interest to others (even if it isn't credit card-related) is dangerous and should be eliminated as quickly as possible. This includes a mortgage on a house in which you are currently living. By applying Money Mastery Principle 4, you can get out of all debt, including a 30-year mortgage, in nine years or less. To see how this is possible, let's first examine the emotions behind the borrowing habits of most consumers and how these emotions must be brought under control before debt can be eliminated.

As a nation, America's collective consumer credit debt, which was $808 billion in 1990, has now climbed to a whopping $1.9 trillion.[1] Total credit card debt is over $727 billion,[2] and total U.S. household debt now stands at $11.5 trillion.[3] A 2004 study by the U.S. Commerce Department's Bureau of Economic Analysis shows that 43 percent of U.S. families consume more than they earn, spending on average $1.22 for each dollar they bring home.[4] That means that for a large number of people, every penny of their income is going towards debt, leaving nothing to save for the future.

Our product-oriented society most assuredly contributes to some of the bad borrowing habits into which many Americans have fallen. Many people have become so accustomed to spending and borrowing that they never question whether a purchase should be made, but only if they can cover the minimum monthly payment, falling victim to what debt counselors call the "minimum-payment-syndrome."

What is contributing to your particular debt situation? Have you become a victim of this "minimum-payment syndrome?" Are bad spending habits, a history of paying bills late, or pushing the limits of your credit cards affecting your debt load? Has your debt resulted from wanting to appear wealthier than you actually are, buying cars and furniture that you simply can't afford or more house than you can reasonably pay for? What about your clothes? Do you feel you must wear designer labels to feel important? Is it hard to turn down offers for retail store credit? Have you found yourself using credit cards to pay for such things as groceries and rent because you spend all your income on vacations you can't afford and on extravagant gifts for others? If you answered "yes" to any of these questions, you've become a complete slave to debt and may not even realize it because of how accepted borrowing on credit has become in today's society.

If it weren't for easy credit and the widespread acceptance of debt (once broadly shunned as an immoral and shameful method of acquiring goods) Americans would not be so enslaved by this debt dilemma. Debt helps makes material acquisition possible on a scale in the U.S. that has never before been seen in any country or at any other time in the history of the world. Savvy media moguls know how readily available credit has become, counting on it as a means to further seduce Americans into purchasing more goods and services through emotional advertising messages. Not only do those who are sick with the Disease of Consumerism listen to these messages and make purchases they cannot afford, but they further compound the problem by going into debt for them, adding an interest payment on top of the expense. This triples the amount of money they should actually be paying for an item. Is it any wonder that the majority of Americans cannot keep most of the money they make? In the U.S., consumer spending has risen twice as fast as income,[5] a fact that James Clayton, a history professor and U.S. economics researcher, confirms in his best-selling book, *The Global Debt Bomb*:

> *Along with the lowest savings rate in the industrial world, the United States has the highest consumption rate. To illustrate, in 1965 the rate of personal consumption as a percentage of net national product was 68 percent; by 1991 that figure had risen to 77 percent. This substantial increase comes at the expense of everything else....As Peter Peterson, who was Secretary of Commerce during the 1970s has long argued, this strong desire to consume is part of our policy of growth maximization and entitlement mentality....Our rapidly expanding entitlements are a derivative of this larger desire to consume [and] debt is the vehicle by which greater consumption is made possible.[6]*

In addition to consumerism, a prosperous and seemingly strong economy during the 1990s added to the notion that high levels of personal debt were acceptable. A somewhat artificial euphoria floated over the United States for years because of a ten-year economic boom — a boom that dampened the stigma of borrowing on credit and contributed to a sense of "entitlement" that many people possessed during that decade. Most Americans didn't worry about getting into debt, believing that it wouldn't really hurt them because they could not imagine an economic downturn. James Clayton notes in *The Global Debt Bomb* that the euphoria surrounding Americans for so many years during the decade of the 90s created a false sense of well being:

> *The message conveyed....by Congress [was] that Americans no longer need[ed] to worry about rising public indebtedness — that a growing economy and a continually rising stock market [would] solve the debt problem that plagued the nation for several generations. This euphoric outlook [was] even more evident regarding the rising private-sector debt. Private-sector debt in the United States in 1999 was about 130 percent of the gross domestic product (GDP), the highest level on record. Equity prices, which have risen faster in the U.S. than in any other major nation since 1990, are often used to justify this level of private indebtedness and unprecedented optimism. A rapidly rising stock market is thought to have increased the net worth of corporations and households, thus justifying historically high levels of debt. This stock-inflated net worth [was] also used to justify a zero household savings rate....In short, [it felt] like good times — people [had] jobs, inflation [had] been tamed, and the stock market [had] been on a roll—but the underpinnings of this late-stage expansion are especially precarious because of the historically high levels of private indebtedness.*[7]

Without fear and respect for money, our current generation is sinking itself into greater debt enslavement by its "gotta-have-it-now" attitude. There are roughly 1.2 billion credit cards in use in the United States,[8] with the average U.S. household carrying 10 credit cards, up from seven in 1989.[9] Average card debt for people who have at least one credit card now stands at $9,205 — triple what it was in 1990.[10] James Clayton, again, makes a very stark observation about this level of debt: "Americans, who invented the shopping mall and the credit card, believe they deserve more than they have. So why shouldn't they continue to prosper even if they do not earn it."[11]

Debt penetrates every part of our lives, with the potential of ruining far more than just our credit ratings — it can break up marriages and destroy future financial happiness. This indebtedness, naturally, is counter to the principles we have already taught about getting spending under control so that you can save for the future. And it eliminates any possibility of preparing for the emotional, emergency, and retirement events we mentioned in the last chapter.

To better see the negative affect that debt and its accompanying compound interest can have, let's review the case of Mark and Joyce, the couple we profiled in the Introduction. Take a look at their "Real Debt Report" which was created using Money Mastery's Master Plan software:

Mark & Joyce
Current Debt

REAL DEBT REPORT
For: Mark & Joyce

Description	Monthly Payment	Interest Rate	No. of Payments	Remaining Debt	Real Debt
VISA	55.00	18.000	9	460.00	495.00
Medical/Dental	215.00	12.000	12	2,420.00	2,580.18
Auto	325.00	9.500	16	4,866.00	5,199.89
AT&T Credit Card	110.00	16.500	24	2,236.00	2,640.47
Furniture	220.00	12.000	32	6,000.00	7,040.95
Home	815.00	7.500	354	116,032.00	288,508.50
	1,740.00			132,014.00	306,465.19

The interest you will pay is: $174,451.18

From this report we can see that Mark and Joyce have six debts, totaling $132,000. If they were to pay all six of their debts using a monthly minimum payment, they will pay an additional $174,451 in interest, bringing their actual total debt to $306,465! That's nearly two and a half times what they borrowed!

Unfortunately, most people don't realize that when the initial loan amount is combined with compound interest, they can end up paying three times the amount they actually borrow! This bears repeating:

When you accumulate debt, you can end up paying
three times the amount you actually borrow!

Credit card companies and other credit issuers thoroughly understand this fact. They know that compound interest is the way to make money. That's why they send out more than 5 billion offers for new credit cards each year,[12] even to those with bad credit or who have declared bankruptcy. Unless you more fully understand the power that compound interest can have over you, you will fall victim to credit card companies, lending institutions, banks, and other entities that wait with bated breath to put to work for them the compound interest they collect from you.

David and Wendy are a good example of how compound interest can ruin a family financially. This couple had 18 credit cards and thought nothing of using them to pay for everything — even groceries. When asked how much they owed on their cards Wendy said quickly, "around $17,000." But David said, "No, I pay the bills, and it's around $22,000 to $24,000." When their Money Mastery coach finished adding up all their credit card debt it was more than $47,000! They were shocked and completely unaware that their debt was so high. Their interest expense alone to service these debts was $950 a month! They had to earn $1,450 each month so that after taxes they would have the $950 left just to pay the interest.

A Systematic Approach to Paying Off Debt

We have painted a fairly bleak picture of the debt problem plaguing most people today, and if you are like the majority of Americans buried under a load of debt, you need to be aware of just how grim your own situation is before you can ever hope to do anything about it. While the situation may seem overwhelming and discouraging, there is hope. We can promise that Principle 4 (Power Down Your Debt) will have the most dramatic ability to change your life because it teaches a direct method for getting out from underneath debt. When you learn how to "Power Down" debt you will be able to eliminate compound interest much more quickly and begin accumulating the money you need for future events.

What does it mean to "Power Down" your debt? Powering Down is a method of eliminating debt through a systematic approach to paying bills. Through this technique, you prioritize debt, then work to entirely pay off the first obligation in your prioritized list. Once this debt with the highest priority is paid off, you then apply that debt's payment amount to the next obligation on your list. As you work through your list of debts, paying off each one, you will continue to add the previous debt payment amounts on top of each other, allowing you to more rapidly pay off loans by gradually increasing the amount available to you to make those payments.

To more fully understand how the Power Down method works, let's go back to Mark and Joyce. Take a look at their "Get Out of Debt" Report, which is Money Mastery's way of showing our clients the benefits of the Power Down method of eliminating debt as quickly as possible.

Mark & Joyce
Get Out of Debt

Loan Description	Principal	Regular Payment	Power Payment	Interest Rate	Total No. Payments	Estimated Payoff Date
VISA	460.00	55.00	158.00	18.00	2	10/21/03
Medical/Dental	2,420.00	215.00	213.00	12.00	7	3/21/04
Auto	4,866.00	325.00	428.00	9.50	10	6/21/04
AT&T Credit Card	2,236.00	110.00	753.00	16.50	12	8/21/04
Furniture	6,000.00	220.00	863.00	12.00	16	12/21/04
Home	116,032.00	815.00	1,083.00	7.50	92	10/21/11
		1,740.00				

	Standard Debt Repayment-	29.5 Years	Accelerated Debt Repayment-	7.75 Years
Original Debt		132,014.00		132,014.00
Total Payments		306,465.19		174,683.48
Total Interest Paid		174,451.19		42,669.48
Savings Balance		0.00		1,159,441.33*

*If you save 1,898.00 per month for 21.75 years at 7.00%

Mark and Joyce prioritized by putting the debts that could be paid off quickest at the top of their list. You will notice on the report that the first debt listed is a VISA credit card. They began working to pay off the VISA card by applying a $55 monthly payment. When that was accomplished after nine months, instead of using that $55 they had been paying to VISA on other needs and wants they began applying it to the second bill of $215. By applying the $55 to the $215 Medical/Dental payment, they were able to pay off this second debt in 11 months instead of 12. If they continue this process, adding the combined amounts from each of the previous paid-off debts to the next prioritized debt, they will be completely debt-free in 7.75 years instead of the 29 years it would have taken them had they not Powered Down.

In addition to applying money from one paid-off debt to the next on their list, Mark and Joyce could also apply an "Accelerator Payment" to their debt, for instance, should they find an additional $158 each month through tracking and re-prioritizing their spending. On top of each of the accumulated debt payments they could add this $158, decreasing further the time it will take to get completely out of debt. They could also sell an asset and apply the proceeds from the sale towards their debt. Regardless of which of these additional methods for Powering Down debt that Mark and Joyce choose, applying them will only add to the amount of interest they will save.

It has been our experience that by using the Power Down method of eliminating debt, you can drop your interest expense by two-thirds.

At the end of the 7.75 years, when all of Mark and Joyce's debts are completely paid off, they will continue to take that same amount they have been applying to debt reduction and put it into a savings plan. This savings will accumulate interest and provide them with an impressive nest egg. That saved interest of $174,451 that they didn't have to pay to creditors can be used to increase their net worth at retirement.

Naturally, in a real world setting many things can occur financially that are not reflected on the reports we have just discussed. For example, it is unlikely that Mark and Joyce will go 29 years without incurring more debt. Eventually cars or appliances wear out and need to be replaced, requiring new debt. When this occurs, instead of getting out of debt in 7.75 years, for instance, it may take nine. But using a Power Down approach Mark and Joyce can see their debt and potential savings as a snapshot in time, and by applying Principle 4, can save an enormous amount of money!

Now of course Mark and Joyce could choose not to Power Down. Will they be out of debt in 30 years? Yes. But if they Power Down their debt, they will not only be out of debt 30 years down the road, but they will also have more than $1 million in the bank. Which should they choose? Which would you choose? The answer is obvious. Using the Power Down method, the money you save by not paying interest for years on end can be put to work in the form of compound interest, which over time will make you more money for the future.

One of the greatest minds of our time, Albert Einstein, certainly understood the power of compound interest — he considered it the greatest discovery of the 20th century.

We like to point out that compound interest is also the greatest opportunity of this century!

That's because it doesn't just work for the bill collector. It can work in your favor, as well, if you understand how to harness its power. Millionaires have learned to harness that power. That's why they receive interest instead of paying it. Rich people may have debt, but it is always the kind of debt that will eventually result in a profit for them (such as real estate holdings or business capital investment). They only engage in borrowing practices that will increase their net worth.

But what about the discipline it will take to stop reckless spending and eliminate debt?

Most people are successful at some sort of orderly approach to paying off debt, and are usually vigilant enough to stick to that system until at least one debt is paid off. But absent a full Power Down approach they might think, "Well, I paid off that debt; now I have extra money I can spend." This is wrong! Without understanding the full impact that interest has, many people lack the discipline to remain committed to debt elimination and are tempted to spend. As we have already noted, that kind of mindset will force them to pay three times the amount they actually borrow. Consider the following statement made in 1938 about the relentless nature of compound interest:

Interest never sleeps nor sickens nor dies. Once in debt, interest is your companion every minute of the day and night; you cannot shun it or slip away from it; you cannot dismiss it; it yields neither to entreaties, demands, or orders; and whenever you get in its way or cross its course or fail to meet its demands, it crushes you. — J. Reuben Clark, Jr.

What happens when we let interest expense silently multiply?

Situation

- Amount owed on a credit card is $3,100
- The card company charges an interest rate of 19.9%
- Cardholder only pays the minimum monthly payment of $51.43

Question 1: How long will it take to pay off the card?

Answer 39.4 years!

Question 2: How much principal will be paid on this debt in the first year?

Answer $0.29!

Question 3: How much interest will be required to pay the card off?

Answer $21,216.10

As *Consumer Reports* has admonished, "Remember, cards are designed to keep you in debt forever."[13] And that's exactly what they will do if you do not understand the importance of the Power Down method of eliminating debt.

Now let's meet a couple who were being choked by indebtedness and how through the Power Down method they were able to take control of their lives again and begin investing in their future.

Tim & Sherri Vest: Plunging Deeper Into Debt

Case History

Tim and Sherri Vest* should have had everything money could buy. Tim was a dentist who had graduated from a top dental school and had been practicing for seven years in California. Sherri had a Master's degree with a successful career in interior design. They had been married three years when they came to Money Mastery seeking help in 1996. Although their gross annual income was close to $600,000, they owned no home, had no savings, and didn't feel like they could afford to have the child they so desperately wanted. They were burdened with 26 credit card debts totaling more than $59,000 in real debt, which did not include interest. The Vests were in arrears three years on their federal income taxes. To make matters worse, they had used eight credit cards attempting to pay for the back-taxes they owed.

Tim had come from a wealthy family who had paid for his dental schooling. As a child he had never been denied anything he wanted and had never been taught any self- discipline when it came to money. To compound matters, Tim had been single for several years before marrying Sherri, so all the money he made as a dentist he felt he could spend entirely on himself. He also admitted that as a medical professional he labored under the delusion that he would always have an endless supply of money, much like he had as a child growing up. Once he graduated from dental school, his family felt he was equipped to manage his own financial affairs. They left Tim to manage his money, ill-prepared though he was to do so. In addition, as a person with a passive personality, Tim sometimes let urgent matters slide. Spending to Tim was something he did without thinking, because it felt good and because he had been raised to think that he didn't need to deny himself.

Sherri, on the other hand, was a fastidious, detail-oriented person with a proactive personality who had fallen in love with a man who was already thousands of dollars in debt. In 1996, when the Vests first came to Money Mastery, Sherri was 36 years old, and very concerned about bringing a child into such a financial mess. To complicate matters they were renting an apartment in a desert region of California and scorpions constantly plagued their home. The Vests could not imagine bringing a baby into such a situation, yet they had no way of moving due to their financial problems.

"I felt so completely burdened," says Tim. "It was unbelievable to me that we could be making $600,000 a year and still be so completely behind. To me the dollar figures said it all. With that kind of money I didn't feel any urgency to hold back on spending. I kept insisting that the figures should have been enough, so I couldn't understand why we were so far behind. With as much education as I had, I had never been taught to consider the emotional side of money. Instead, I just spent without thinking of the consequences."

Finally, at their wits' end, Tim and Sherri began tracking their spending and learned just exactly where all the money was going. They also began working with Money Mastery coaches to prioritize their huge list of 26 credit card debts. Using Principle 4, Tim and Sherri were able to apply Power Down payments to their debt load. Using the "Get Out of Debt" Report, the Vests projected that they would be debt-free in 2.8 years if they used Power Down techniques as opposed to 15.5 years if they only used a minimum monthly payment plan.

With 15 years of debt ahead of them, should they have chosen not to Power Down, they would never have been able to get their spending and borrowing under control to the point that they could start a family. Three years later, in 1999, the Vests had purchased a house and were expecting their first baby. Today, after the birth of their son, the Vests are well on their way to total financial freedom, having paid down every single credit card and meeting their IRS tax obligations. They are now saving $21,000 a year.

"It was difficult to sort out all our debt issues at first, but we are so thankful for the principles we learned through Money Mastery," says Sherri. "We are so grateful to have been empowered by these principles [which help us make] serious decisions about our financial future. Now we are looking with hope at where we are today, and where we can be tomorrow, and it means so much to us!"

*Names have been changed to protect privacy.

Fortunately, the Vests were able to get out of debt and get their lives under control. But let's stop and ask why the Vests found themselves in such a financial bind in the first place. Since most people don't make $600,000 a year, you might find it hard to believe that they could be in debt to 26 credit card companies. You can probably think of a lot of things you would be able to do with that kind of money. But that's precisely what Tim and Sherri were thinking, too. They mistakenly assumed that since they made that much money, there should always be enough, regardless of how they spent or borrowed.

As we instruct our clients about Principle 4 and the power it can have in their lives, there are two very important messages we like to emphasize:

1. The Long-term Picture: As you get your spending under control and pay off the first debt on your prioritized list, you must choose to think long-term so you can pay off the next debt on your list. Only you can decide if you want to continue to be in debt or out of debt with a lot more money in the bank. You must learn to think about what kind of long-term emotional impact the choices you make today will have on you tomorrow. Remember...

> *Every dollar paid in interest today is one less dollar*
> *to invest in your future.*

2. Opportunity Cost: Spending money always comes at a cost. If you choose to spend money on consumable goods rather than towards paying off debt, you must understand the consequences of that decision because it eliminates opportunities for the future. Remember the Time/Value of Money and that debt decreases you ability to put money to work for you over time so that it can have more value in the future. As we noted in Chapter 3, it is up to you to make a choice about how your money will be spent, but remember...

> *You can have anything you want,*
> *you just can't have everything you want.*

If you choose not to Power Down, not only will you remain in debt, but you will deny yourself future opportunities to make money because you will continue to pay interest to someone else. As James Clayton notes, "Traditionally, persistent increases in [private] debt levels have often been compared to termites in the house. You can ignore these pests for quite a while, but eventually you will have a very big problem."[14]

How big is your problem? To find out, ask yourself the following questions:

1. Do I argue with my partner over bills?
2. Is an increasing percentage of my income being used to pay off debt?
3. Am I near or at the limit of my lines of credit?
4. Am I extending repayment schedules — paying bills in 60 or 90 days that I once paid in 30?
5. Am I chronically late paying bills?
6. Am I borrowing to pay for items I used to buy with cash?
7. Do I put off medical or dental visits because I can't afford them?
8. Do I know my total debt, or am I afraid to add it up?

If you are struggling with any of these concerns, now is the time to get your debt load under control. It's your choice. You can continue spending like crazy while trying to pay down debt for another 30 to 40 years, or you can be empowered to get out of debt now so you can reap the following wonderful rewards:

- Get completely out of debt within nine years, including your home mortgage.
- Begin saving, on top of eliminating debt, at least 1 to 4 percent of your monthly income.
- Begin to maximize your retirement income by making compound interest work for you instead of against you.

All this is possible if you want to make it happen! If you have five or more debt items, it is mathematically predictable that you can be out of debt in nine years or less, even including a 30-year home mortgage. And the best part is that it's easy and effective, requiring no additional out-of-pocket money. What's more, it's literally worth "millions" once you learn how to stop paying someone else so you can begin paying yourself!

Decide today that you will no longer be a slave to the power of compound interest! Incorporate the Power Down system today by taking the challenge found on page 94.

As you begin this challenge to Power Down your debt, we hope you will find great strength and encouragement from the personal and inspiring story of one of the Money Mastery authors, Peter Jeppson. Peter tells, in his own words, how through a tragic accident he learned first-hand the power and peace that comes from eliminating debt:

"As a young man just starting college, I was in a serious car accident. I was hit head on by another car and trapped in my Volkswagen Bug, almost burning to death, until three drivers in passing automobiles stopped and pulled me from the wreckage. I spent over two years in the hospital, depressed, broken, blind, and burned beyond all recognition.

At first I went in and out of a coma, fighting for my life. The doctors told my mother privately that I had no chance of living. Once I did stabilize, the doctors informed me that I would never walk again, and that there was no chance I would ever see again, having lost my eyelids and most of the skin on my face.

"As the days came and went, I recovered enough to be out of danger of losing my life. But I became very despondent and discouraged. While in this terrible situation I received help from so many caring people who read to me, bathed me, played checkers with me, and gave me pep talks to buoy up my spirit. From this service I learned some of the most important lessons in life. I discovered that self-worth and self-esteem come from within and that beauty is what is on the inside.

"Over time, my health gradually began improving. Eventually I did walk again, and thanks to the many medical professionals who worked with me, my eyesight was saved. But as I lay in ICU for months, the medical bills began to pile up. I did not have health insurance and every Friday the hospital accounting office came to my room to review my bill with me. After every Friday's meeting I would become so upset about the thousands of dollars of debt I was incurring and knowing there was nothing I could do about it, I would schedule a morphine shot for pain relief. Just a little calculation and anyone can figure that seven months in ICU was costing me a literal fortune. Add to this another two years mostly in the hospital and 28 major surgeries, and I began to stagger under the weight of this tremendous financial burden. It was while under this incredible pressure that I learned the lesson that would change my life forever.

"While in the hospital I had my visitors read me the book *The Richest Man In Babylon* by George S. Clason. The chapter on the 'Clay Tablets' about Powering Down debt was so impressive to me. At first the methods described in the book seemed too simple and too good to be true. I couldn't fathom ever paying off all my debt. But then I found myself asking, 'Yes, but what if this system really works? I certainly have nothing to lose! It's easy to test the math — I can do that in my head.' What I found by doing the math was that if I applied a Power Down system to my debt load, I could completely eliminate it in five years. Then, I had different members of my family write down the math when they came to visit. Their numbers checked out with what I had figured in my head. In time, I was released from the hospital. But even with those debt reduction methods still fresh on my mind, I was so overwhelmed by what I owed (besides my hospital bill, I owed money to seven different doctors) I didn't know if I could ever get out from underneath it all. However, I once again tested the figures and found that I could, indeed, be out of debt in five years if I applied Power Down principles.

"Bankruptcy was mentioned over and over by many friends and family members as a way to start a new life financially. My own father, who now had been divorced from my mother for three years, told me he was going to file bankruptcy himself. Because I was still a minor when the accident happened, I could be included in his bankruptcy if I wanted, and wipe my slate clean.

"His suggestion caused me to review all the work the wonderful doctors and nurses had done to save my life and restore my eyesight and I realized there was no way that I could bail out on my obligation to them. As I declined my father's invitation, he told me he thought I was making a stupid decision, but I then thought about how money had ruined his marriage to my mother. I thought of all the arguments he had had with her about money. I thought about how upset it made me feel every time I heard them fight and I determined to do something different financially with my own life. It was then that I committed myself to applying the systematic Power Down approach to my debt.

"Five years later, I paid off my last medical bill. Even though my body was terribly scarred, those scars began to stand as a symbol of victory over my own personal debt and as a sign of triumph at beating impossible odds, both physically and financially.

"Although most people do not carry any outward scars, so many individuals today have scarring on the inside caused by a lack of self-esteem due to financial worries and crushing debt. I have learned, over 30 years of taking every opportunity to teach thousands of people about the Power Down approach, that if you have five or more debts it is possible to eliminate all of them in nine years or less using this method. I learned it for myself personally all those years ago, and I have seen it work over and over again in the lives of countless people. It simply works — no matter how much debt you have, no matter how bad it is, no matter how high the interest rates are, no matter what! It works! If I can do it, you can too! Gaining the victory over debt is a huge accomplishment that I strongly encourage you to work towards. Begin now! Don't wait another day to relieve yourself of this terrible burden that scars, destroys, and maims your life."

✓ CHALLENGE #4: Prioritize Your Debt

This week, gather information on all your debts, including interest rates, monthly payments, and balances. Then begin to prioritize each debt using one of the three following choices:

1. List debts by maturity (shortest to longest debt period)
2. List debts by interest rate (highest to lowest)
3. List debts by size of debt (smallest to largest)

We usually suggest that debt be prioritized by maturity date because for most situations, this will get people out of debt the quickest. However, because each individual situation is different, be sure to check out all three methods for prioritization and then choose the one that will eliminate debt the fastest for you. Once you have prioritized debts for payoff, determine to begin paying off the first debt on your list by allocating an amount of money towards the bill that will help eliminate it as quickly as possible.

Also, you may want to review your spending to see if you can find additional money that you are wasting on unneeded items that you could apply as an Accelerator Payment. Money Mastery's Master Plan software is specifically designed to help you prioritize debt and to visualize the impact that interest will have on your finances over time. It was used to create Mark and Joyce's debt reports featured in this chapter and can help you play "what if" scenarios to determine the best way to Power Down your own debt. (If you would like to obtain the software, refer to Appendix A for more information.)

CHAPTER 5

Know the Rules

When Einstein said that the greatest discovery of the 20th century was compound interest, he was right. Compound interest has had far-reaching effects on the modern world, making millions (even billions) of dollars for some people, while costing others a fortune in debt interest. Whether it works positively or negatively in your life depends on how well you understand and apply it, As the old saying goes:

"Those who don't understand interest pay it — those who do, earn it."

At the end of Chapter 4, we gave you the challenge to prioritize your debt and then begin powering it down so that you can learn how to stop paying compound interest and start earning it instead. Once you see how quickly you can actually become debt-free, you will begin to experience strong feelings of empowerment. You will be appalled at the thought of paying someone else and work to begin paying yourself, instead!

Remember Mark and Joyce? As they began looking at their real debt situation it became apparent that they had a choice. They could either get out of debt in 29 years, or in the same timeframe, they could be totally debt-free with more than $1 million for retirement from the debt interest they saved by Powering Down. Just like Mark and Joyce, you too can become more informed about the reality of interest working either for you or against you, and then make some important changes in your life. Taking advantage of the tremendous benefits that being informed can bring to your life leads to the next Money Mastery Principle.

Principle 5: Know the Rules

Initially, the value of this principle should seem very obvious. It isn't. If it were a concept that more people truly understood, there would not be nearly the amount of emotional heartache over finances that most people experience.

Take a look at the picture below of a die. Notice the four dots on the front side of the die. How many dots are on the opposite side of the four dots? If you're familiar with dice, you probably know. The answer is three. What is on the opposite side of one? The answer is six. The rule with dice is that opposite sides of a die always add up to seven. Therefore, on the opposite side of the five are two dots. When you know the rules it is really easy to predict what will be on the backside of the die.

How many times do you make a financial decision when you are not able to really examine that decision — pick it up, so to speak, turn it around and look at what is on the back side? Many financial choices are very difficult and not being able to see the final result can make us feel frustrated, even out of control. Has not being able to see the final outcome of a financial decision ever made you feel at the mercy of what others know over your own basis of knowledge? You can see from this little example with the die that knowing the rules can be very powerful.

Here's another example of why it is so important to know the rules. Sandy and Bart came to us very upset about refinancing their debts. They found, as they went through the process of consolidating some of their debts, that a pre-payment penalty of $2,200 had been written into the agreement for their mortgage loan. This stipulation was clearly stated in the agreement Sandy and Bart had signed when they obtained the loan. It was easy to read and understand yet they had never known it was there because they didn't take time to read the contract before signing it. Now, when it came time to consolidate, they could not do so without paying the $2,200 penalty. Not knowing the rules in this case cost them.

Knowing the rules is just like playing the game of Tic-Tac-Toe. If you have played it before you can pretty much predict who will win within the first few plays of the game. If both parties know how to play Tic-Tac-Toe, usually there won't even be a winner — the end result is "CAT" or a tie. In the case of Sandy and Bart, the lending institution was adept at Tic-Tac-Toe while neither of them ever took the time to learn the rules of the game. If they had learned the rules, even if they couldn't win, they would have had at least had an equal advantage. In this case, they ended up the losers.

> *When you know the rules of the game, you have a much*
> *higher chance of winning or of at least playing even.*

Now let's meet another individual who lost big time because he did not know the rules of the game he was playing.

Michael Marchant: Paying a High Price for Not Knowing the Rules

Case History

Michael Marchant* provided financial planning for medical and dental professionals. For over 25 years he counseled many people who had improperly invested their money and had subsequently lost large portions of their retirement funds. To better serve his clients, Michael became licensed in insurance and securities and placed the license with a broker whom he had worked with in financial planning. Over the years, this broker helped Michael with securities issues, and Michael helped the broker with insurance and real estate issues. At one point in their working relationship, the broker asked Michael to perform some simple functions as the secretary/treasurer of a small, private investment fund. His duties in this position were simply to pay out money when clients asked to redeem their shares. But as Michael said, "Never in my wildest imagination did I realize the tremendous liability in which I had placed myself by accepting the broker's request to become secretary and treasurer of this fund."

That's because over time the broker began making improper trades on the stock market. When the market crashed in October of 1987, a large portion of the money the broker had traded was lost. He did not disclose this to Michael or to his clients. The clients just continued to redeem their shares with the money that was left, until finally it ran out. The last few clients couldn't get their money so they filed complaints that eventually resulted in law suits. An investigation by the state division of securities was then launched.

When the securities division first approached Michael, he was completely unaware of the broker's fraudulent behavior. Michael was helpful, openly discussing the activities of everyone involved. He had not been in a position to invest this money or control it. He didn't see any reason to be concerned about the investigation because he was not one of the broker's owners, nor was he one of his directors. Michael was completely unaware that anyone had ever lost any money until the securities team came calling. He had not been in the least involved with anything that would require him to be responsible for the investments, so he didn't see the danger he was placing himself in by not knowing everything that had happened up to that point. Answering each inquiry started a chain reaction creating a "domino affect," which only made matters worse. Michael recalled: "This securities team then began asking me searching questions for which I had no answers."

In the end, Michael forked out more than $160,000 for attorney's fees and court costs in order to defend himself against the lawsuits, not to mention having to endure incredible humiliation and damage to his reputation. "Unfortunately there are so many people that, like me, don't realize how serious it is when they don't know the rules," says Michael. "Take time to understand the rules of the game you are playing before you begin to play it. Put forth the effort to find out what is happening on the inside. Hire an attorney or other professional if necessary, be sure you read everything before you sign, and keep a copy of all papers you sign your name to!"

*Names have been changed to protect privacy.

Financial Games of Choice

As we have pointed out, every game has rules. The games we play in the financial world should not be games of chance — they should be games of choice. If you know that money is emotional and not mathematical, you will be less likely to take your money for granted and will give it the respect it deserves. If you know the rules about tracking your spending, you will begin to use your money more efficiently. If you know the rules behind properly "spending" into appropriate savings categories, you will not be blindsided by emergency and emotional events that are sure to occur in your life. If you know the rules about compound interest, you will become empowered to eliminate debt as quickly as possible and learn how to make interest work in your favor instead. Knowing the rules has all kinds of valuable consequences, especially in today's complex world.

It wasn't too long ago that the world of personal finance was much simpler. Prices were similar between competing goods and services, taxes were easier to calculate, mortgages and loans were structured with less complexity, and there were less consumer products from which to choose and fewer methods by which to buy them. But today we live in a very complicated and dynamic world economy. We have so many choices! There are thousands of vendors and literally millions of products we can choose from. What was once purchased at the corner drugstore is now available on the Internet. Not only can we evaluate products and services right in our own backyard, but we can choose from those being produced on the other side of the world. All of this complexity makes understanding the following especially important:

> *It's no longer possible to simply assume the vendor or lender*
> *has fully disclosed everything that we may need to know*
> *to make a wise financial decision.*

Today, more than ever, we must become fully informed about how our spending, borrowing, and tax-paying choices will impact our life over the long term. Historically, sellers of goods and services had the advantage over the consumer because these sellers knew more than the buyer. But today, the tables have turned. With all this available information, we are now in a position to structure financial decisions to best meet our needs — but only if we become informed. Learning the rules can help you become more efficient with the money you already make and shifts the focus away from earning more money to learning how to use more wisely that which you already have.

Unfortunately, we have found that the vast majority of people we deal with are more concerned with making money than with understanding how to be more efficient with the money they already have.

Without seeing the value of efficiency and how that efficiency is tied to understanding the rules of the financial games you play, you may be losing those games. This is perfectly illustrated in a *Parade* article entitled, "What We Need to Know about Money" by Lynn Brenner. Brenner notes that a test sponsored by the National Council on Economic Education found that many adults and teens in the U.S. today don't understand the most basic concepts about money. "The economy affects everything in our lives: how we earn a living, how much we earn, the availability, cost and quality of what we buy, and how we invest for our future," says Brenner. "Unfortunately, its importance is the only thing many of us know about the economy."[1]

The article further notes that 1,010 adults and 1,085 high school students took the National Council's test of their knowledge of basic economic principles. "Both groups flunked resoundingly," says Brenner. "Almost two-thirds of those tested did not know that in times of inflation money does not hold its value. Only 58 percent of the high school students understood that when the demand for a product goes up but the supply doesn't, its price is likely to increase. Half of the adults and about two-thirds of the students did not know that the stock market brings people who want to buy stocks together with those who want to sell them."[2]

Hard to believe isn't it? Those findings are alarming, especially in the face of what we have already noted as a time of complexity and opportunity. Now, with that said, you may be thinking, "Well, the amount of information that is thrown at me on a daily basis is overwhelming. With everything else I have to do, I can't afford the time to stay on top of all this, too!" When we hear such complaints, we like to point out that you can't possibly afford not to become informed. In today's world of easy credit and vast consumable goods, many people feel they are entitled to play a very complex economic game, like owning a credit card or mortgaging a house for instance, without paying the price to learn the rules of that game. As the old saying goes:

"If you want to play, you have to pay."

What we are required to "pay" is a little bit of our time and effort so that we will go into the game fully informed and on the same level as all the other players. Those who will not take the time to do this should therefore not be surprised when they are unable to work the game to their advantage. It simply follows that without knowing what you're doing when you enter the playing field, especially where there is a lot of risk involved, you will probably be trampled by those who do.

Following are some of the typical objections to Principle 5 and how we council our clients to overcome them.

Too Much Information

It goes without saying that we live in an era of information overload, a time when there's so much information it's easy to become confused. There is so much coming at us each day that it's impossible to take it all in. We are forced to choose between that which we will absorb and that which we will discard. So how can we possibly learn what we need to know without becoming overwhelmed? What we teach our clients is that they do not have to know everything, but it is important that they get on the road to knowing something. When people realize that there is a limit to that which they personally need to learn they begin to relax and feel empowered by their newfound desire to become informed and to continue that process. While not requiring that a person learn about everything, this requires a commitment to continual learning,

We encourage you to make a commitment to continual learning. Doing so will help you learn a little bit about a lot of things so that you can determine when you need to get extra help. Consumer affairs writer, Carma Wadley, offers some tips on how to start this learning process: "The important thing is not so much knowing all the answers as knowing where to find them."[3] She suggests keeping a list of resources handy to which you can refer including favorite Web sites, government agencies, and lists of people you know who have expertise in particular areas. Another way to get on the road to knowing only that which you need to know is to get in the habit of reading all documents related to the product or service you are evaluating. Sources of information about the rules of that product or service are contained in the documents the vendor or lender provides you. Read all documents. The value of Principle 5 is that it motivates you to study all contracts.

One of our clients we'll call Maria learned the importance of knowing the rules and reading all documents after her Money Mastery coach helped her better understand the tax filing process. When Maria received her tax forms from her CPA at tax time, she felt "comfortable" with the return but because of Principle 5 decided to look everything over carefully. In the process Maria found a $1,700 error in her favor. The CPA then refiled, and instead of receiving $1,800 tax refund from the IRS, Maria got back $3,500. Knowing the rules and reading the documents in this case really paid off!

Not Enough Time

The second objection to Principle 5 is the notion that there's not enough time to know the rules. What people don't realize is that most of us are very close to knowing what would save us a lot of grief, but we don't want to make that little bit of extra effort to find out the last little bit of information that we need. Unfortunately, the cost of avoidance can eventually greatly exceed the cost of trouble, time, and money devoted to proactive self-education. Most people are within 30 minutes or about $300 from getting all the information they need to make informed financial decisions. It usually takes no more than 30 minutes to thoroughly review a legal document. And, if upon examination of those documents you find that further advice is needed, a $300 fee will usually hire a knowledgeable attorney or specialist to review a financial decision to ensure that it is right. Here's what can happen when people don't take the time to be responsible for making sure a deal is secured properly:

Two startup business professionals, who eventually became Money Mastery clients, asked their CPA for help in restructuring their new business from a Sole Proprietorship to a Sub-S Corporation. The CPA said she had prepared everything required by the IRS that would let them operate legally as a Sub-S, allowing them to get some significant FICA tax breaks. Four years later, they began working with Money Mastery in order to more efficiently run their business. As they began getting organized they discovered their Sub-S election had never been filed by the CPA, creating an additional tax liability of $47,000.

After learning Principle 5, the two men understood the importance of taking the time and money necessary to unravel the problems created over the previous four years. They hired a tax attorney who was successful in relieving $30,000 of the taxes due, but they still had to pay an extra $17,000. If these two men had just taken the time in the first place to do a simple review of the Sub-S filing papers with a tax attorney, they would not have lost the $17,000.

Trusting Others Instead of Taking Responsibility

Another reason people don't bother to become informed is that they think other people should know the rules for them. They often trust their economic well being to so-called financial "experts," making the assumption that these individuals will be as concerned about them as they would be about themselves. Of course, as we go about making financial decisions, we are required to trust others to some degree. However, trust is comprised of two elements:

1. Trust that the person or entity providing the service won't try to cheat us.
2. Trust in the competency of that person or entity to deliver as promised.

Our experience shows that people must be on guard in both areas.

Although vendors are not generally trying to cheat the consumer, the biggest risk we take when interacting with providers of goods and services is the incompetence of those providers. Humans make mistakes, as in the case of Maria's CPA. When you know the rules of the transaction in which you are engaging, you protect your dollars and your economic well being.

It has become quite popular these days to leave finances in the hands of automatic savings and debt-paying programs or to trust a financial advisor or investment broker to handle money matters. But we must strongly advise against such practices. Many people who encourage these practices do so with the claim that the average consumer is not intelligent or disciplined enough to manage their own finances. They claim that consumers will not take the time nor will they apply the actions necessary to get their spending under control, pay off their debt, or save for the future. They advocate "automatic" programs that are set up to pay off debt or power up retirement funds by having a portion of a person's income deposited or transferred from accounts on a monthly basis. While this may seem like an easy way to get finances under control, it does not take into consideration the fact that such programs do not "automatically" protect against excessive taxation, market downturns, and unscrupulous vendors. You must know the rules of each financial game you play so that you can withdraw your money from investment programs, for example, when you become concerned about market downturns, or change your automatic retirement deposit programs in order to protect against excessive taxation. Knowing the rules, while requiring a bit more time and attention than just dumping your money in an automatic electronic pay-out or pay-in program, protects against theft, loss, extortion, and a whole host of other problems that you cannot foresee.

Remember, no one will care about your money as much as you do.

A physician by the name of Alan Marcus* provides a prime example of the damage that can be done when we trust others to take care of our money instead of watching over it ourselves. Dr. Marcus had employed a trusted secretary/nurse for over 25 years. According to him, she was a "gem." She not only headed up the office, but was also responsible for making all disbursements to vendors, handling all the accounting, and making deposits into Dr. Marcus's pension plan. When the doctor was thinking of retiring, he contacted his pension administrator who noted that there was less than $20,000 in the pension plan! The "trusted" nurse had been embezzling money for years. This situation could have been avoided if Dr. Marcus had stayed on top of his own financial affairs and hired more than one person to handle his accounting and pension disbursements.

* Name changed to protect privacy.

Dale and Shellie Tamaki: Trusting Others Rather than Learning the Rules for Themselves

Case History

Dale and Shellie Tamaki* are another example of what can happen when you trust others rather than learn the rules for yourself. Dale Tamaki was a professor at a local college in South Carolina and Shellie worked in human resources. When their children were mostly grown, the Tamakis decided to refinance their home in order to lower their monthly payment and to consolidate their consumer debt. The couple's credit was immaculate and they chose a qualified mortgage lender in their area to process the loan. Rates at the time were at 7 percent. When it came time to close the loan, they were told the best rate they could get on the refinance was 9 percent. This shocked the Tamakis since they thought their credit was good enough to get the 7 percent interest rate. The loan officer's response to their shock was "there were a few glitches on your credit report that caused the interest rate to go up." This embarrassed the couple so they didn't question it, nor did they check their own report. They simply signed the loan papers and started to make the payments.

Dale and Shellie were then introduced to Money Mastery Principle 5. It made them think back to the time they refinanced their home and the 9 percent interest rate they were paying. Their coach counseled them to send all the closing documents to a mortgage specialist for review. Upon examination, this specialist found that with their perfect "A" credit rating, the Tamakis were totally qualified for a 7 percent interest rate. Unfortunately, they had been charged three percentage points (which had been completely disclosed at the time of signing) for originating the loan, and six points on the back end, providing a brokerage fee of nearly $14,000 on a loan amount of $126,000. Basically the Tamakis' "A" credit should have entitled them to pay no more than $1,000 in brokerage fees. But because the broker had disclosed the three percentage points and Dale and Shellie had been too embarrassed to question the higher rate, the lending broker was able to arrange for a much larger brokerage fee than he was entitled to, ripping off an extra $13,000. (Some lending brokers will do this if they can see that the borrower is not going to question it.) The Tamakis then went back to the lender and cried foul, at which point the lender promptly revised the loan and negated the excessive fees saving the Tamakis nearly $11,000.

Not knowing the rules and trusting that others would tell them what they should have known themselves made the Tamakis prime targets. A little bit of research could have saved the couple the emotional trauma of "being taken."

*Names have been changed to protect privacy.

Knowing the rules and not being afraid to question are vital in today's world where many people will deal with you legally, but not always ethically.

Other people who know the rules will often take advantage of those who don't.

Not Wanting to Do First Things First

An additional objection our clients sometimes have is that they don't want to learn the financial basics, but would rather experiment with more sophisticated and risky financial games before they have taken care of the fundamentals. They are tempted, for instance, to dabble in the stock market before getting out of debt. Knowing the rules suggests that you do "first things first." In our experience, it is a good idea for an individual or family to do the following in the order prescribed as outlined in the chart below.

As you play each of these financial games in the order that is best for you, you will naturally be led to an understanding of the rules governing the next game. Each step you take will build confidence until you understand how to play even the most risky financial games and have the economic wherewithal to afford to play them. Because every financial game we play comes with a certain amount of risk, knowing the rules means understanding what those risks are. Some financial decisions are less risky than others; nevertheless, each one can be a gamble. (We will discuss these risks in more detail in Chapter 6.)

The Basics

- Consider getting an education or learning a skilled trade.
- Secure vocational income.
- Avoid getting into debt (Principle 4).

Cover Risks

- Buy basic life and disability insurance.
- Build emergency and emotional savings (Principles 2 and 3).
- Purchase a house.
- Minimize taxes (Principle 9; refer to Ch. 9 and Part II for information).

Invest Surplus Money

- Consider investing in guaranteed investments such as CDs or Money Market accounts.
- Consider investing in low-risk options such as mutual funds.
- Consider investing in individual stocks. (Covered in greater detail in Chapters 8 and 10.)

We have seen too many instances where vital savings have been put in jeopardy due to high-risk investments. In general, we recommend that vital savings be invested in low-risk opportunities and that disposable savings be set aside for higher-risk programs, as shown in the illustration on page 108.

From this example you can see that you can make more money the higher the risk you take — but you can also lose more, as well. That's why a person with debt should not be investing in high-risk oppor-

Passbook Savings: Has most flexibility because it allows you to deposit and withdraw money from one account to another easily; has the lowest interest rates.

↓

Certificates of Deposit and Money Market Accounts: Has higher interest rates but usually for a specific term so these are less flexible; requires more money to open than a savings account.

↓

Mutual Funds: Spreads risk out over many pools of stock so the gamble is less than buying specific stock, but these funds are not guaranteed.

↓

Individual Stocks: Allows the buyer to pick something with which they have interest (like dot-com companies or high tech industries) with potential for making large sums but is much more risky; no limit to the downside.

↓

Startups in Closely-Held Companies: Highest risk; only for those who can afford to lose money; examples of such are Angel Investors, venture capitalists, and philanthropists.

tunities because they are not in a position to lose money. Too many people, because they do not take the time to know the rules, try to invest their way out of debt. This is unwise. Remember, debt interest is unrelenting and it's not a good idea to borrow money (that has interest costs) in order to invest in something else (that has speculative returns).

Investment returns for the indebted disappear like smoke.

We see people in their late 50s get panicky about retirement and then become tempted to invest in high-risk programs instead of trusting in a moderate plan. One of our clients, Sam Bennett*, is a good example of this. At age 58, Sam had accumulated more than $300,000 in savings over the course of his career as a mechanical engineer. While it wasn't a meager sum, Sam and his wife knew they still needed more money before Sam could retire. He planned to continue with his retirement savings until he reached age 65. Right before his 59th birthday, however, three of his friends presented him with an opportunity for investment. While he did not have to contribute any money personally to the deal, he did have to co-sign on the loan to secure the funds they needed to launch the venture. Sam decided to jump at the chance, looking at it as a way to more quickly accumulate retirement wealth.

A year later, the investment went bad and the creditors went after Sam's friends to collect on the loan. None of these men had the money to cover the debt, so they came to Sam looking for money. As the only person with anything to contribute to the delinquent debt, Sam lost his entire $300,000 retirement nest egg. His wife was so hurt and angry that she began divorce proceedings. Sam came to Money Mastery desperate for help. Using the Money Mastery Principles, Sam began tracking his spending and found an extra $3,000 a month he could put into savings. Although his plans of retiring at age 65 were severely altered, he will be able to retire at age 72. In addition, he has used his engineering expertise to design slot machines that have been installed in the Las Vegas casinos near his home. He receives a royalty fee from these casinos that will provide him and his wife with a perpetual source of income, even after he retires. Both Sam and his wife are pleased with the results they are getting by applying the Money Mastery Principles and have reconciled their marital differences. However Sam could have avoided all the heartache if he had resisted the temptation to invest in a risky business venture late in his career.

The Credit Card Game

Credit card debt is another area where it is important to know the rules and to do first things first. As we have already stated in previous chapters, it is important that you get out of this kind of debt first because it is usually the most costly. If you have ever taken the time to read the unique set of rules that govern a credit card, you know they can be complex and numerous. Of course the banks that provide credit cards know their own interest rules; they know their own averages, and they know their own risks. If you are going to borrow money from these banks, you had better know their rules as well. Many of these institutions have begun to loosen their requirements and extend the length of credit card loans, causing consumers to go into further debt. Without understanding the gimmicks that can be used to get more money out of you, you're probably losing far more than you think to a credit issuer.

For example, many credit card companies warn in fine print on their card contracts that they will bump up your interest rate by as much as 1.5 percent if they see a derogatory credit report appear on your record. But what constitutes a derogatory report? It has been our experience that credit card companies may consider any check done on your credit as "derogatory." Some of our clients who have gone to the bank seeking a loan for a new car, for instance, and had the bank run a routine credit check as part of the loan fulfillment process, later had that check interpreted by their credit card company as a negative report. The card company then felt legally justified in raising their interest rates. Unfortunately, because most people don't bother to check their credit card statement each month, they have no idea whether their card company is raising interest rates.

Upon learning the various methods card companies have for getting more interest expense out of their cardholders, many of our clients feel that card companies have taken advantage of them. But as we mentioned previously in this chapter, in today's society you are not automatically entitled to play a very complex financial game, like owning a credit card, without paying the price to learn the rules of that game. Some people feel the solution is to get rid of every card they own. While we strongly recommend that you get credit card spending under immediate strict control if you are in debt, there are rules about the value of using credit cards that could actually hurt your credit if you don't use one. And did you know that some credit card companies allow you to earn interest from their credit card rather than pay it? Select cards allow you to earn as much as $.05 on each dollar you charge on that card if you pay it off completely each month. If you were to spend $1,500 per month for 12 months, you could earn $900 if you spend wisely. Some cards even offer rebates on purchases such as gasoline, like the AAA Diamond Advantage credit card. This card offers a 5 percent rebate on all gasoline purchases anywhere in the world if the card is used at the pump and not swiped separately.

Of course most of us know that it usually costs us money to use a credit card. That's why knowing the basics about credit card borrowing could save you (or earn you) thousands of dollars. It's worth the effort and we strongly urge you to take the time to learn more about your own credit card situation.

Here are a few startling observations about credit card borrowing from an article in *Consumer Reports* entitled "The New Rules of Borrowing." It may help you see the value of knowing the rules.

> *Say you paid $19 for a pepperoni pizza by charging it to your card. If you carry no balance on your credit card and pay your bill within the 20- to 25-day grace period, the pizza won't cost an extra dime. But consider instead the cost of that pizza if you are already carrying an unpaid balance of $5,000 on your credit card. If you simply add the cost of the pizza as a topping to all your other revolving debt, that "inexpensive" dinner out would have cost a total of $40.04. Did you really want to pay so much for a pizza? Probably not. Next time [when carrying balances] pay cash. And what about perpetual payment? Lenders would prefer you didn't worry how much a debt will cost or how long it will take you to repay. All they want you to think about is the minimum monthly payment that will keep your account current. At a recent meeting of the International Credit Association in Wilmington, Del., Peter McCorkell, senior vice president of Fair, Isaac, warned credit card industry executives of a proposed law that would require lenders to disclose how long it takes to pay off a balance with minimum payments. "In some cases, the answer would be darn near infinity," he announced to a ripple of giddy laughter. Paying off balances with the minimum now takes longer than ever because, over the years, credit card companies have downsized monthly minimum payments from between three and five percent of the balance to between 1.5 and two percent.[4]*

The article also urges consumers not to wait for a credit card offer, but to choose what's best for them. "That can only be done by getting out your magnifying glass and scrutinizing the terms and conditions in the fine print on the back of the offer. Does the low introductory rate apply to new charges, cash advances, or balance transfers — and how long does that rate last?"[5] Even a low introductory rate on a credit card offer of say 2 percent could end up costing you money if you don't know the rules of the game the credit card company is playing with you.

When making crucial financial decisions, such as which credit card to carry, it's always wise to give yourself 24 hours or at least overnight to think about the decision and re-read anything related to the rules that will govern the contract once you enter into it. Never make on-the-spot decisions without first giving yourself time to thoroughly consider the issue.

What You Don't Know Can Hurt You

What about home mortgage refinancing? In today's credit-laden world it's become very popular to consolidate debt through a home mortgage loan. However, as the "The New Rules of Borrowing" article suggests, "even the new math of mortgage refinancing can add up to trouble for many of the hundreds of thousands of borrowers who rolled over a higher-interest-rate-mortgage for one charging today's lower rate. Had you bought a house in 1992 and financed it with a $100,000, 8.3 percent, 30-year mortgage, for example, you would still have $93,020 in principal left to pay by 1999. You could decide to refinance that loan with a cheaper 30-year loan at today's prevailing rate of 7 percent. You would have to pay 2 percent in closing costs, or $1,860. However, your monthly payment drops from $752 to $619 — not bad. But what looks like a big win for the borrower can end up costing plenty. If you had left the old mortgage in place, your 360 payments at $752 per month would add up to $270,700 by the time the house was paid off. Your new mortgage will cost $222,800. But that figure doesn't include the nearly $54,700 you already paid over the seven years of your first mortgage. *A refinancing restarts the clock on your payments*, so that new loan will end up costing a grand total of about $277,500 over a period of 37 years — an additional cost to the borrower of $6,800."[6] The article suggests that if you decide to refinance, try to make the same monthly payment you made under your old loan. "That way you'll shave years — and tens of thousands of dollars in interest payments — off your debt obligation."[7]

In the case of refinancing, most people only care about the immediate, short-term savings, failing to see the real costs they will incur over the long run. This comes from not taking the time to learn the rules.

Knowing the rules about your FICO score is another area of financial game-playing that is becoming increasingly more important, since the score is being used not only by creditors to see if you qualify for a loan, but also by utilities, employers, insurers, and a growing host of others. An Associated Press article quoting a 2004 study conducted by the Consumer Federation of America noted that the lack of knowledge most Americans have about their FICO score is costing them a lot of money. The survey of more than 1,000 Americans found that only one-third correctly understand that credit scores indicate the risk of not repaying a loan, and more than half incorrectly believe a married couple has a joint credit score. The survey also found that a majority of Americans don't know that credit scores are being used for purposes beyond borrowing, such as evaluating potential tenants, setting deposits for utilities and determining the rate on auto insurance policies.

The report looked at the likely interest rates consumers would be charged for mortgage loans based on different FICO scores, which are developed by the Fair Isaac Corp. of Minneapolis. A borrower with a FICO score of more than 720 could expect to be charged a 5.72 percent interest rate, with a monthly payment of $872 on a 30-year fixed-rate mortgage of $150,000. But a borrower with a score below 560 will likely face a 9.29 percent rate with monthly payments of $1,238. That's a different of nearly $4,400 a year in mortgage payments.[8]

If you are unsure about how your FICO score is either helping or hindering you, it's time you got educated. To learn more about your FICO score, visit www.myfico.com.

Following is a summary of how best to start learning the rules of the financial games you play:

1. **Don't get overwhelmed by the amount of information you need to know.** Remember, you don't have to know *everything*, you just need to begin by knowing *something*.

2. **Take the time to learn the rules.** It usually only takes 30 minutes to learn what you absolutely need to know in order to make informed decisions.

3. **Don't trust others to know the rules for you.** Take responsibility for your own financial well being and do what is necessary to ensure success; hire a professional if needed to help you understand the rules. This can usually be done for as little as $300.

4. **Do first things first.** Avoid the temptation to dabble in risky behavior before you are secure enough financially to afford that behavior. Pay off high-rate credit card debts first and know the rules of the credit card game before you play it.

5. **Give yourself 24 hours to consider a financial decision.** Never feel pressured to make an important financial decision on the spot. Take 24 hours or overnight to consider all the issues to which you will be obligated by signing a contract, and re-read anything related to the rules of that contract before signing.

Knowing the rules is a simple concept that in today's world is more important than ever. Once again we encourage you to become more proactive and make that little bit of extra effort to protect yourself and your financial future. The amount of material you will need to study is not enormous, though an ongoing time commitment devoted to continuous learning is vital. To help you make that commitment, we recommend the following reading list as a place to get started. You will be enthused, empowered, and inspired by the books on this list.

Money Mastery Suggested Reading List

1. *The Richest Man in Babylon*, George S. Clason
2. *The Consumer Report Book*, Consumer Reports
3. *Lower Your Taxes Big Time*, Sanford C. Botkin
4. *The Wealthy Barber*, David Chilton
5. *Your Money or Your Life*, Joe Dominquez & Vicki Robin
6. *The Millionaire Next Door*, Thomas Stanley & William Danko
7. *Die Broke*, Stephan M. Polan & Mark Levine
8. *Millionaire Mindset*, Gerry Robert
9. *One Minute Millionaire*, Mark Victor Hansen & Robert Allen
10. *The Intelligent Investor*, Benjamin Graham (updated with new commentary by Jason Zweig, preface and appendix by Warren E. Buffett)
11. *Trading in the Zone*, Mark Douglas
12. *Quadrant Theory*, Robert Kiyosaki

✓ CHALLENGE #5:
Understanding Your Important Financial Contracts

We challenge you this week to locate all of your important financial documents. These could include home mortgages, warranties, credit card agreements, car loans, insurance contracts, tax returns, etc. Take time to review each of these documents carefully. Make the extra effort to read the fine print where necessary. Once you have reviewed these documents, evaluate your understanding of them based on the following:

1. Do I understand the rules of the contract?

2. Do I understand the amount of risk I have taken by agreeing to the contract?

3. Where the IRS is concerned, do I understand the tax laws surrounding this contract?

4. Do I know my own priorities and do my priorities fit the contract?

5. Can I afford to lose part or all of my money by engaging in this contract?

We also encourage you to seek counsel from a professional if needed. Money Mastery offers extensive coaching for those who need more information about how to learn the rules. (Please refer to Appendix A for information regarding Coaching Services.) In addition, refer to Part II of this book for more information on tax laws and tax relief.

CHAPTER 6

The Rules Are Always Changing

A n ancient Chinese proverb affirms:

He who knows not, and knows not that he knows not,
*   is a fool — shun him.*
He who knows not, and knows that he knows not,
*   is a student — teach him.*
He who knows, and knows not that he knows,
*   is asleep — wake him.*
He who knows, and knows that he knows,
*   is wise — follow him.*

Which level of consciousness best describes you? If you've come this far in the book, we're certain you don't belong in the first category. As you have begun tracking and controlling your spending and are now more aware of your true debt situation, you're becoming more conscious of your true financial and emotional state. If you now see the value of Money Mastery Principle 5, "Know the Rules," which we outlined in the last chapter, you are probably moving ever closer to the fourth and most significant state of being with regard to finances — that of knowing what you need to know in order to make wise decisions.

Awareness of that which you really need to know brings a newfound confidence and an exciting sense of your own potential for being in control of your money. Examples in every aspect of life demonstrate how this kind of knowledge brings empowerment. Take for instance a college student who, as he goes through the process of learning, will either become very aware of that which he knows he still needs to learn, or feel satisfied that he now possesses enough knowledge to build a career. Both levels of awareness are key to rising above the foolishness of ignorance. Upon graduating from college, this student has basically learned how to learn. If you, like the student, have "learned how to learn" by embracing Principle 5, you are well on your way to the incredible emotional freedom and happiness that come from being in control of your finances.

But "Knowing the Rules" is only part of the equation. If, for example, after completing his education a physician felt that he could stop learning simply because he thought his knowledge was complete, he would soon be unable to properly heal the human body. That's because he would not remain current with the latest technologies and improved medical procedures. Likewise, if you stop learning about money and how it can affect your life simply because you think your knowledge is complete, you will make foolish financial decisions that you cannot afford. Remember the old bumper sticker: "If you think education is expensive, you ought to try ignorance." Knowing the rules coupled with understanding that those rules can change introduces the sixth Money Mastery Principle.

Principle 6: The Rules Are Always Changing

We live in a world where change is a constant. Fields such as technology, politics, medicine, agriculture, weather prediction, and education are continually evolving. Though many changes are positive and promote the well being of society, others are troubling. Taxation by the federal and local government, for instance, has evolved insidiously, regularly, and subtly. As we noted in the Introduction, government has grown to an astronomical size over the last 60 years, causing the tax system designed to support it to grow with it. To keep up with this growth, more and more tax laws have been changed or added, making the overall tax system extremely cumbersome and complex.

To see just how much tax law has been altered over the last several years, take a look at only some of the major tax changes that have occurred since 1993.

1993: Revenue Reconciliation Act

- Created four tax brackets: 15%, 28%, 36%, 39.6%
- Retroactive taxation
- Further deduction limitation and phase out of personal exemptions
- Increased estate tax
- Reduced qualified retirement plan compensation limit
- Social Security included in gross income for tax purposes

1996: Small Business Job Protection Act
Health Insurance Portability and Accountability Act
Personal Responsibility and Work Reconciliation Act
Taxpayer Bill of Rights II

1999: Financial Freedom Act

2001: Economic Growth and Tax Relief Reconciliation Act

- Increased the equivalent exemption for estate tax purposes to $1 million
- Phased-in increases to contribution limits on pension plans
- Phased-in additional pension contribution limits for those 50 and over

2003: Jobs and Growth Tax Relief Reconciliation Act

- Accelerated increase in the child tax credit
- Accelerated marriage penalty relief to 15-percent bracket for couples filing joint returns
- Accelerated provisions of the 2001 EGTRRA
- Provides capital gain and dividend tax relief

2004: American Jobs Creation Act

- Repealed foreign sales corporation/extraterritorial income tax
- Provided far-reaching business tax breaks for U.S. businesses
- Revenue-raising provisions to offset the cost of enacting the new law

Other, less obvious tax administrative changes that have had a major impact on Americans include treasury regulations that supplement the

Internal Revenue Code; revenue rulings and transactions governing state procedures, which the IRS will follow in specific situations; and private letter rulings issued to taxpayers by the IRS dictating how tax code may be interpreted by individual taxpayers.

Did you know that Americans spend 5.4 billion hours each year just trying to comply with the 46,000 pages of federal tax code? Basically those hours are equal to three million people working full-time all year deciphering tax law.[1] According to Walter Williams, professor of economics at George Mason University, "If it were employed in productive activity, the labor now devoted to tax compliance would be worth $232 billion annually."[2]

Although legislators are trying to cut down on tax laws, an Associated Press article reported that the U.S. tax code "now stands at more than 1.5 million words...thanks to more than 12,000 changes enacted by Congress...in the past two years alone."[3] The report went on to say that the IRS developed 11 new forms and revised 177 others in one year alone.

Naturally, all those changes can make the average American feel very overwhelmed by what they know they don't know. As we noted in Chapter 5, information overload and the sheer volume of material can make us feel very anxious. But our intent in sharing tax law changes is not to discourage you; as we noted in the last chapter, you can get a handle on that which you need to understand personally in order to make informed decisions. We'll talk more about that later in this chapter and in Part II of the book. For now, we simply want to illustrate the importance of at least being aware that the rules don't stay the same, and that it's vital that we know how changes will affect us financially.

Subtle shifts in the banking industry also demonstrate how the rules are always changing. Years ago, when a person bounced a check, the bank would charge a dollar or two for overdraft fees, which was the actual hard cost for the bank to provide the service of returning the check and informing the customer that funds were insufficient. Today, however, banks charge on the average $25 for bounced checks, plus will often hit the customer with an additional interest fee if the charge goes on a credit card. Banks have found by experience that people are embarrassed when they bounce a check, so the customer will not usually challenge the high cost of these fees, even though it still only costs the bank about $3 to process such checks. This results in a very lucrative source of profit revenue for financial institutions. Customers who took for granted that banks have changed the rules subtly over time are now locked into paying ultra-high bounced check fees. Such fees are now accepted as the "new rule" and nobody disputes them. Even though the change has been slow, it has also been very dramatic.

Of course, taxes and the banking system aren't the only things that can affect our money over time. Other changes in our world, which have seemingly little to do with financial matters, can also have a huge impact on what happens to cash flow. For example, with advances in medical technology, people are living longer. This longevity is now introducing the possibility that most will actually outlive their available money. Individuals in their 40s today will add another 10 years onto their life expectancy, which means most people will live well into their 90s. Will they need money past age 65? Of course — 30 more years worth! This need for more money is greatly affecting the way people are forced to plan for retirement and whether they will be able to retire at all.

Explosive changes introduced by the growth of the Internet and e-commerce have altered the way we buy and sell goods and services, opening up opportunities to more rapidly make or lose a profit. Fortunes in the high-tech computer and consumer electronics industries are made and lost every day. And what about the events of 9/11? The incidents of that day changed the way we conduct business both here and abroad. International opportunities for sophisticated financial deal-making with the rest of the world, while much broader than they were 60 years ago, have also diminished since 9/11. Security, privacy, and the nation's overall financial health were just a few of the things that were affected by the events of that day.

Other things that are in a constant state of change that can also affect our financial well being include:

Attitudes	Income	Marriage(s)
Health	Debt	Environment
Government	Laws	Desires
Relationships	Goals	Emotions

With 52 percent of American marriages ending in divorce, a large number of people are finding themselves facing a change in their marital status. Alimony, child support, and attorney fees can drastically change the cash flow situation.

How was money affected the last time you had to deal with a change in your marital status, health, or income level? When you experienced one of these life changes, you may have felt a bit unprepared because (like most people) you probably weren't expecting a shift in your situation. But since change can take place on a daily basis, it's something we're required to deal with continually.

Life's only constant is change.

The fact is, the only thing we can really count on is change itself. That's why it's so important to learn the value of Principle 6, because just as people, attitudes, taxation, and world markets can change, so do the rules that govern these things. Knowing that the "Rules Are Always Changing" will help you avoid being blindsided by change when it does occur — especially changes that can affect whether you keep or lose your money. Remember Joseph and Gentry Meckling whom we profiled in Chapter 3? When Gentry was diagnosed with cancer, their lives were changed drastically by this unexpected and highly emotional event. When an emergency like the Mecklings experienced occurs, we can be caught off guard, unless we are prepared for these unexpected events with emergency savings and adequate insurance to help offset the impact of the event. When we expect the unexpected by anticipating change, we are better prepared to meet that change without affecting our ability to take care of the daily expenses we must deal with on a regular basis.

The Risks of Change

When the world changes, many times the rules change as well, and these alterations introduce a certain element of risk into our lives. Change brings uncertainty. When something changes, it can take a while to adapt to its new form and function and requires a bit of time to distinguish how the modification will affect a situation.

For example, say your old car is on its last leg and it's time to purchase a new one. You have grown accustomed to your current financial situation that does not require making a car payment. But now you've purchased a new car. It's beautiful, but you're not quite sure yet how paying for this car is going to affect your current spending situation, not to mention all the other debt in your life. Purchasing a car isn't necessarily a huge risk but, of course, that depends. Let's say you don't choose well and end up with a lemon that requires a lot of unexpected car repairs. Or let's say that you can afford to make the car payment, but you get sick and incur some medical bills that make it difficult to meet your car loan obligation. Since you have introduced change into your life by bringing the unknown (the purchase of a new car) into your financial situation, you have also introduced a certain amount of risk, which you must then deal with.

Change forces us to take risks during that period of adjustment between the known, comfortable past and the new, uncertain future.

Regardless of how hard you try to avoid it, change will occur, and that change will bring risk with it. It is your job, therefore, to determine the degree of risk that is acceptable for you to take by keeping up with the rules, and how much risk you should avoid based on the financial games you are currently playing.

Let's meet an individual who did not understand the reality of change within the stock market and took unnecessary risks that put her in financial jeopardy.

Lori Jones: Taking Unnecessary Risks

Case History

Lori Jones* was an account executive for a national network marketing company. Lori had done well at her company, earning bonuses, commissions, and a high-paying salary. In the first two years of her career with the company, she had invested heavily in the stock market and developed a sizeable portfolio worth $500,000. Although she was doing well in her job, Lori was still battling emotionally with the recent death of her husband, whom she had been married to for

25 years. Because he had handled all their finances before he passed away, Lori had no idea how to really track or control her money. Without him by her side, she began relying on others, including an investment broker who called her about an opportunity worth $75,000. She trusted the advice of this broker and purchased the stock right over the phone. Lori was also spending $5,700 more per month than she was making, drawing off her savings to indulge her children and do financial favors for family members. The one thing she felt proud of in her financial life was the large and impressive investment portfolio she had built. Adding to it with the $75,000 investment made Lori feel empowered.

As her spending became more unmanageable, she came to Money Mastery seeking help. Her coach explained to Lori the considerable risk she was taking by owning stock in light of her poor spending habits and the market's continual ups and downs. "Lori, investments can increase but they can also go down in value, and based on your goals and objectives you cannot afford any losses," her coach told her. "But my broker told me the stock will go to $60 per share!!!" Lori said. Her coach then responded by saying "Yes, but the stock market could change and you're spending more than you have each month, putting yourself in terrible risk." That was in November. By June of the following year, the value of Lori's stock had dropped to just $6,800.

Lori's failure to take seriously the risks of being involved in a changing market proved to be an extremely costly error. She lost thousands of dollars, which forced a big change in her circumstances and lifestyle.

*Names have been changed to protect privacy.

Here's another example of a client who underestimated the impact changing rules can have on finances. This man was a dentist who had invested close to $31,000 in mutual funds. By the time we started working with him and his wife, the value of his initial investment had dropped by $9,000. The amount of debt he had incurred over time did not allow him the luxury of losing that kind of money and he was emotionally unprepared to handle the difficulties he had brought upon himself and family through his own shortsightedness.

Investing in mutual funds or any other higher risk stock is not necessarily wrong, especially if you are in a position to lose a bit of money with the hopes of making more. But if you don't have that luxury of losing money, investments can be risky. Because the market rules that govern those investments are constantly changing, timing is extremely important. The following graph illustrates this problem.

Take a look at Line A-B. This line very closely represents the stock market's success over the last 40 years. Many investment brokers point this out, demonstrating that the stock market beats inflation. Line C-D shows the value of the general market in January 1986 when a couple we'll call Harry and Sarah invested $10,000 in mutual funds. They took their money out in May 1988 at which point they lost 41 percent. Why did they sell? Their daughter was diagnosed with leukemia and they needed the funds for medical bills. Line D-E shows the value of the stock market in February 1988 when another couple we'll call Tom and Judy invested $10,000 in the same mutual funds. They took all their money out in May 1996, gaining 43 percent.

Two families who invested $10,000 each had results that were very far apart, even though they invested at the same time. Mutual funds have grown in popularity over the last 25 years because of their good overall returns, and we take no issue with this apparent success. But there are rules and risks in buying mutual funds or investing in any other higher risk option. While many popular financial gurus of our time represent mutual funds to the buying public as a modest risk and a predictable investment, the real issue is timing. Circumstances can force a decision, wise or not....profitable or not. That's why it's so important to apply the Money Mastery Principles we have already covered. Controlling spending, saving into emergency funds, and powering down debt as we have outlined in Principles 2, 3, and 4, all work *together* to minimize cash flow problems when the rules do change.

Another risk that people sometimes take is trying to invest their way out of debt. Many fortunes have been built on taking big risks, but a far greater number of fortunes have been lost because risks were not understood. Ask yourself this question: If I were the head of a family who made $5,000 per month, had an emergency savings fund of $5,000, and $1,500 in an emotional fund — but had nothing saved for long-term retirement — should I invest in my brother's new software startup company? We have coached many couples who have engaged in pursuits very similar to this scenario, often losing every bit of money they put into the new venture and placing heavy burdens on their families. The reason they lose their money (and sometimes their families) is that they don't control any of the variables of that investment and how those variables can change.

Relying so heavily on the investment game, which it seems most financial "experts" encourage consumers to do, only invites trouble for such individuals. Though the average American today has not been taught how to manage the fundamentals of personal finance first, many of today's financial wizards don't bother to enjoin caution on that sizeable group. They fail to differentiate between people who can and should invest (those whose finances are under control and have enough money to risk) and those who should be a little more conservative for the time-being. Thus, though the message they preach about the benefits of investing is sound advice for a small minority of people, the eager majority (whose lack of financial stability should temporarily disqualify them) can end up dabbling in financial games which they are not prepared to win — often with disastrous results.

In addition, relying heavily on the latest pop financial adviser can cause individuals to turn management of their finances over to another person or program. This removes the responsibility and therefore the control over what happens to their money. When markets change and loss occurs, excruciating frustration is the result. We often hear our clients complain about how much money their stock portfolio has lost or is not really making and how powerless they feel to ever build up a cash surplus, given the fact that they do not fully control the forces that affect such programs.

If you are deeply in debt or are not yet prepared for retirement, we recommend that you invest in much more conservative programs. The opportunity to make money can be found in many savings or investment options, but knowing that you don't always control all the variables, and thus all the rules, will go a long way in helping you to invest wisely. It will also help you time those investments so that you will lose the least amount of money should things change. In addition, by doing so, you will avoid losing more than just money, since bad investments can also place you in emotional risk and jeopardize relationships with loved ones. Efficient use of money goes a long way toward protecting what money you already have as well as those emotional relationships in your life worth far more than anything money can buy. Efficient use of money ensures that you will be able to safeguard sacred family relationships and keep your emotional life intact.

The Lack of Control that Change Can Bring

Another issue with change, in addition to the risk it introduces into our lives, is the way it can sometimes make us feel completely out of control. As we discussed in Chapter 5 and earlier in this chapter, the fact that we need to know the rules and to know how those rules are always changing can be overwhelming. It is natural in today's world to feel compelled to learn about everything that comes across our path. But this is unnecessary and definitely discouraging. The important point to remember is:

> *You don't have to know* everything,
> *but you do need to know* something.

Here's an example of one couple who paid a high price when they became overwhelmed by changing tax laws and thus failed to master even a few basic rules about capital gains.

Margaret and John Jacobs* wanted to sell their home, which they had originally purchased for $100,000, at its current appraised value of $600,000. From what they thought they understood of capital gains law, they assumed they could rent it out for a while if it didn't sell as long as they constantly had their home on the market. They decided not to take the time to review the law and went ahead with their plan, renting the house for several years. Finally, the market turned around and a buyer came forward willing to pay their asking price. To the Jacobs' shock, however, their accountant told them that they would have to pay tax on the entire capital gain because they had not lived in their home for at least two of the previous five years. Because John and Margaret were not aware that the laws had changed pertaining to capital gains, their entire profit from the sale of their home was subject to tax. Not knowing the rules and how they had changed over the years, in this case, cost the Jacobs over $100,000 in taxes! This was a costly mistake, to say the least — a $100,000 opportunity cost that need not have been if the Jacobs had relied on someone who knew the tax law instead of on their own ignorant assumptions

* Names changed to protect privacy.

As you can see from this example, it always costs more to be overwhelmed than it costs to learn a few things that will help avoid catastrophe. Making a commitment to begin learning at least a few things — and to continue the learning process — is the only way to maintain control in the face of an ever-changing world. By doing so, you will feel empowered by the confidence that even a little bit of knowledge gives you. Begin today to learn just a bit more than you knew yesterday. A good place to start is with your insurance policies, credit card contracts, and bank notifications. Read notices about changes that have been made to these documents over the previous year. One of our clients took this advice and read carefully a bank notification she had received. It stated that due to changes in the bank's policies, in order for her to keep her Money Market account she would be required to open an accompanying checking account by a certain date or be charged fees. The bank's new policies, she felt, were inconvenient and annoying, so she took her money and invested it elsewhere.

The Perceived "Lack of Time" to Deal With Change

We often hear our clients complain about the perceived lack of time in keeping up with how the rules are always changing. We like to point out at Money Mastery that once you understand your own emotions behind money and then put a system in place that helps track, control, and save money, the amount of time it takes to stay on top of the rules and their changes is minimal. We find that most people spend a greater amount of time worrying and stewing over finances than they would ever need to get informed and stay that way. Unfortunately, many people would rather spend time fretting than doing anything about their situation. These same people are more comfortable swimming around in the stressful familiarity of their seemingly hopeless financial circumstances than in investigating how a slight modification in their behavior could completely change their lives. If you find that you are someone who frets and stews over finances, find the courage to break away from the enslaving power of your own cycle of helplessness so that you can make changes for the better. Decide today to spend less energy on money matters and more time on those things that will bring you the most satisfaction by getting informed and staying that way.

Keeping Up With Changing Rules

The best advice on how to stay abreast of changing rules is simply to start! Begin today to take a more proactive approach to this principle. We're confident that with just a bit of effort to learn how rules can change, you will improve your life in ways you never thought possible. Following are some additional ideas to help you implement this principle more fully:

Don't be afraid of change. We have already established that change occurs on a daily basis and that the only thing we can really count on is change itself. Consequently, there is no reason to fight it. We can be cowards, constantly worried about how a variation in our lives will affect everything, or we can face those variations head-on by learning how to alter our lives to meet those changes.

Set aside time to become informed about change. You should plan to devote a certain amount of time each year to reviewing such things as modifications in life and medical insurance, new lending policies surrounding your loans, new bank policies, changes in tax laws that may affect you personally, and changes in any other area that you think might affect your financial situation. An annual financial review at the first of the year or around the time of your birthday will help you remember to do this.

Subscribe to information sources and commit to study. We have already noted that the time it takes to become informed and continue the process of learning is minimal compared with the time most people waste fretting and worrying over their financial situations. Subscribe to those publications and listen to news sources that will provide you with information on changes you need to know. Get in the habit of seeking out knowledge and then asking the important questions specific to your case. (See the Money Mastery Suggested Reading List found in Chapter 5.)

Seek professional council. If you are unable to find answers even after holding an annual financial review and asking the important questions, it may be necessary to tap a knowledge source greater than your own. Meet with an attorney, tax advisor, insurance agent, or other professional as suits your particular financial situation. As we noted in Chapter 5, most professional advice can be secured for a very small amount of money compared to the risk you take by not seeking such counsel. In today's extremely complex world with its myriad of options, what you don't know can hurt you, so you may also want to consider financial coaching. While there are many financial advisors and investment brokers out there who are willing to share bits and pieces of the financial puzzle, unfortunately many of them are unwilling to paint the entire picture. Instead, they make you dependent on their advice and sell you expensive financial products that line their pockets. This does not put you in the driver's seat. Financial coaching does just the opposite. It helps you learn for yourself how to best manage your own money and the changes to your financial situation that are bound to come along. It also puts you on an even playing field with others so that you can take the emotional confusion and frustration out of your financial decisions.

In addition to receiving financial mentoring from a literacy expert, we recommend that you also meet with a qualified accountant or tax planner at least once a year. Doing so can help you avoid conflicts with the IRS. For example, did you know that when you prepare your own tax return, you generally increase your chances of an audit? The reason is that the IRS has found that people who do their own tax return have 11 times the error rate as that of professional accountants. In addition to helping you properly prepare your tax return, have them explain changes in tax laws that can affect your family or estate and let them suggest some tax planning strategies. Every couple of years, you should also meet with your insurance professional to evaluate policies and premiums.

And finally, we suggest that every two to three years you go to a new accountant or insurance agent to assess what your prior advisor has recommended. Getting another opinion is just as important when it comes to money matters as it is to your health. We strongly encourage you to look outside yourself for some of the answers by seeking qualified financial coaching and the advice of other professionals who can best help you understand how the rules can change and what to do when that change occurs.

Develop a Master Plan. We like to point out that in the absence of a plan, most people make financial decisions they cannot afford. We will discuss the importance of a Master Plan in more detail in Chapter 7. For now, the illustration on the right may help you see how having a goal or plan can assist you in staying on track and free of fear even in the face of continual change.

The post in this illustration represents your plan for reaching desired goals. At the top of this post is your desired goal, of say, retiring at age 65 with $900,000. You stand at the bottom of this post, intending to climb the rope that will lead you to your desired goal. By having a post (or a plan) in place, you are tethered to the desired goal at the top of the post and can climb with confidence towards it. Even as the winds of change blow you about while you climb the pole (represented by the dotted lines in the diagram extending out from the pole), you will still be tied to your desired end result because of the pole. Without a plan, you are tethered to nothing and the winds of change and the relentless march of time may carry you completely away from your desired goals altogether.

Decide today to be proactive in your approach to the rules and their constant change. Do as the ancient Chinese proverb advises: make a commitment to become wise by being one who knows that he knows all that he should to stay on the path to financial happiness. You can do it!

✓ CHALLENGE #6:
Learn About Services that Can Keep You Informed

We challenge you this week to spend some time becoming familiar with the following services that can keep you informed about pending financial change:

1. Money Mastery (www.moneymastery.com)
2. Free tax tips (www.taxreductioninstitute.com)
3. The "Money" section of your local newspaper (provides a quick and easy resource)
4. The Wall Street Journal (www.wsj.com)
5. Kiplinger Report (www.kiplinger.com)

Find out through these services which tax law changes (and other changes to financially related law) will have the most impact on you and your family. In addition, we further challenge you to investigate one other source that can keep you informed about changes to tax law and other financially related laws by visiting your local library or surfing the Web.

CHAPTER 7

Always Look
at the Big Picture

Imagine for a moment that your financial situation is like a puzzle to which you have been fitting various pieces. The pieces are providing descriptive details that help the puzzle take shape and create an overall image that becomes clearer and more exciting every day. You began putting together this "financial puzzle" the moment you applied Principle 1 by examining your emotions about money. You then applied the pieces of Principles 2, 3, and 4 by tracking your spending, saving more money, and powering down your debt. With a firm grasp of these principles, you are now beginning to make more sense of your financial life. In Chapters 5 and 6, we encouraged you to work on piecing together more information about the puzzle by knowing the rules of the financial games you play and understanding how those rules are always changing.

Let's imagine further that applying all the Money Mastery Principles we have covered thus far is like fitting small, detailed pieces into several sections of the puzzle — like adding the piece that represents feathers on the wing of a bird for instance, or pieces that signify light refraction on water. While that detail is very important to the overall appearance of the puzzle, every so often you must step back and view the entire puzzle in order to stay focused on what you're piecing together and how that detail is affecting the picture's overall image. The importance of stepping back so that you can view your entire situation leads to the next Money Mastery principle.

Principle 7: Always Look at the Big Picture

Just as we begin to lose touch with the puzzle's overall image if we don't step back and look at it, most people lose touch with their financial situation if they are not always "stepping back" to look at the big picture. Looking at the big picture means understanding where you are now, as well as having a very solid plan for where you want to go financially and exactly what it will take to get there.

This map of the United States helps further illustrate why Principle 7 is so important.

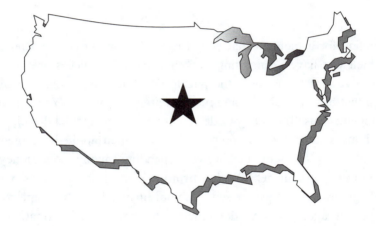

Notice that a star has been placed right in the middle of the map. In order to get to the point on the map that the star represents, there are two things you must find out. First, where is the star located? Is it in Des Moines or Santa Fe? If the point on the map is neither of these two places, then you must identify where the star is located. Second, you must know where you are in order to get to the star. If you are in Maine you will have to take a different route to get to the star than if you are in California.

Now let's analyze this illustration from your own financial situation. If you don't know how much money you spend each month or what your real debt load is, you don't know where you are on your financial "map." In addition, if you don't know when you want to retire (or even what retirement means to you), or how much money you'll need at retirement, then you don't know where you are on your map. Further, if you don't know how you're going to reach any of your other financial goals for the future, then you don't know where your star is located on your financial map.

The two most important things you need to know
are where you are and where you want to go.

To reach your own "star," or your future financial goals, you must know how far away those goals are and where you are financially in relation to those goals. Everything we have been doing together up until now has been preparing you to be able to step back from your "financial picture" and see just exactly where you are. If you don't understand the emotions behind your money, you aren't ready to look at the big picture. If you don't have spending under control, you are not ready to look at the big picture. If you have not begun saving at least 1 percent of your income and started powering down your debt, you are not ready to look at the big picture. Why? Because doing these things helps you understand where you are on the "map." In the beginning, as you took the challenge to get your "bearings" it may have been hard to see, for example, how it can be possible to get completely out of debt in just nine years or less. But if you've been successful at applying the Money Mastery Principles, we are confident that it's becoming much easier to see the effects of your efforts.

The next thing you must determine is where your desired financial star is located and what it will take to reach it. We have found through years of coaching that most people have a very vague idea of where their financial star is located. They have the thought somewhere in the back of their mind that they will reach their "star" when they turn 65 and that hopefully they will have enough money to quit working at that time. Their ability to see what their true financial situation is going to look like 15, 20, or 25 years down the road is usually clouded by the inability to accurately predict or forecast how their spending, debt load, and taxes will affect their money over time.

What about you? Are you caught in the same unpredictable circumstance that many of our clients are, unsure about where your star is actually located, and feeling anxious and out of control? Do you lack the ability to accurately predict what you need to reach your long-term financial goals, and feel uncertain about your ability to look at the big picture so you can make plans to get there? If you could accurately predict where your star is located, what would it be? Early retirement at age 60? Having the choice whether or not to work by a certain age? A trust fund for your kids? Travel? As *Money* magazine writer Denise Topolnicki asks: "What will it be? St. Thomas in January with daiquiris at the 19th hole and a pile of dividend checks waiting for you back home? Or a part-time job at the local mall, macaroni four nights out of seven, and a stack of bills that will overwhelm your next Social Security check?"[1] Only you can decide. Achieving your financial goals for the future does not magically happen when you reach the "fixed" retirement age of 65. Instead, it happens at the point when you have enough passive income to wake up in the morning and elect to work or not. This idea bears repeating:

You will have reached "retirement" at the point
when you have enough passive income
to wake up in the morning and elect to work or not.

What will it take to get you to the point that you can accurately predict the amount of passive income you will need so you can have the freedom to make the choice to work or not? How old will you be when you can make that choice? Will you be dead long before you can make it happen? So many financial problems occur in our lives because we refuse to look at the big picture, not realizing where we are now and where we want to go, ending up on the road to Nowhere.

In the absence of long-term goals, you will make
financial decisions you cannot afford.

It's astonishing that close to 84 percent of people retiring today are totally dependent on Social Security for their monthly income,[2] and yet they have made on average more than $2 million over their lifetime! How is it that a person can make that kind of money and have little to show for it at age 65? The answer is simple — they don't plan to fail, they just fail to plan. This is further evidenced by the Social Security Administration's 2002 study of the aging U.S. population. The report revealed the following about the total population for people age 65 and over:

- 4% have achieved financial success
- 55.2% have annual incomes between $6,000 and $35,000
- 88% are living on Social Security and some other small pension
- 10.4% are living below the poverty level with the average income for those aged 65 and older at just $26,796.[3]

Again, we have to ask why only 4 percent of those who have reached retirement age are financially successful and the average income for those aged 65 and older is just $26,796?! The answer is that people are not looking at the big picture in time to alter it and before it gets too late.

Now let's meet a couple who had no long-term goals for the future. Take a look at the emotional heartache that a lack of planning brought into their lives.

Deena and Leon Hansen: No Map, No Plan

Case History

The Hansens* were from a rural community in the western United States and had built a loving family around their five children, whom they adored. Leon was a cabinetmaker and Deena was a receptionist. They had purchased a big home that was a bit larger than they could afford, and because their children were heavily involved in athletic competitions, had also purchased a large pickup truck to pull a fifth wheel trailer so they could follow their kids to tournaments. Buying these expensive recreation vehicles, reasoned Deena and Leon, "would save on motel bills and meals while traveling." In addition to these vehicles the Hansens also decided a boat would make a nice addition to their family's trips. Leon was sure that he could pay for the vehicles with the sales deals that he promised himself were always going to "come in next week." While the Hansens were a good, hardworking couple, they were constantly out of control financially. Leon owed close to $50,000 to vendors with whom he had contracted as a cabinetmaker. Their home, which because of a debt consolidation was mortgaged for $220,000, appraised at only $190,000. The ultimate result was 20 years of highly charged financial frustration between Deena and Leon and the eventual loss of their home, trailer, pickup truck, and boat.

With these financial losses, Leon began to feel terrible guilt. He realized that through his indebtedness he had cheated his loyal vendors because he couldn't pay them. Over the course of receiving coaching, the Hansens began to realize that they had been operating under a false premise, believing that their overspending would not catch up with them and that without any thought for the future they would still be able to retire comfortably. For years they had lived from one day to the next, spending any money that came into the family. As their coach explained Principle 7 and how the Hansens had not stepped back over the last 20 years to take a look at the big picture, Leon Hansen, a big, burly man who rarely showed emotion, began to sob. He put his head in his hands and cried uncontrollably for about 10 minutes.

"The realization of what I had done to myself and my family began to sink in, and I just couldn't deny the consequences of those decisions any longer," says Leon. "Deena sat there smiling...I think in relief, because she saw that finally I was seeing the big picture, one that she had been trying to get us to look at for years."

*Names have been changed to protect privacy.

The Hansen's case is unfortunate and need not have happened. If they had known and understood the Money Mastery Principles, paying particular attention to Principle 7, they could have avoided the absolute heartache of the situation.

Look at the Long-Term Picture

If we as Americans, living in the most affluent society in the history of mankind are to avoid the all-too typical and tragic mistakes that the

Hansens made, it is imperative that we begin to look at the long-term picture.

To discover how willing you are to do this, ask yourself the following fundamental questions about your future financial goals (regardless of your current age):

1. At what age do I want to "retire" (or in other words, have enough passive income to wake up in the morning and elect to work or not)?

2. How much money do I want to receive each month at this "retirement" age?

3. Do I have specific plans to assure I will receive this desired income?

As anyone who has actually asked themselves these hard-hitting questions knows, it is extremely difficult to look into the future and predict what you will need and what you will want 20, 30, or even 40 years down the road. Because of that, most people procrastinate, never discovering where they really are today and leaving their future in hands other than their own. Looking at the big picture for our young clients seems particularly difficult. As we mentioned in Chapter 3, many individuals under the age of 40 don't want to admit that they will actually get old, assuming that youth is eternal. But stepping back to look at the big picture has nothing to do with age — it's just good common sense. No matter how old or young you are you must have a firm grasp on where you are and where you want to go. As John Pierson states in his article "Thirty Years of Retirement," which appeared in both *Fortune* and *Money* magazines, "the sooner you start planning and saving, the sooner you start benefiting from 'the miracle of compound interest.'"[4] The longer you wait to start planning for the future the harder it becomes. This is illustrated in the following graphic which shows, through the Master Plan Software, the rate of saving you will need to maintain if you begin putting money away at 30 as opposed to age 50.

Begin saving at age 50:

	Retirement Age: 65			
Description	Current Amount	Annual Rate	Annual Deposit	Retirement Amount
IRA	75,000.00	5.00	2,000.00	199,076.74
Residence	125,000.00	3.00	0.00	194,745.93
Savings	6,000.00	4.00	1,800.00	46,848.12
			Total:	$440,670.79
			Percent Taxable:	62.36

Amount you will have to retire on at age 65: **$440,670.79**

Begin saving at age 30:

	Retirement Age: 65			
Description	Current Amount	Annual Rate	Annual Deposit	Retirement Amount
IRA	75,000.00	5.00	2,000.00	594,341.76
Residence	125,000.00	3.00	0.00	351,732.81
Savings	6,000.00	4.00	1,800.00	156,250.53
			Total:	$1,102,325.10
			Percent Taxable:	75.03

Amount you will have to retire on at age 65: **$1,102,325.10**

The difference is astonishing isn't it? When you truthfully answer the three questions we posed earlier, and then write down your responses, you will become instantly aware of 1) whether you even have any long-range goals, and 2) what you are doing today to accomplish those goals. You must learn to think about what kind of emotional impact the choices you make today will have on you tomorrow by asking yourself these important questions. Don't wait until you get older. Consider Leon and Deena Hansen. They thought "later" would never come and paid dearly for it when it did. Nothing stays the same, the world doesn't remain constant, and you will not always have time to say, "I'll do something tomorrow."

*Remember, there are no future decisions, only decisions
made today that will affect the future.*

Plan today as if tomorrow is already here because it will be upon you
sooner than you think. Commit yourself to take control now!

Look at Short-term Behavior in Order to See the Big Picture

While asking the tough questions about long-term financial planning is
important, it isn't the only way you should be stepping back to look at the
big picture. You must also realize that the future depends on controlling
your spending and borrowing today. Many times, the ability to be farsight-
ed (or see the "big picture") is thwarted by the nearsighted need to spend
money right now. The Disease of Consumerism contributes to this near-
sightedness. Today's society is being devoured by the need to consume but
it doesn't understand the impact of its consumption. It's easy to exchange
coins for goods and services — it does not take talent or skill — even little kids can spend money. It's learning how to prioritize the spending of
that money that most people find difficult. The childishness of spending
money thoughtlessly and without a plan can be attributed to a lack of
respect towards money that has permeated our culture. We find that many
of our clients are still acting irresponsibly about spending, as if currency
could be passed around like paper money from a Monopoly game.

One of the best ways to combat this irresponsible and shortsighted
behavior is to become more aware of the process we all go through when
we spend money. This process is called the "Spending Decision." Every
time a person makes the decision to buy, they either consciously or sub-
consciously consider the following three fundamental criteria of the
Spending Decision:

1. **Utility:** Do I need or just want this item? Do I like the color,
    taste, size, power, dependability, performance, etc., of the item?

2. **Availability:** Do I have the money "available" to pay for the
    item? Do I have cash in my pocket, can I write a check, should I
    use my credit card, will the bank give me a loan?

3. **Affordability:** Can I "afford" the item? Does it fit into my long-range goals? What impact will this purchase have on my financial future?

Each of these criteria should be carefully considered every time you buy something. However, most people do not give the third element any real conscious consideration. In fact, most of the time they think that because they have access to money in the form of cash, a check, or a loan, that they can afford a purchase. Nothing could be further from the truth! The most critical question of the three you should be consciously asking yourself is whether you can afford to make the purchase. Understanding the definition of "affordability" will enhance your capacity to see the big picture like nothing else and is essential if you are going to make wise spending decisions. "Affordability" can only be determined based on the following two criteria:

a) Long-term Financial Goals

If you can achieve your personal long-term financial goals and spend money in this instance too, then you can "afford" it. Remember, in the absence of long-term financial goals, you will make financial decisions you cannot afford! For example, you might decide to buy a third car today at a cost of $20,000. You have the means to purchase the car and it seems harmless enough, right? Maybe not. Without looking at the big picture and your long-term financial goals, you might not see that you truly cannot afford the extravagance of this automobile because a $20,000 loan obligation today will rob you of all the interest you would have earned at retirement had you not obtained the loan in the first place. Remember the Time/Value of Money — purchasing the car will end up costing you $112,000 you could have had in your long-term savings for a later date when you really need it. Can you afford the car when you consider your long-term financial goals as part of the "Spending Decision"?

b) Opportunity Cost

The second way affordability must be determined is by being aware that spending money always comes at a cost — we call this "opportunity cost." This means that you only get to spend a piece of money once. If you choose to spend a dollar in one place, you will no longer have it to spend in another. Of course you can replace that dollar, but you will still only have one dollar, whereas you could have had two.

Let's suppose that you feel compelled to stretch your financial situation so you can get into the largest home possible. Can you "afford" to do so? Perhaps you can qualify for the loan, but does that mean you can really afford it? To determine that you must weigh the opportunity cost of purchasing the house. Let's take a look at Mark and Joyce's "Get Out of Debt Report" which we first introduced in Chapter 4 to get a better picture of what the actual opportunity cost of buying a new home might be.

Get Out of Debt Report

GET OUT OF DEBT REPORT
For: Mark & Joyce

Loan Description	Principal	Regular Payment	Power Payment	Interest Rate	Total No. Payments	Estimated Payoff Date
VISA	460.00	55.00	158.00	18.00	2	10/21/03
Medical/Dental	2,420.00	215.00	213.00	12.00	7	3/21/04
Auto	4,866.00	325.00	428.00	9.50	10	6/21/04
AT&T Credit Card	2,236.00	110.00	753.00	16.50	12	8/21/04
Furniture	6,000.00	220.00	863.00	12.00	16	12/21/04
Home	116,032.00	815.00	1,083.00	7.50	92	10/21/11
		1,740.00				

	Standard Debt Repayment-	29.5 Years	Accelerated Debt Repayment-	7.75 Years
Original Debt	132,014.00		132,014.00	
Total Payments	306,465.19		174,683.48	
Total Interest Paid	174,451.19		42,669.48	
Savings Balance	0.00		1,159,441.33*	

If you save 1,898.00 per month for 21.75 years at 7.00%

You can see from this report that because they are Powering Down their debt, that somewhere between now and age 65 Mark and Joyce are going to have more than $1 million available to them. Does that mean that they have enough money to buy a newer home twice the size of the one they are living in now? Yes, they can do whatever they want with more than a million dollars. But, if they choose to take $300,000 out of their accumulated savings and buy a new house, that will cause their savings to shrink to less than $300,000, decreasing the amount of cash available to them at the point when they had planned to stop working. If they spend the money on the house now, will they have money later when they want to travel around the world? If they buy it now could they be forced later to sell it because they can't afford it any longer? What will Mark and Joyce do then? Move into a tiny condo or worse yet, in with their children?

What we have found is that most people have trouble weighing the actual opportunity cost of the big-ticket items such as cars and houses. Imagine how hard it is for them to weigh the opportunity cost of more consumable, disposable goods about which they don't think they need to be so conscientious. But opportunity costs are just as important to consider when determining the affordability of a less expensive item as they are when deciding whether to purchase a new home. When we understand that everything we purchase has an opportunity cost attached to it, then we can make better spending decisions.

*Remember, you can have **anything** you want,*
*you just can't have **everything** you want.*

If you choose to spend money on consumable goods rather than using it to pay off debt or accumulate wealth, you must understand the consequences of that decision because it eliminates opportunities for the future. Affordability, then, can ultimately only be defined within the context of your long-term goals and opportunity costs.

To help you more consciously consider your long-term goals, recognize that almost everything you do will either move you towards your goals or away from them. The key is to prioritize the way you spend money so that you move toward your goals and eliminate those things that deter you from achieving them. For example, if you buy the jacket you saw in the mall without consciously asking yourself whether you can actually afford it based on your long-term goals and the opportunity costs, then you are at a moment in time where you are risking the chance to move closer to those goals. Almost every decision you make in life has its affect on your goals — the task is to recognize that the moment to make a decision has arrived and carefully consider it.

What is the best way to ensure conscious decision-making about your spending, future goals, and your overall big picture? Following are some strategies that might help you begin thinking about your short-term behavior as it relates to your long-term goals.

Develop a Master Plan

A Master Plan is like a "snapshot" in time, representing all that your financial life is comprised of today, and what its possibilities are for the future. In order to develop a Master Plan, you will need to:

1) Combine that which you already know about spending and borrowing (which includes creating a spending planner, tracking system, and debt payoff prioritization plans as we have already outlined) with long-range planning for the future (which includes setting long-term goals, developing savings and retirement plans, and projecting how taxes and inflation will affect the value of that retirement money over time). Using forecasting, planning, and tracking tools and seeking advice from qualified financial mentors will help develop this Master Plan.

2) Then, you will need to forecast what you must do today in order to achieve those future goals. Examining where you are today and what you want to do to get where you are going tomorrow is how a Master Plan can help you look at the big picture.

We have found that our clients, once they have a Master Plan in place, begin to get a real sense of what their financial future looks like. In the areas where they come up short they make plans to make up the difference. When people can see the reality of their retirement and their financial future as it's really going to be, they make serious changes!

A Master Plan is like the post

we mentioned at the end of Chapter 6. By having a post (or a Master Plan) in place, you can be tethered to your desired goals. Even as the winds of change blow you about and time carries you forward, you will still be tied to your desired end result. Without a Master Plan, you are tethered to nothing and the winds of change and the relentless march of time may carry you completely away from your desired goals altogether.

Now let's meet some individuals who did some long-range planning and forecasting in order to develop a Master Plan. See how taking a "snapshot" in time helped bring power and financial control into their lives.

Sherri Long: Planning for Retirement

Case History

Sherri Long* was a 45-year-old postal worker from Jacksonville, Florida. She had recently divorced and was very concerned about her big financial picture. She wanted to make sure that when she was 65, she would have enough in savings so that she could retire. We began working with Sherri using the Money Mastery Retirement Worksheet from the Master Plan software, which is shown on page 147.

The first section of this worksheet helped Sherri identify what she thought her retirement needs would be. At the time she was grossing $35,000 a year. She estimated that she would need about 80 percent of that to retire comfortably, which meant she would need $28,000 per year at 65, her desired retirement age. The worksheet further helped her assess what funds would be available to her in the future. She determined that she would be getting $13,300 from Social Security annually, a $5,000 per year company pension, and $2,400 from a duplex she owned, from which she collected a monthly rental fee of $200. When all of these outside sources of income were combined, Sherri found she would have $20,700 in annual income she could count on at retirement. This meant that she would be $7,300 short each year in order to reach her retirement goal of $28,000 annual income. With the help of the Retirement Worksheet, Sherri now realized that she must save a grand total of $161,330 by the time she reached age 65 in order to retire as she desired. Based on what she had already saved, she had to come up with a total of $141,330. After sub-

Money Mastery®

Principle #7 - Retirement Worksheet Report

This worksheet is designed for anyone to obtain a basic understanding of financial needs at retirement. The numbers and estimates will not be exact, but can be used as general guidelines toward retirement planning.

Retirement Needs

			Example	You	Spouse
1.	Enter your current annual income. This is your gross income, before taxes and other deductions.	1.	$35,000		
2.	Estimate the percentage of your income that you will need at retirement. This estimate should be between 70% and 90%. Enter the percentage on line 2.	2.	80 %		
3.	Multiply line 1 by line 2. This is your approximate annual needs at retirement. The higher the percentage in line 2 the more comfortable you will live at retirement.	3.	$28,000		

Retirement Income from Outside Sources

			Example	You	Spouse
4.	Enter the annual amount from Social Security. Use the Social Security Estimate worksheet on page 2. Enter the amount from line C.	4.	$13,300		
5.	Enter the annual income from company pension plans (not 401(k) or personal savings.	5.	$5,000		
6.	Enter other annual income (like rental income, annuity income, etc).	6.	$2,400		
7.	Add lines 4, 5, and 6. This is the total income received from outside sources for your retirement.	7.	$20,700		

Retirement Savings Goal - How Much You Will Need

			Example	You	Spouse
8.	Subtract line 7 from line 3. This is the amount of income you will need to generate from personal savings. If this number is less than zero, you have planned very well.	8.	$7,300		
9.	Use the Retirement Needs Table on page 2. Enter the total amount you will need from line F.	9.	$161,330		
10.	Enter the amount of your current savings balances for retirement. Include any savings accounts, IRA's, 401(k) balances, etc.	10.	$20,000		
11.	Subtract line 10 from line 9. This is the amount of savings you will need to accumulate by the time you retire.	11.	$141,330		

Annual Savings Amount

			Example	You	Spouse
12.	Use the Savings Factor table on the back to determine the savings factor for your retirement savings. Enter the factor here.	12.	0.034		
13.	Multiply line 11 by the savings factor on line 12. This is the annual amount you will need to save in order to maintain your desired standard of living.	13.	$4,805		
14.	Enter the amount your employer contributes to your 401(k) annually.	14.	$1,200		
15.	Subtract line 14 from line 13. This is the annual amount you need to be saving.	15.	$3,605		
16.	Divide line 15 by twelve to determine the monthly amount. Find room in your Spending Planner for this amount.	16.	$300		

Factors in this worksheet assume an average 4% inflation rate and a 5% growth rate during retirement. It is also assumed that the participant will live to age 90, which is longer than the statistical life expectancy, and that there will be no retirement money remaining for heirs.

tracting the $1,200 a year that her employer contributed to a 401(k), the Retirement Worksheet helped Sherri see that she would need to be saving $300 per month in order to reach her retirement goals.

Sherri was very pleased with these findings, and even though she realized she was quite short of the funds she would need to retire, she was excited to have a plan in place and that she was in control of it. Because of Principle 2, she knew how she could save $300 per month and now felt in charge of her future, which gave her much needed peace of mind.

*Names have been changed to protect privacy.

Joe Barcone: Funding Retirement

Case History

Joe Barcone* was from Des Moines, Iowa and was 49 years old when he became alarmed about how little money he would have at retirement. He had always planned on retiring at age 65, but had not put away any significant amount of money into a savings program. When his Money Mastery coach asked him to look at the big picture, he realized he was not in control of his smoking habit and the money it was costing him. As he kept track of his spending, he found that he was smoking three packs a day and it was costing him $251 per month. After looking at his situation closely, he realized that if he could stop smoking and put the $251 into a savings account every month for the next 14 years, he could accumulate more than $88,000 towards retirement. This motivated Joe and he immediately quit smoking. When he applied Principle 2 and Principle 7 he was able to make a major effort towards solving a big financial problem. That problem was one that he didn't even know existed until he stepped back and took a hard look at where he really was and where he really wanted to go.

*Names have been changed to protect privacy.

Both Sherri and Joe learned the value of developing a Master Plan, which is bringing more control and peace of mind into their lives than they ever thought possible. However, creating this kind of plan requires some tools, which up until now have been very limited. Most people do not own a financial calculator or know how to use one to figure the Time/Value of Money. Knowing how to calculate the numbers needed to predict the future can be very complex when such things as interest, growth, risk, maturity, and taxation must be considered. Fortunately, there are myriad of tools available today that make it easy for the average consumer to develop a Master Plan. The Retirement Worksheet that Joe and Sherri used, which is featured on page 147, is just one of the tools Money Mastery offers that makes master planning easy because it gives a greater view of what will be available at retirement. Use this worksheet to complete Challenge #7 at the end of this chapter.

Become Aware of Things that Can Affect the Master Plan

In addition to developing a Master Plan, another way to ensure that you are able to see the "big picture" is to become aware of those things that can affect your Master Plan and what you may need to do to adjust it in order to stay on track.

Changes to Social Security

Did you know that according to the Social Security Administration, by 2029 the Social Security trust fund will not have enough money to pay benefits to the wave of aging Baby Boomers? In 1951, there were 20 workers for every one person retired. Today there are 2.5 workers for every retiree. By 2015, the ratio will be 1 to 1.[5]

A *USA Today* article also states that by 2032 the entire Social Security fund will become totally insolvent.[6] Many people are baffled by this bankruptcy. They mistakenly think that their payroll taxes deducted for Social Security go into a personal account at the Social Security Administration, which will be paid to them as soon as they retire. This is not so. The *USA Today* article "For Boomers, Social Security Is Near Bust" explains: "What [payroll taxes] are not spent on benefits are used to buy Treasury bonds. That means the Social Security surplus is being loaned to the federal government to cover its other expenses."[7]

In other words, your FICA taxes are not being set aside for you. Instead they are being spent in other areas of government where policies on spending are not fiscally sound. That means that with the influx of Baby Boomers making huge draws on the system, if you will be 65 in the year 2032, you may not be able to count on any Social Security income at all. What will you do to make up for those lost funds? How will you modify your Master Plan to offset those losses?

If you, like many other Americans today, are planning to use Social Security as a default source of retirement income, perhaps it's time to rethink things, especially in light of the changes to the system which are sure to occur. According to Kenneth S. Apfel, former commissioner of the Social Security Administration, "Social Security can help support your family in the event of your death and pay you benefits if you become severely disabled. But it was never intended to be your only source of income when you retire or become disabled, or your family's only income when you die. Social Security supplements the income you have through pension plans, savings, and investments."[8] As we have already noted, it is important to know where you are on your financial map and where you want to go in the future so that you can revise the Master Plan in case these Social Security funds are not available to you at retirement.

Extended Life Expectancy

According to the article "Thirty Years of Retirement" by John Pierson:

It used to be that people retired at 65 and died by 72. Seven years of retirement. Not anymore. Thanks to advances in medicine, quite a few folks will live to a ripe old 85 or 90. Instead of seven years of retirement, many Americans can now look forward to 30 years of life after work. Thirty years! These words can strike terror into the heart...or joy. Joy for those who've planned fun things to do with the last third of their time on earth and have saved enough money to pay for them. Terror for those who haven't planned and haven't saved. As it happens, far too many people feel terror, or would feel terror if they only knew how ill-prepared they are for 30 years of retirement. Or for 20 years. Or for 10.[9]

How prepared will you be if you should live at least 30 more years after your desired retirement age? Because of medical intervention, it is possible that you will live much longer than your money will last. You must take this extended life expectancy into consideration and adjust your Master Plan to help prepare for the future.

Deteriorating Health

Although Americans are living longer, statistics show that the last ten years of a person's life are the most expensive because many times they are spent in a nursing home or long-term care facility. Close to 50 percent of all Americans will need long-term care at some point in their lives[10] because even though Americans live longer, their quality of life in the later years is not very good. Again, John Pierson puts it best in "Thirty Years of Retirement":

"By the time members of the Baby Boom generation have reached retirement, in about 2020, an average year in a nursing home will cost $160,000. Crushing expenses like that can soon destroy the best-laid retirement plans and nest eggs."[11]

Charles E. Gerrard, a financial adviser columnist, points out that we plan well for other risks and catastrophes, but we don't often think about planning for poor health in old age: "How does the risk of long-term care compare to other major risks that we insure against?"[12] asks Gerrard. Take a look at the following chart to see how he answers the question:

Home Fire	Auto Accident	Major Medical	Long-term Care
1 out of 1,200 homes	1 out of 240 automobiles	1 out of 15 people	*1 out of 4 people*

Obviously you can see from these figures that your risk of needing long-term care is much greater than an auto accident, for instance. Are you taking that risk seriously by making medical expense a part of your Master Planning? Many individuals are living on the edge financially, without adequate emergency reserves in case a catastrophic illness strikes or they need long-term care as they age. We have found that most people are able to manage financially from day to day, but if confronted by a major catastrophe, such as illness or injury, most are unprepared to handle the extra strain. This is illustrated by a 2005 Harvard study that links medical expense with bankruptcy. The study — "Illness and Injury as Contributors to Bankruptcy" — reveals that more than half of the bankruptcies filed in the United States each year are associated with medical expense and that close to 75 percent of those who filed because of medical debt were covered by health insurance.[13] This indicates that the coverage offered by many medical insurers is not enough to protect against serious illness and that out-of-pocket medical expenses are pushing many people over the edge.

Unfortunately, health is one aspect of our lives that is hard to control, especially as we age, so it's vital that you anticipate that your own health may deteriorate and take steps to plan for it.

Bad Investments

As we have already outlined in previous chapters, investing money in mutual funds and other ventures comes at a risk, and you may not always be able to predict how those investments are going to pay off. Naturally everyone makes mistakes and sometimes we may lose big on those bad investments. According to an article entitled "Ten Problems that Often Hit Investors if They Lose Track of the Big Picture" by Jonathan Clements, "investors often parcel out their dollars, without comparing the likely return from different investments. In pursuit of market-beating returns, many investors single-mindedly search for the best investments." Clements cites Pittsburgh financial planner, Jonathan Kuhn in the article as saying, "They [investors] look at one mutual fund or one stock at a time, rather than looking at the whole portfolio."[14] Other investments that may not always make sense include loading up on lots of stock of the company for which you work. If the company makes it big, then the payoff can be an important part of your retirement future. But if the company goes belly-up, you will have lost those funds that could have been invested in more stable options. Being aware of the many ways you can invest wisely will help you stick to your long-range goals and keep the Master Plan on track.

Disappearing Company Pension Plans

It wasn't long ago that most full-time employees could look forward to some sort of company pension at retirement. Those days are fast disappearing and for the most part are largely gone. That's because most employers can no longer afford the expense of paying retired employees a full pension with health insurance and other benefits. Today, most employers offer their employees the opportunity to contribute to their own retirement program through a 401(k) plan and will match any contribution to that plan up to 100 percent. If, at one time, you were counting on a company pension to fund your retirement and it has now been eliminated, you will need to revise your Master Plan to make up the difference. You can still make good headway towards saving for retirement (provided you are applying Principle 4 to power down existing debt) by taking full advantage of 401(k) programs. Unfortunately, many people do not see the value of these programs and are not contributing to them. Don't be one of them. While 401(k) contributions are certainly not the only way in which you should be saving for retirement, plan to offset any loss of pension plans by contributing enough to your company's 401(k) plan to get the maximum matching contribution from your employer. If you are self-employed, plan to contribute the maximum amount allowed by law into your IRA or Roth IRA accounts.

Other factors you may want to consider that can affect the Master Plan include inflation, life insurance proceeds that can be taxed, estate taxes, and changes to IRA plans.

The illustration below representing a river depicts why it is so important to adjust your Master Plan so you can always see the big picture. Let's say you are standing on the banks of this river at point "A." You wish to cross the river to reach a point marked "B" directly opposite of where you are standing. Although you will make efforts to cross the river by walking, swimming, or boating directly across to the other side, it is not possible to reach this point due to the river's current that pulls you slightly downstream, landing you further downriver at the point marked "C." To get to the point marked "B," you will need to adjust your plan by starting up stream from the point marked "A" just a bit farther. Although it is difficult to anticipate every factor that may pull you "downstream" and affect your long-term big picture, becoming aware of at least some of these factors will help you stay in control and on track.

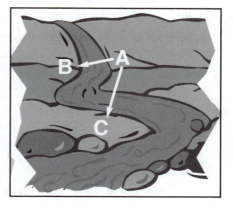

Most people spend more time planning a party or vacation than they do planning their lives. Don't be one of them. Take the following challenge so you can see your big picture more clearly.

✓ CHALLENGE #7: Plant the Master Plan "Post"

Stepping back to look at the big picture will be eye-opening. We can promise that if you will take a serious look at your long-term goals and analyze how your short-term behavior is affecting those goals, you will take even more control of your financial life. This will bring a sense of well being and peace of mind that you have never known before. To help you achieve that peace of mind, we challenge you this week to decide where you are on your financial map and where you want to ultimately go in the future.

1. Create a "Vision Statement" for your life. What is it that you really want to achieve overall, and what will you need financially to get there?

2. Review the following definition of "retirement" and record your feelings about what this means to you personally: *"Retirement" is the point at which you have enough passive income to wake up in the morning and elect to work or not.*

3. Reach out and plant the Master Plan "post" solidly into your financial ground by answering the following questions:

   a) At what age do I plan to "retire" (or have enough passive income to elect to work or not)?

   b) How much money do I want to receive each month at "retirement"?

   c) What plans do I already have in place that will help me receive my desired monthly retirement income?

4. Using the Money Mastery Retirement Worksheet on page 147, determine in what areas you fall short of your desired monthly retirement income. Consider what you may need to do to make up for any shortfalls. Visit http://www.moneymastery.com/Savings.aspx for more help on completing the Retirement Worksheet.

CHAPTER 8

Organize Your Finances
to Create More Wealth

W e invite you to begin this chapter with a moment of reflection. Think about the way you felt about your financial future before you began reading this book. Now, after learning 7 of the 10 Money Mastery Principles, consider your feelings today about your current financial situation and your retirement plans for the future. How have things changed? In our experience, once our clients get to this point, the synergistic nature of each of the Money Mastery Principles energizes and empowers them to take further control and brings more prosperity to their lives than they ever thought possible.

We are confident that you, too, are becoming more optimistic about your options for future financial success and security, including the opportunity to create more time and resources required to make your deepest desires a reality. With a "big picture" view of how everything can work together for your good when you apply each of the principles, you are now ready to embrace the next Money Mastery Principle. This principle will help you see the value of arranging and coordinating all aspects of your financial life so that you can keep more of what you make and create an optimum amount of new wealth.

Principle 8: Organizing Your Finances Enables the Creation of Additional Wealth

What does it mean to organize your finances in order to create more wealth? As you have gained greater control of your spending and borrowing and have begun planning and saving for the future, you have naturally been led towards more opportunities to create wealth. As this new wealth accumulates, your overall financial picture (though perhaps better understood by you now) is also becoming more complex. Without organization it is impossible to continue piecing that picture together because you will not understand how to order and control some of the complex issues that can surround wealth creation and retention within that big picture.

The following image of a "junk" drawer helps illustrate why Principle 8 is so important in light of everything else you have learned thus far.

If you're like most people, you probably have a junk drawer in your home where you keep odds and ends. You most likely store items in this drawer because you haven't decided where they really belong and figuring out where to put them is time-consuming. Consequently nothing in the drawer ever gets properly organized.

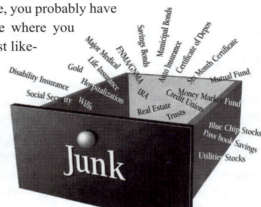

Most people have a "financial junk drawer" as well, like the one illustrated here. If you were to examine your own "financial junk drawer" what would it look like? Perhaps it would resemble this picture, where a mishmash of important financial and legal documents have been carelessly tossed. Like the junk drawer in your home, this "financial junk drawer" only exists because you haven't taken the time to order and arrange important financial issues or to sort and review documents as necessary.

Organize Your Financial Life

If you are going to continue piecing together your financial puzzle, you must adopt an organizational system that will help you arrange and order your financial affairs, including your wills, trusts, investments, assets, important financial paperwork, and other critical documents. Once a system is in place, disorganization and procrastination will diminish. You will then find it much easier to maintain that "big picture" view so you can better see how to create additional wealth.

Although you have just been introduced to the idea of organizing your finances, you've already begun practicing good financial organization by taking each of our previous seven challenges. For example, when you begin to understand your own feelings about money (Principle 1) you are actually getting mentally organized about your financial situation. When you track your money (Principle 2) you are implementing organization in a big way! Remember Stan Harbrecht, who until he became organized through tracking did not see the amount of money he was wasting on Big Gulps? When you spend your money into Emergency, Emotional, and Long-term Savings categories (Principle 3) you are implementing the kind of ordered financial organization that brings real peace of mind and long-term rewards. When you Power Down your debt (Principle 4) you are executing a very strict form of organization by prioritizing debt and working systematically to eliminate it, saving thousands of interest dollars. When you take the time to know the rules and are aware that they can change (Principles 5 and 6) you are mentally organizing the information you need to play complex financial games and come out the winner. And when you develop a Master Plan (Principle 7) and set measurable long-term goals, you are practicing one of the most important forms of organization, evaluating your short-term and long-term objectives so that you can accurately predict when you will have enough passive income to wake up in the morning and elect to work or not.

As you can see, organization helps you sort out complex emotional thoughts and feelings related to money. Organization helps you make good spending decisions. Organization helps you make good investment choices. Organization helps you get out of debt — quickly! Organization creates additional wealth because it helps you make the most out of the hard-earned assets you create through good long-term planning. Most importantly, organization gives you the ability to accurately predict what the future will look like, helping protect money from excessive taxation, theft, and loss, and opening up a host of opportunities for financial growth and prosperity that would never be available otherwise.

Once you have organized every other aspect of your financial life by following each of the seven preceding Money Mastery Principles, it is vital that you continue on that path in order to take full advantage of the wealth you create through organization. If you do not make the effort to do so, you will not be able to forecast how time will influence what happens to the value of your money, how taxes may eat into the worth of your assets, or how to make informed decisions that will allow you to keep the wealth you are building. A disorganized mind keeps people in poverty.

> *Without an organized approach, you will make*
> *financial decisions you will regret.*

Eliminating "financial junk drawers" so that you can create more wealth is an idea that needs more attention. Most popular financial leaders today claim the secret to financial control and wealth creation lies in making more money and investing in the stock market. But at Money Mastery we believe that fixating on a bigger income and on playing financial markets is like adding more "stuff" to the junk drawer rather than ordering and optimizing that which is already there.

Thomas J. Stanley, co-author of *The Millionaire Next Door*, makes a good case for this in his article for *Medical Economics* entitled "Why You're Not as Wealthy as You Should Be." Stanley's research indicates that of all the high-income occupations in the U.S., physicians are the worst at holding onto their money. "The fact that so many MDs are millionaires — by estimates printed in *Medical Economics* magazine (nearly 40 percent have a net worth of $1 million or more) — is a testament to how much doctors earn rather than how well they manage their money. Simply put, doctors could and should accumulate much more and at a much younger age but they don't."[1] Stanley also notes that after surveying people in posh neighborhoods across the country, he discovered something odd: "Many people who live in expensive homes and drive luxury cars don't really have much wealth. They may earn a fair amount of money, but they spend it all."[2] Stanley also points out in his article that if you make $1 million a year and spend $1 million, "you're not getting wealthier, you're just living high. Wealth is what you accumulate."[3]

Accumulating wealth requires financial organization because if you're not organized you won't be able to keep much of the money you make, regardless of how little or how great the amount may be. Although a higher wage certainly helps create greater opportunity to accumulate wealth and covers a multitude of mistakes, it doesn't automatically guarantee a person will be rich. It has been our experience at Money Mastery that high-wage earners are just as apt to create financial "junk drawers" as anyone else, becoming disorganized and unable to control some of the complex issues such as estate distribution, investment losses, and capital gains tax that surround financial planning and organization. Organizing how you spend and save the money you have already earned is the real secret to creating and retaining wealth.

Financial organization helps you learn how to get more
out of the money you already make.

Now let's meet a family whose financial disorganization and lack of planning made it impossible to control the complex issues surrounding the disbursement of assets during an estate settlement. See how this family lost more than just money because they had no organized plan for keeping highly valued and sentimental property safe within the family circle.

The Judds: Unable to Keep it All in the Family

 Sam and Janice Judd* had been married for 25 years and were parents of four children when their marriage finally broke apart. The Judds parted on friendly terms and decided that Janice would take the house, which had been Sam's childhood home. In exchange for the home and all furnishings and other assets that Sam left Janice, Janice would continue making payments on the home until the mortgage was paid in full. The house, besides having sentimental value for the Judd children and a 70-year history in the family, sat on over five acres

Case History

of prime property. Its real estate value was very high and all during the years that Sam and Janice had been married, a nearby developer had hounded the Judds to sell the house and property. The Judds always refused to sell to the developer, wanting to keep the house within the family and to possibly pass it on to their children. Because Sam and Janice had not taken the time during their marriage to do any financial planning or estate organization, when they divorced there was no plan in place to ensure that Janice would disburse of the house in due time in a way that would best suit their children. Within five years of the divorce, Janice remarried. Because she wanted to get on with her new life, she was anxious to get away from the old house where she and Sam had spent so many turbulent years together and where there were often sad and painful memories.

With a new husband and life, Janice no longer had a desire to be tied to the Judd family home in any way, even changing her desire to pass it on to her children. Janice hastily sold the house and property for almost half its market value to the same developer that had hounded her and Sam for over 20 years.

Within four years of her new marriage, Janice became ill and passed away. Janice had no will and proceeds from the sale of the Judd family home, which were being paid out yearly, were subject to probate fees and state and federal estate taxes. In addition, Janice's second husband inherited half of the remaining monies from the sale of the Judd family home that did not go towards paying the estate tax. The remaining half went to the Judd children, each of whom only received $3,000, when in fact they should have received a far greater sum due to the extremely high real estate value of the home. The Judd children, while not that interested in the actual monetary inheritance from their deceased mother's assets, were somewhat resentful over the loss of the home to a powerful developer. The sentimental value of the home, coupled with its tie to their father, continues to be a constant source of bitterness for the children.

*Names have been changed to protect privacy.

Of course Janice Judd did not set out to hurt her children, but because she and her first husband did not take time to plan and organize their financial and legal affairs during their divorce, their children experienced a great monetary and sentimental loss. All that regret could have been avoided with a little organization on the part of Sam and Janice Judd.

Why Don't More People Get Organized?

Naturally, financial organization makes sense. But why is it that so many people fail to do it? As we have already noted, many individuals simply do not want to face their own mortality or to take the time to sort through the issues surrounding their assets and liabilities. We have also found that people don't get organized because they simply do not know how! That's because many of the issues related to financial organization are emotional and the amount of energy and effort it will take to resolve these issues can sometimes seem overwhelming. Without an understanding of where to start the process, fear sets in, making it difficult to draw up a will or create a trust, for instance. Attorneys have reported to us that on average only two in seven families have a will made out in writing, and of those, only 20 percent are wills that have been updated in the last five years.[4] But how important is a will? As illustrated by the Judd family, if you don't have a will and you pass away, your assets will go to a court for processing (probate) and there will be fees and expenses that will come out of your assets to pay for this processing. In addition, if you leave minor children behind for whom you have not appointed a legal guardian through a will or trust, your children could end up wards of the state or worse yet, caught in a legal battle between family members who must decide how to provide and care for them.

Without the knowledge of how to start, where to turn for help, or what resources to utilize, many individuals go about handling all aspects of their lives without any semblance of organization, creating great stress and tension. Much of this tension is due to an inability to make decisions and resolve concerns. In *A Guide to Confident Living*, Dr. Norman Vincent Peale teaches that the main ingredient in tension is mental disorganization: "The mind refuses to make decisions about many different things and as a result always carries around numerous burdens, never really resolving any of them. The mind in this situation reacts somewhat like the body when shivering. One shivers when passing suddenly from a warm to a cold area; the body attempts to accommodate itself quickly to the sudden change in temperature. It has been estimated that as much energy is expended in a half-minute of shivering as in several hours of work. This results in depletion of vigor. In a similar way, shivering in the mind depletes its force when one fails to practice the fundamental principle of mental organization."[5]

We find that most people spend far more time worrying and stewing over financial planning and organization than necessary because they are in the process of this "mental shivering." Unfortunately, many people would rather spend time fretting than learning a few simple skills that will help them improve their situation. These same people are more comfortable with the stressful familiarity of their financial situation than in investigating how a slight modification in their behavior could create an even better economic outcome for them and their families. It goes without saying that if you take the time to get your spending and borrowing under control, then work very hard to build up a sizeable nest egg, you should also take the time and effort to learn how to protect that nest egg through good financial organization.

One of our clients we'll call Bob is an excellent example of how getting organized and implementing Principle 8 can help protect hard-earned money. As Bob reviewed his company pension plan, he found that the company was under no obligation to make a contribution to his pension if the company made no profits. Bob hadn't paid any attention to the annual reports in the past, but he now carefully reviewed each of them and found that the contributions to his retirement plan had been very small in three years out of five. If this trend continued, Bob knew he would have a very small accumulation at retirement. He approached his employer and inquired about the small contributions. "We're sorry, but we have not been very profitable and in the future it will be unlikely that the company will contribute any more than we have this year," his boss said. Bob realized he better examine all his options. In his case, he pressed for more income and got it. He then took this money and established his own retirement plan.

We've demonstrated the importance of getting organized, but perhaps you're thinking, "Well, I'd like to get my financial life in order, but I'm one of those people who just doesn't know how." Don't worry. Getting organized is easier than it seems and can bring tremendous rewards to your life.

Ideas for Good Financial Organization

Getting that "financial junk drawer" in order doesn't have to be difficult. Besides giving it the time it deserves, following are some basic ideas that will make organizing your financial life a little easier.

Get mentally organized. The first thing to consider when getting organized is your own mental state. Ask yourself if you are mentally disorganized or mentally calm. If you are a person who constantly "shivers" because you cannot make decisions about financial concerns, now is the time to learn how to organize your mind. Dr. Peale suggests an excellent way to do this:

> *Get the calm selective ability to take up one thing at a time and concentrate upon it. Deal finally with it, if possible before passing to the next matter. When you organize your mind, a sense of power will come to you, and you will soon wonder at the ease with which you can handle responsibilities. Your capacity for work will increase, so will your pleasure in what you are doing. Strain and tension will subside.*[6]

As Dr. Peale notes, the best way to begin getting organized is to calm your mind first by doing one thing at a time. Trying to tackle your entire financial situation in one sitting will simply overwhelm you. Organization requires patience and steady persistence, but it does not require that everything be done at once. Getting organized is like the man on an African safari who came across a pygmy who had just finished eating an elephant. "How on earth did you manage to do that?" the man asked. The pygmy replied, "I didn't swallow him whole, you know. I ate him one bite at a time!"

Know what to keep and what to throw away. After you have organized your own mental processes, you should next consider how to sort through important paperwork. Some people save almost everything they come across. Others can't stand to keep anything. But not saving and organizing the right documents can cost you and your family thousands of dollars. At the same time, preserving the wrong documents ensures that you'll go through life heavily burdened by worthless material. The American Institute for Economic Research published an article entitled "How to Avoid Financial Tangles" which gives important tidbits of wisdom on what you should keep and why.

> *The problem most of us face is the avalanche of paper we must deal with each year. What to keep and for how long? What you need to ask in order to decide what to keep is: Why am I keeping this? The second question you might ask is: What would be the worst thing that would happen if I did not have this and I needed it? And finally, is it likely that someone else will be keeping this record and could I get a copy of it if I needed to? There is only one fundamental reason to keep any given document: to prove something. Some things you might need to prove to yourself. What these are is left up to personal discretion....There is, however, far less flexibility and discretion for the things that you might be called upon to prove to others. These include records of payments and receipts, especially those that substantiate the legitimacy of exemptions, deductions, or credits taken on income tax returns. One broad category of things you need to keep is composed of items that you may need to refer to in order to prepare your tax return for the year.[7]*

Once you have determined what to keep so that you are not barraged by worthless material, you should organize important documents into a simple, yet efficient filing system. We have found that 95 percent of our clients when asked where they keep their automobile policy cannot accurately pinpoint where it is located in their house — 95 percent! That means that most people do not have a filing system by which they can quickly and easily locate all the important documents they may need at a moment's notice. We suggest filing paperwork using the following categories in the order they appear:

Automobile
Debt
Home Improvements
Income Tax
Investments
    Taxed
    Tax-Free
    Tax-Deferred
    Life Insurance
    Capital Gains
Medical/Dental
Miscellaneous
Property Tax
Utilities
Warranties
Wills/Trusts

Organize based on what's left after taxes. Once you have filed important documents in your home so that they can be easily located, it is important to go one step further by organizing all your financial assets. Most people have been taught to organize their investments using one of the following six criteria:

1. Risk of the investment.
2. Liquidity of the asset, i.e. how easily can I convert this asset to cash?
3. Timing, i.e. when will it be wise to sell this investment?
4. Valuation, i.e. dollar value.
5. Income of the asset, i.e. how much income does it provide me?
6. Taxation of the investment.

Of these six ways, we have found the most financially efficient way to order assets is based on the way they are taxed.

By suggesting this, we in no way wish to minimize the importance of organizing based on the other five criteria. But first ordering assets based on the way they will be taxed, and secondly based on the other criteria, makes predicting how much those assets will be worth much easier. While each individual's situation may vary according to risk, liquidity, timing, etc., everyone's situation is universal when it comes to taxation. Unlike the other criteria, taxation does not vary greatly depending on your individual circumstances. Taxation is definable and absolute.

The taxes we pay are demanded of us before we do anything else. That's why we teach our clients to organize their finances around what they get to keep after paying taxes. By doing so, it becomes easier to understand what you need to do to plan because you absolutely know what's going to be left over. If you organize based on risk, for instance, you may never be quite sure what you have to work with because that risk will always vary. But taxes are sure. By organizing based on taxation you can know either how to hold taxes to a minimum, thus keeping more of your wealth, or know how much money you will have left after paying taxes so you can feel free to work with the balance in order to create additional wealth.

To organize based on taxation, important documents should be ordered in what we call "Tax Drawers." Because there are only five ways you can be taxed, financial affairs should be organized based on the following five dimensions of taxation.

Drawer #1: Taxed – savings and checking accounts, reserve funds, etc.

Drawer #2: Tax-free –municipal bonds, Roth IRAs, etc.

Drawer #3: Tax-deferred – 401(k)s, IRAs, and so forth.

Drawer #4: Life Insurance – Life insurance is taxed differently than those items in Drawers 1, 2, and 3, and depending on how it is structured, it can be taxed in any one of the other three ways described above. For this reason it is organized into its own drawer for better efficiency in dealing with it.

Drawer #5: Capital Gains – real estate,

mutual funds, stocks that appreciate in value, fine art, precious jewelry, classically restored automobiles, antiques, stamp and coin collections, etc.

Organizing your financial assets into these five "Tax Drawers" will help you find a lot of extra money you didn't know you had and will help you more accurately predict the amount of passive income you will need to reach your long-term financial goals. How is this possible?

1. It makes it easier for you to visualize your assets in terms of what you get to keep for retirement.
2. It provides a basis for calculating and projecting the accumulation of your wealth.
3. It helps you understand the impact taxes have on long-term savings.

The following example illustrates the importance of organizing into "Tax Drawers." Suppose you put all your money in a 401(k) program for retirement. This money should grow depending on where you invest it because you will be able to defer paying taxes on it all those years you are working. However, when you begin withdrawing this money, 100 percent of it will be subject to income tax. If you organize your assets into the five "Tax Drawers" and use a forecasting tool like Money Mastery's Master Plan software, you will be able to play "what if" scenarios with your money. "What if" you put this money into a tax-free municipal bond rather than a 401(k) or capital gains account? "What if" you put it into a Roth IRA, or "what if" you put it elsewhere? Of all the tools available to get and keep oneself organized financially, a forecasting device that can help project your debt, income, and assets over time is among the most valuable.

Staying organized is a function of being able to sweep
all financial elements (spending, borrowing, saving, and taxation)
to a future date and evaluate the results.

By doing this, it is easy to play "what if" so that you can test how a financial decision made today will impact your future. Using organizational and forecasting tools can help you determine the best way to accumulate money so that you can maximize your assets. And since there are no future decisions, only decisions made today that affect the future, this knowledge allows you to make much better choices. You can make the necessary changes today and not get down the road and have to look back and say "Oh, I wish I had known!"

Now meet Susan, a woman whose husband could not see how his actions would affect his family over time because he did not properly organize his life insurance. Susan and her husband Bob had set up a trust and conveyed most of their assets to it. Each would be the beneficiary of the trust if one of them died. After their deaths, the trust assets would be used for the education and support of their minor children until the children were 35, at which time they would receive their inheritance outright.

When Bob completed life insurance forms at his place of employment, he named as beneficiaries "my wife and children." Bob was killed in an on-the-job accident soon after. His company insurance totaled $600,000, and although Susan expected to inherit all of it and manage it for herself and her two teenage sons, she was shocked to find that because Bob had named "my wife AND children" as beneficiaries, Susan was only entitled to one-third of the proceeds. Her two sons were entitled to the other two-thirds. Because they were minors, Susan had to become appointed by the court as custodian for her sons' $400,000 and manage it under strict court supervision. She was also dismayed to learn that when her sons turned 18, they would be entitled to receive their money to spend as they chose. Bob's lack of care in naming his beneficiaries left a large sum of money in the hands of his children instead of his wife.

Take advantage of estate organizing tools. As we have already noted, creating and retaining additional wealth can be complex. Estate and asset organizational tools can help manage that complexity. Look for an estate planning and financial organizing system that is designed to help you easily order and store, in one place, all essential information and copies of wills, trusts, and important documents that you'll need to manage the major financial events in your life. At your death, using such a system, your heirs should be able to easily find all the necessary documents and financial information they'll need to quickly and inexpensively settle your estate. Once you have gathered all pertinent information into a good estate planning system, you are then prepared to meet with a qualified estate-planning attorney. Using a quality estate organizer will give you easy access to all the information you will need, assuring the most cost effective meeting and keeping the time you need to retain a lawyer to a minimum.

When looking for a good organizational system, make sure to select one that not only helps you collect and organize everything you will need to manage your estate, but will also help you organize all areas of your financial life. Such organizers will include sections for planning and organizing how you spend, save, pay down debt, pay taxes, and run small business operations. Select an organizer that includes checklists, storage, and helpful tools for each of these areas. To get an idea of what kinds of things to expect from a financial organizer, review the contents page of the Money Mastery Master Planner located on page 170.

What happens when we don't use planning tools like the Master Planner Organizational System? A man we'll call Frederick declined to use the Master Planner as had been recommended to him saying, "I've already got a great organizational system that I'm sure will help my family when I die." When he did pass away, his "great organization system" had little of the information the family really needed. His daughter, inexperienced in settling an estate, spent countless hours listing assets, getting appraisals, and updating financial information — much of which could have been expedited by proper completion of the Asset Schedules in the Master Planner. Was this costly? Her accountant and the estate planner estimated that the settlement costs could have been reduced by thousands of dollars had proper financial information been maintained by her father. Because Frederick didn't feel the need to do estate planning and organization while he was still alive, his daughter was burdened with doing it later.

And what about getting organized in order to avoid the legal and emotional battles family members may wage over your health and well being if you are ever incapacitated? A good organizational system will prompt you to put in order all required legal documents, including a medical power of attorney and living will, necessary to protect you in case of physical or mental incompetence.

Dan Sorenson* is an example of one of our clients that understood the power of proper organization. As he learned about Principle 8, he began organizing all his assets according to the five "Tax Drawers" and then fur-

🐦 Money Mastery®
Master Planner
Comprehensive Annual Organizational System

Overview of the Master Planner Sections and Contents

Introduction
How to use the Master Planner
How Money Mastery® Works

Section 1: Money is Emotional
Checklist of action items for Principle 1
Self-discovery questions
Sample Spending Planner
Spending Emotion Q&A

Section 2: When You Track You Control
Checklist of action items for Principle 2
Tracking observations form
Dealing with a variable income

Section 3: Saving Is Delayed Spending
Checklist of action items for Principle 3
3-Category savings observations
Wealth accumulation account
Case studies

Section 4: Power Down Your Debt
Checklist of action items for Principle 4
How interest expense multiplies
Case studies

Section 5: Know the Rules
Checklist of action items for Principle 5
How Much Risk? form
First Things First
Suggested reading list

Section 6: The Rules Are Always Changing
Checklist of action items for Principle 6
Risks that change can bring
Case studies

Section 7: Always Look at the Big Picture
Checklist of action items for Principle 7
Big Picture observations
My financial map
Predicting purchases
Money Mastery Retirement Worksheet

Section 8: Organizing Wealth Creates More
Checklist of action items for Principle 8
What to keep and what to throw away
Money Mastery Life Insurance Calculator
Tax Drawers
Subsection 8: Personal Organization
Personal & family information forms
Personal and family medical records
Personal and family history outline
Subsection 8: Estate Organization
How to organize your estate
Asset schedules
Real property
Cash accounts
Life insurance
Homeowner/Auto/Medical Insurance
Retirement benefits
Personal Net Worth Summary
Estate planning & distribution guide
Subsection 8: Estate Settlement
How to settle your estate
Estate settlement checklist
Death notification
Funeral and burial arrangements
Incapacitation
Legal instruments (wills/trusts)

Section 9: Understanding Taxation
Checklist of action items for Principle 9
Accumulation stage taxation explanation
Form 1040 and Schedules A, C, and K
Subsection 9: Business Organization
Separating business from yourself
How to set up a business checklist
Legally structuring your business
Accounting procedures and terms
Business tax deductions list

Section 10: Money in Motion
Checklist of action items for Principle 10
Creating a surplus of money
Principle 10 leverage ideas

ther arranged his important documents using the Master Planner. While reviewing his various titles, deeds, and contracts, he came across his home deed and noticed it had never been legally assigned to him. The home that he lived in had been built in the 1860s and had been handed down to members of his family from generation to generation. Around 1920, it was sold to someone outside the family. Later, Dan arranged to buy the house back and raise his own family in it, never realizing that the deed hadn't been signed over to him.

Dan sought legal counsel and an attorney ended up charging him a little over $5,000 so the home could be reprocessed and recorded properly at the county seat. The man who had previously owned the house was now 92. The attorney mentioned to Dan as they completed the transaction that if Dan had not been able to accomplish the transfer before the 92-year-old man had died, it would have taken nearly five years to clear the title at an expense of well over $15,000. Because Dan took the time to begin organizing his assets and estate documents he saved himself a lot of trouble and several thousand dollars.

* Name changed to protect privacy.

When we get organized we find that emotional issues can arise and we learn many things about ourselves and our financial situations that we didn't previously know. This knowledge, while eye-opening, can also be very encouraging, building a motivating fire underneath us.

Hold annual reviews. It is always a good idea to hold an annual review of every area of your financial life, including your spending plans, debt elimination plans and schedules, and your Master Plan and long-term retirement plans. In addition, it is also important to review paperwork related to your estate distribution, vital documents such as wills and trusts, and asset schedules to be sure they are in order. Set a specific time to hold this meeting with yourself and/or your companion once each year. It may be a good idea to hold it on your birthday or at the first of the calendar year so that you don't forget it. Using an organizing system like the Master Planner, begin gathering all the important papers for each of the sections within the organizer. For example, one year you may want to complete and/or update the personal and family information section by gathering dates, household information, medical records, and family histories. Another year you may want to concentrate on life insurance, will preparation, trusts, etc.

Holding annual reviews can save thousands of dollars and maximize the wealth you have already created. Take for instance Laurel, who was browsing the index in her Master Planner during an annual review when she remembered her father telling her 30 years earlier that he had some stock set aside for her. She had forgotten all about it, but did some checking and found the certificates. Laurel took the certificates to a brokerage house, which determined the stocks had a value of $45,000. Because Laurel took the time to hold an annual review, her memory about the stocks was triggered and she was able to retrieve the money from the certificates to use as a down payment on a new house.

Another client, we'll call Harold, began reviewing all insurance policies on his house, cars, and professional practice during an annual review. He then took the policies to his Money Mastery coach who pointed out that Harold no longer needed half the insurance he was carrying. Eliminating this insurance saved Harold over $7,000 annually in premiums.

George Briggs* had tried to be careful in the way he had organized the disbursement of his assets through a well-planned will. Unfortunately, George had inadvertently disinherited his own children when he titled his assets for the children in "joint tenancy" with Joan, his second wife. When George died, Joan, being the surviving joint tenant on the assets, became the sole legal owner. It didn't matter that her late husband's will left his assets to his children — the wording of the jointly titled assets prevailed over the wording of George's will. Because Joan despised the Briggs children, she instructed her lawyer to transfer all of the newly acquired inheritance from George's assets to a living trust she had created for her own children from a previous marriage. "George's children always treated me like the Evil Stepmother, and I don't want them to get anything!" Joan told her lawyer. Ethically bound to be Joan's advocate, the lawyer did as she was instructed. When Joan died, George Briggs's legacy did not get passed on to his own children; instead, it went to the children of his second wife, leaving the Briggs family with nothing. Although Joan's lawyer felt bad about the outcome, the law was clear. Even though the Briggs children hired an attorney, they ended up empty-handed. If George Briggs had been better organized, he would have learned that the way assets are titled at death determines who inherits those assets. If he had held an annual review of his important documents, George might have caught the dangerous wording in his will and changed it in order to protect his children.

* Names changed to protect privacy.

Be Aware of Things that Can Affect Your Estate Organization

Becoming organized and staying that way not only requires a good estate organizing system, but also demands that you be aware of those things that through change, can affect your assets over time. By applying Principles 5 and 6 you can stay ahead of any changes that may affect your ability to keep and maximize wealth by becoming informed and staying that way. Following are just some of the things that can affect your estate planning and organization:

- Changes in estate tax laws
- Changes in capital gains tax laws
- Tax laws that affect real estate purchases
- Newly created retirement accounts
- Living trusts, wills, and probate
- Changes to marital status
- Health and medical issues
- New asset purchases

By implementing Principle 8 you can keep more of your assets secure. We can promise that if you get organized, you will see financial rewards you never thought possible and you will thank yourself later for having the forethought to plan ahead. More importantly, your loved ones will be grateful to you for caring about them enough to plan for their future through solid organization. If you haven't done so already, decide today to put your financial affairs in order!

✓CHALLENGE #8:
Implement a Financial and Estate Organizing System

We challenge you this week to obtain a comprehensive financial and estate organizing system. We recommend a comprehensive system that includes everything you will need to get fully organized in each of the four areas of personal finance: spending, borrowing, savings, and taxes (including a section on business organization and estate organization and settlement). Once you have a good financial/estate organizer, take the challenge to do the following:

1. Review financial documents that you are still unsure about and identify areas that need greater clarification. Seek professional counsel about these issues.

2. Review each of your current savings and investment programs and determine if they are taxed, tax-deferred, or tax-free.

3. Begin organizing each of your savings accounts, life insurance policies, and capital gains items into the five "Tax Drawers."

4. Begin completing asset schedules for the assets that comprise your estate (i.e. real property, cash accounts, investments, life insurance, vehicles, retirement benefits, etc.).

5. Summarize the worth of your assets to get a better idea of your personal net worth.

CHAPTER 9

Understand Taxation to Keep More Money

Having come this far, you should be astounded by the way your financial life is being transformed into one with the potential for creating an abundance of time and resources. There is still more work to do, but you are well on your way to achieving goals that you probably thought were impossible only a few short chapters ago. By now you should be in better control, better informed, better prepared, and a whole lot more organized. By ordering your assets, wills and trusts, and other important financial papers, and organizing your investments into the five tax drawers we outlined in Chapter 8, you're now ready to take the last few steps towards complete money mastery. To do this, consider carefully the ninth Money Mastery Principle that deals with the subject of taxation and the serious impact it has on your financial well being.

Principle 9: Understanding Taxation Allows You to Keep More of Your Money

As we mentioned in the Introduction, Excessive Taxation (along with Consumerism and Indebtedness) is a force at work in the world today that you must learn to control if you want to create or maximize any kind of wealth. It goes without saying that taxes are a huge part of our lives and have a pervasive affect on everything we do. Not only do they have an impact on how much money we keep, but they also affect what we can and

175

cannot do with that money. Almost all Americans* pay a fortune in taxes over a lifetime, but most don't fully understand the true extent of their tax bill. Consider the following illustration of this massive tax obligation.

First, we must pay income taxes, both federal and state. The amount Americans pay in this category is extensive, especially when you consider that those taxes are being collected for close to 40 years.

Add Medicare, Medicaid, and FICA (Social Security). When these taxes are added to income tax, the average American is required to work until approximately June 3 of every year for the government before they can begin earning any money they can keep for themselves.

Next, add to these taxes the burden of property tax on homes and cars, along with federal estate tax, and state inheritance tax. When you combine these with all the other taxes, some Americans are paying as much as 55 percent of their annual income in taxes!

Don't forget the quiet taxes that slip in unnoticed: sales tax, use tax, gasoline tax, import tax, and excise tax.

Finally, add to all of these

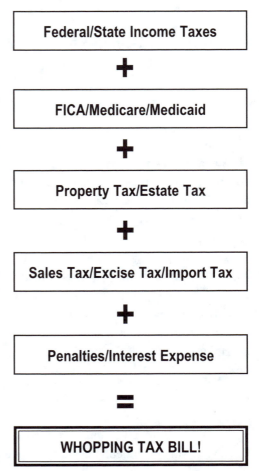

* It is recognized that the principles and strategies that are being treated herein are applicable to both U.S. and Canadian citizens; while there are minor differences the basic principles still apply to both countries. For more information on Canadian tax law and the Canada Customs and Revenue Agency (CCRA) contact Money Mastery: (888) 292-1099 or the Tax Reduction Institute at (800) 874-0829.

taxes the penalties (which are also a tax) and interest expense for late fil-ing and excess distribution from retirement plans.

What do you get? A staggering tax bill that makes it very hard for the average American to get ahead!

This gigantic tax bill now exceeds what most Americans pay for food, clothing, housing, and transportation combined![1] Hard to believe, isn't it? Most people have no idea how much they are actually paying in taxes. In addition, they have no idea how taxes affect every other area of their finan-cial life, including their spending and borrowing, and especially their sav-ings. How income is taxed at the payroll level affects how we can spend money now. How we are taxed at the cash register when we purchase goods and services affects whether we will be able to purchase more goods and services later and whether we will have the financial wherewithal to obtain loans for future goods we may need to buy. How our assets and investments are taxed affect how much money we can save and whether that money will be available in the quantities we assume it will be when we need it for retirement or for the benefit of family members. How we are taxed affects the type of cars we can afford to drive, the size house we can get into, the type of vacations we can go on. It affects the amount of money we can put away for kids' college education, whether we will have any-thing after 40 years of working to show for all our efforts, and a whole host of other issues.

Taxation affects everything we do, and yet many individuals do not understand just how pervasive its influence on their finances can be. Even though taxes are the first thing we must pay, it seems that the only time most Americans give taxes any real consideration is around April 15 when they must file their income tax returns. But as we have already pointed out, income tax is only a small portion of the tax burden we are currently bear-ing. The following quote by the 17th century French finance minister, Jean Baptiste Colbert, very aptly sums up the subtle ways that taxes are exact-ed from us:

"The art of taxation consists in so plucking the goose as to obtain the largest amount of feathers with the smallest amount of hissing."

Why is it that our feathers are being plucked so extensively? Based on our work with thousands of clients, we believe it's because most people have bought into a host of dangerous tax myths that keep them perpetually yoked to a relentless tax machine.

Tax Myths

Rather than "hissing" at government, which some preach as the answer to the tax problem, the objective of Principle 9 is to help dispel these myths and motivate you to spend the time and effort necessary to understand taxation so that you can learn how to keep the government from plucking as few of your feathers as possible.

Let's take a look at some of these tax myths:

Myth #1: A huge tax bill is inevitable and inescapable.

This pernicious myth has evolved over the years due to the continual expansion of government, which has required more taxes to sustain its girth. As we have already mentioned, taxes have become the largest expense for most people, exceeding what they pay for food, clothing, housing, and transportation combined. While many people grumble over the high cost of taxes, few seem to question what they can do about it, assuming they must pay such ridiculous sums of money. The truth of the matter is the IRS gets away with taking far more money from you than is required by law simply because you don't know any better. This chapter and the subsequent chapters in Part II will help you learn the rules you need to know to escape an unnecessarily large tax burden.

Myth #2: A large and complex government supported by citizen tax dollars is necessary.

Through an attitude of "entitlement" many Americans are unknowingly subjecting themselves to larger and larger tax burdens. As we have already noted, over the last 65 years, post-Depression generations have held their hands out in expectation, demanding more services and greater benefits from government than at any other time. But tax-supported social programs are getting harder to fund as more people sag under the financial burden of such programs. Now is the time to ask yourself if you can really afford to continue believing the myth that a large and complex government is necessary, especially when it is getting increasingly more difficult to support it. Abandoning an attitude of "entitlement" and embracing the Money Mastery Principles that promote self-reliance and self-control will go a long way towards reducing overall tax burdens.

Myth #3: Questioning the system and trying to take the most advantage of it increases my chances of getting audited.

This is absolutely untrue. The people that believe this myth only do so because they don't know about all the "good" tax laws and are therefore living in fear of the IRS. Remaining in the dark about tax law and just paying what you think you must pay without learning what is really expected might seem like the "safe" path to take, but it's actually a foolish one. By applying Principle 5, you no longer need to cower in fear — knowing the rules changes everything because it puts you in control.

Myth #4: My tax refund gives me extra cash I can use to purchase things I've been waiting for all year.

Because automatic payroll tax withdrawal has become so common-place, most people don't ever think to question the way they are taxed at this level, defaulting to the notion that it's acceptable to have a large amount of income tax withdrawn from their paycheck each month. "After all," they reason, "I'm going to get most of it back at the end of the year." Many people look forward to their tax refund as some sort of "rebate" or "gift" the IRS is giving back to them without considering that the government has had use of their money all year, preventing them from using that cash to make themselves even more. Instead of waiting on the IRS for the use of your own money, it's always best to have access to as much of it as possible throughout the entire year by ensuring that you do not have too much income tax withheld from your pay. Turning more of your money over to the IRS than is necessary, to use interest-free for 12 months, is foolish. Paying only as much income tax as you are required by law throughout the year, even if that means being prepared to pay a little more on April 15 to meet your tax obligation, is the smart way to manage your finances. This gives you control over your money and lets you have more available cash that you can use to pay off debt, invest in your future, and so forth. In addition, by expecting a tax refund in one lump sum at the end of the year, most people are tempted to spend that money on disposable consumer goods they've been waiting to purchase all year rather than increasing savings or paying off debt. (Refer to Appendix B for information on how to properly calculate your W-4 withholding.)

Myth #5: My accountant takes care of my taxes

As we noted in the Introduction, this is the most pernicious tax myth of them all. It is also one of the worst wealth killers and makes more money for the IRS than anything else. Believing such a myth is like eating nothing but fat-fried foods, ignoring the symptoms of heart disease, and then going to your doctor and expecting him to make you well. Likewise, if you don't know the rules for good "tax health," you can't go to your accountant and expect him or her to save you thousands of dollars in taxes at the end of each year. If you don't know what to tell your accountant by December 31, there is very little he or she can do for you. In addition, accountants will usually err on the side of conservatism with regard to deductions in order to avoid the severe IRS penalties that they will incur if they wrongfully counsel their clients. This protects their pocketbook but not usually yours. If you want to stop wasting money on excessive taxes, it is up to you to learn the rules and make sure your accountant helps you take full advantage of them. If you believe that your accountant takes care of your taxes, you will end up paying more to the government than even it requires!

Remember, your accountant is only as good as you are.

This does not mean that we are dismissing professional advisors because, as we have already counseled there are numerous times when we cannot function without their expertise. But you can save yourself a lot of money by knowing the rules and what you personally need to understand about your own situation so that your accountant can help you save every tax dollar possible.

Which of these tax myths are keeping you in a cycle of Excessive

Taxation? If you want to keep more of the money you make and prevent as few feathers as possibly from being plucked, you must see the futility of such myths and get out from underneath them.

In addition to this, if you want to keep more of the money you make, you must understand more fully how it is taxed today, tomorrow, and even after you die. To do this, let's examine each of the life phases you will pass through and how your money is affected by taxes within each of these stages.

Accumulation Stage

During this stage, a person usually works 40 or so years to provide for his own needs and the needs of his family. If you are still in this stage, you spend the majority of your time working to earn money. During this stage, you should be applying all of the Money Mastery Principles we have covered in previous chapters in order to keep as much of that money as possible. If you are, we can guarantee that you are amassing far more wealth than you ever have before because you are in control. But now it's time to take things a step further by understanding how taxation can affect how much of this accumulated money you actually get to keep. To do this, you must understand that in the Accumulation Stage, your money is taxed in one of two ways:

1. **The W-2 System:** This system of paying income taxes is for W-2 employees who work for an employer. Most people fall into this category. The taxes on W-2 income are easy to calculate because they are automatically withheld from a paycheck. Under this system, there are certain tax deductions that are allowed when filing the standard 1040 tax form. These deductions are provided for on Internal Revenue Service form "Schedule A."

2. **The Self-employed System:** The second system for paying income tax is prescribed for the self-employed. These individuals use IRS form "Schedule C" to determine taxable income. This Schedule C allows for business expenses to be deducted before taxes are figured. When a person uses Schedule C, the rules allow for many more deductions than

are listed on Schedule A. In fact, self-employed taxpayers get to take deductions before they figure out various taxes, such as Social Security. This is different from employees who are taxed on dollar one. After a self-employed individual uses Schedule C, they still get to itemize their deductions on Schedule A (just like W-2 employees) before calculating their income tax.

Schedule C: Expense Section

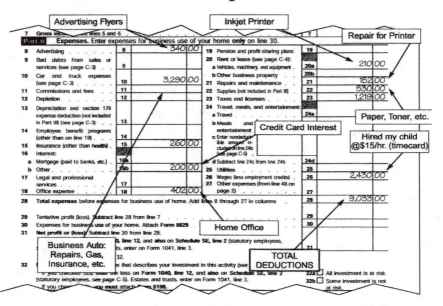

Example: On Schedule A, medical expenses must exceed 7.5 percent of adjusted gross income before you can deduct these expenses. However, the self-employed are allowed to deduct 100 percent of all medical expenses if they have provided for them on line 13 of Schedule C. Many kinds of expenses that cannot be deducted on Schedule A are deductible on Schedule C.

If W-2 employees knew how to move normal expenses to Schedule C, thus making them tax deductible, they could keep more of their money. If you take advantage of the self-employed tax system, you could put an extra $2,000 to $5,000 in your pocket every year. That also applies to self-employed people who rarely take full advantage of all the business expense deductions available to them through Schedule C.

If you are not self-employed you may be asking how it's possible to take advantage of the self-employed system. It's simple — the tax rules allow for it! The reason most W-2 employees don't use this system is because they don't know that the rules allow any person, even those who are W-2 employees, to take deductions using Schedule C.

Don't miss out on this valuable tax saving point: All W-2 employees can make use of the powerful deductions on Schedule C.

To the extent that you take advantage of this rule, you could be deducting anywhere from $3,000 to $19,000 in expenses. Let's take a look at some of the misconceptions that most W-2 employees have about the Schedule C system that keep them from taking full advantage of it:

Misconception #1: I am not self-employed. Many W-2 employees don't think they can use the Schedule C system because they incorrectly presume that they are not self-employed. What we tell our clients is that there are many hobbies and activities they are already engaging in that could be converted to a viable business venture if they would consider them as such (just as long as they run their business like a business and not like a hobby). Here's an example of a Money Mastery client who learned how to take advantage of the self-employed tax system by examining their own lifestyle for tax-saving opportunities.

Perry & Michelle Kamboris: Becoming "Self-employed"

Case History

Perry and Michelle Kamboris* were from a small Midwestern town and liked to go boating at many different lakes and reservoirs with their two registered Husky dogs. The couple loved meeting new people and making friends from all parts of the country. After learning about Money Mastery Principle 9 and the significance of Schedule C, the Kamboris' immediately applied this new information to their travel lifestyle. They realized that their knowledge and interest in Huskies, along with their love of travel, could be turned into a "self-employment" business opportunity.

They arranged for a referral fee with the same person from whom they bought their dogs to begin promoting the sale of the Husky breed while on their boating trips. They then took pictures of their dogs and prepared an inexpensive advertising flyer that they placed on all windshields of the trucks at the boat docks wherever they went boating. The response was overwhelming! They not only made some money on the referral fee, but because they were running a small side business, they were able to deduct the veterinarian bills on their dogs, travel expenses for their boating trips and even the food for their Huskies on Schedule C. Veterinarian's bills alone for their two dogs averaged $300 each month and the travel expenses to various lakes and reservoirs were sizable. Combining these Schedule C deductions with all their other deductions, Perry and Michelle began saving $300 on their taxes each month. By putting this saved tax money into a retirement savings plan, the Kamboris' will have nearly $178,000 extra interest income in 25 years simply by forming a viable small business.

"We were thrilled when we actually saw the results of our actions on paper," said Perry. "We had no idea that developing our hobby with the dogs into a little part-time business venture could bring such valuable dividends. Plus we love going out on the boat and meeting new people anyway. To us it was a no-brainer!"

*Names have been changed to protect privacy.

The Kamboris' little "self-employment" opportunity took very little of their time to operate and brought tremendous tax savings to their family. Since they were already heavily involved in the Huskies as a hobby, it seemed only logical to them to take advantage of that interest by converting it into a legitimate business and then into a viable tax write-off. If you are a W-2 employee and think that you cannot be "self-employed," it's time to think again.

If you don't have a side business, it's time to start one!

Important Note: The IRS expects all business operations to be run with an honest expectation of profit and that business expenses be ordinary, necessary, reasonable, and directly related to the business, and that any tax deductions be documented correctly. How to launch a new business and take advantage of all the tax write-offs a self-employed person is entitled to will be covered in complete detail in Part II of this book. Please be sure to refer to it after reading Chapters 9 and 10.

Misconception #2: I can only deduct expenses up to the amount of income I made in my self-employed activities. This is false. You do not have to make a profit in order to take advantage of Schedule C deductions. While the IRS does expect you to operate your business with the honest expectation of making a profit, it also understands that in the first year or so you might have losses. In fact, if your business generates a loss, you can use that loss against any form of income such as dividends, wages, pensions etc. If your loss exceeds your income, you can carry back business losses two years and get a refund from both federal and state taxes for the past two years or you can carry forward all business losses up to 20 years! And did you know that expenses for advertising, car and truck maintenance, commissions and fees, insurance, legal and professional services, office equipment, supplies, travel, meals, utilities, and entertainment can all be deducted from the self-employed activities you itemize on Schedule C, regardless of whether you turn a profit or not? These Schedule C deductions can also affect W-2 income, reducing the overall taxes paid as a W-2 employee. In Part II, we will show you all the airtight ways to take these business deductions using Schedule C. Using a tax diary, we'll explain how to keep accurate substantiation records that are IRS bullet-proof.

Misconception #3: I feel like I am cheating by taking deductions for simple activities I was going to pay for anyway. This, too, is an incorrect assumption. The tax laws provide for these deductions, even if you were "planning to do them anyway." As was illustrated by the Kamboris', it makes no difference where the source of "self-employment" comes from, the tax laws provide for those deductions. Even though the Kamboris' were going to travel around and show their Huskies to new friends and acquaintances "anyway," they might as well have used that time and those resources to conduct a viable business, make a little extra money, and thereby take advantage of available tax write-offs. The tax laws that allow for those simple activities to be deducted are available to all who will learn them and apply them appropriately. Naturally there are certain requirements in order to consider activities as viable business ventures and to claim deductions from Schedule C, as noted previously. But the law is very clear about the required protocols, making it possible for anyone to take advantage of these laws. (Please refer to Chapter 13 in Part II for information on how to properly structure and set up a business.)

One of our clients we'll call Karen dried flowers as a hobby. After learning the value of Principle 9, she decided to turn this hobby into an actual business. She set up a separate bank account and obtained a business license from her city government. Today Karen makes a few sales per month, and although her business is not a large source of income for her and her husband, Karen is making extra money and now writes off all her flowers and drying chemicals on Schedule C. She is able to continue developing her skills in flower arranging while enjoying some added income and saving valuable tax dollars all at the same time.

Misconception #4: I don't want to trigger an IRS audit. This is another naive comment we often hear. People incorrectly assume that if they take the deductions allowed on Schedule C and then have a big loss, that this will spur the IRS to come after them. Not so. As long as you know the rules and apply them fairly, there will be no problem. The way to legally and ethically pay taxes while taking advantage of tax laws for the self-employed is fully covered in Part II of the book.

From each of these examples it is clear that these fearful misconceptions are the product of ignorance about the real tax laws and how they work. There are numerous ways to minimize the amount of feathers plucked from you during the Accumulation stage if you will only take the time to learn about them. Once again, we strongly encourage you to explore the detailed treatment of these tax-saving strategies in Part II of this book.

Conservation Stage

After a person spends 40 years earning money during the Accumulation stage, they eventually begin to slow down and prepare for retirement. This retirement period is called the Conservation stage. If you are no longer accumulating money, you are now using that which you have already saved as a means of support. As we mentioned in Chapter 7, because people are living longer most individuals will need at least 20 years of funds in order to live comfortably during this stage — some may even need money for as long as 30 years. But knowing how to project into the future how much your assets will be worth so you will have this 20 to 30 years of income can be difficult. Predicting how much your assets will grow, how much risk will be carried with each investment, and how inflation will affect those funds can be hard. Not only will each of these factors influence your assets over time, but trying to predict how taxes will influence the overall worth of your investments can also be tricky. Following is a common example used by industry experts to examine the value of investments.

Let's suppose you invest $10,000 for 40 years in a long-term savings plan that receives an average annual rate of return of 12 percent. At the end of 40 years you will accumulate $930,000 right? Wrong. Take a look at the following graph:

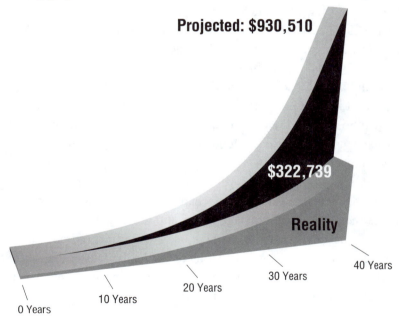

You will notice from this diagram that if you were taxed at a 22 percent rate on that gain, year after year right out of that savings plan, the amount of money you would actually earn in 40 years is only $322,000.

You will lose two-thirds of your wealth to taxes even paying in a low-end tax bracket of 22 percent. Losing $600,000 to taxes is a huge amount of money, don't you think?

When investment values are presented to you, you must consider whether the growth figures of that investment reflect the amount of taxes you will be required to pay over the life of the investment. Remember the Time/Value of Money and how certain factors such as taxes can affect the value of money over time.

Now let's use that same $10,000 to illustrate another way that the true impact of tax obligations on "conservation" money can be hidden from plain view. Suppose that same $10,000 was deposited into a CD which paid 8 percent interest. If you received the 8 percent on $10,000 in one year, the bank would owe you $800. If your tax bracket is 25 percent, then you will pay $200 in taxes on that $800 interest the bank pays you. At the beginning of the second year, how much money will you then have in the CD? The answer should be $10,600, right? Actually the amount is $10,800. The reason for this is because at tax time we generally do not withdraw the $200 from our CD and deposit it in our checking account to cover the check we write to the IRS for taxes. We come up with that $200 from other sources. The $800 of interest income will just stay in the CD and that $200 tax liability will be absorbed into our entire tax obligation. In other words, what really happens is that we compound our taxes in savings, camouflaging the true tax impact.

Taxes have such a subtle, yet profound affect on our money. That's why, as we mentioned in the last chapter, we encourage our clients to organize their Conservation stage funds into the five "Tax Drawers." By doing so, it becomes easier to see how taxes will affect retirement money over time. In addition, using calculating tools like the Master Plan software can help you project how much money you will have at retirement age, the total value of all your assets at retirement, and what percent of them will be subject to taxation.

Without the tools to play "what if" scenarios with your money, it may be easy to get caught up in popular retirement and savings programs touted by the news media, politicians, and financial advisors, which may or may not help save the most tax dollars. Take 401(k) retirement programs, for instance. Most people today are very enthused about these tax-qualified deferment plans because they can be a great way to benefit from an employer's matching contribution. The argument for these plans is that when a person begins to withdraw funds at age 65, he or she will usually "be in a much lower tax bracket" than they were in during the "accumulating" years so theoretically they should pay much less in taxes on those funds. But that may not actually be the case. Bart Croxford, a CPA writing for the *Salt Lake Tribune*, spells out what may be closer to the truth about tax-deferred plans like 401(k)s:

> *I have never seen anyone who promotes tax-qualified plans run the figures through [the entire period of] retirement. They run the figures to age 65 or [just] beyond and show how much more you can accumulate if you use a tax-qualified plan, such as an IRA or 401(k), and defer your taxes until retirement. But in savings, as in sports, it's the final score that counts, not the score at half-time or even after three quarters. The real clincher in the whole plan is the fact that with tax-qualified plans, one must pay taxes on the entire amount taken [during] retirement, including the growth, which accounts for the largest portion by far. Whereas on tax-free plans, one pays no taxes on the growth at all. In other words, one can be taxed either on the seed or the crop. With tax-qualified plans, one pays on the crop and on tax-free plans, one pays on the seed. One does not receive the tax deduction now but he or she receives a far greater benefit by not having to pay taxes on the amount received at retirement.[2]*

Of course we do not automatically dismiss 401(k) and IRA accounts as a way to save for retirement, and we strongly encourage you to take advantage of matching contributions your employer may make towards a fund. However, Croxford does make an excellent point about saving valuable tax dollars:

You can be taxed either on the seed or the crop. Which would you prefer?

The only way to determine what you prefer is to organize your assets into the five "Tax Drawers" and use a forecasting tool that lets you predict more accurately exactly what kind of affect paying taxes on the seed or paying taxes on the crop will have on your various retirement plans.

As an example, take a look at this graph that compares taxed, tax-deferred, and tax-free investments over time.

This illustration shows the value (after taxes) of your $10,000 investment over a 28-year period. If you invest that money today at 7 percent and just pay the taxes along the way, you would have $41,900 at retirement. If you defer the taxes and pay them at the end of 28 years, the amount you would

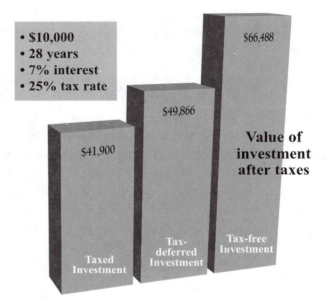

earn is $49,866. But if you accumulated the money tax-free, the investment would be worth $66,488 in 28 years. That's a big difference. As Croxford notes:

> *"In savings, as in sports, it's the final score that counts not the score at half-time or even after three quarters."*

Understanding how your money can grow and how you can reduce your tax obligation dramatically if you invest in tax-free savings programs such as life insurance, municipal bonds, and Roth IRAs can make a big difference during the Conservation stage of your life. To gain that understanding, apply Money Mastery Principles 5, 6, and 7 so that you can become informed about various retirement plans, the rules that govern them, and which plans would be best to integrate into your financial big picture.

Joe and Miriam Stein* are a good example of how investing wisely during the Conservation stage can save a lot of tax dollars. The Steins were in their 50s when they decided to buy a duplex and rent it out. The experience was so good they decided to buy additional duplexes located on adjacent parcels. They took the rental cash flow from these duplexes and paid off all their debt. Over the course of a year, the value of the property on which the duplexes sat went up. Joe and Miriam decided to trade the group of parcels for one large commercial piece of land and were able to build a 42-unit rental property without going into debt for it. The new property is now appraised at $1.2 million. The Steins have created a trust, have retired, and are now living on the income from their real estate business. The interesting part of this story is that Joe was a "traditional" W-2 employee and decided to use the management of the properties as his side business in order to claim as many Schedule C tax deductions as possible. The Steins are now making a decent income off what was once their "side business," and saving taxes along the way.

*Names changed to protect privacy.

Distribution Stage

At some point, we all die. When it comes time for you to pass away, whatever assets you have built up during the Accumulation stage and the Conservation stage will be distributed either by way of your own plan, or if you have not planned, according to the laws in affect at the time of your death. You've heard the statement, "You can't take it with you." Well, either you spend your money before you die, or it will be spent by others after you pass away during this Distribution stage. All states have laws specifically treating how to distribute money and assets of a deceased person. The reason for this is because only two out of seven individuals have pre-planned how they want to distribute their wealth after their death.[3]

As we noted in the last chapter, without a Master Plan and good estate organization, your money will be handled in a way far different from that which might be the most beneficial to your surviving loved ones.

Remember the Judds we profiled in Chapter 8 who made no provision for the sale of the family home, and lost it to a powerful developer? And what if you die unexpectedly and leave minor children behind? If you have not made provisions to care for them, any money available in your estate could be eaten by court costs as legal battles about how to care for your children ensue. Without tax planning and estate organization, following are only some of the ways that money and assets can be devoured by the state:

Probate Fees	If you have not planned well by preparing a will before death, every bit of your money and any property or accumulated assets will be subject to probate fees and court processing costs. These can eat into your assets considerably.
Appraisal Fees	These are charged to appraise your property and to assess taxes at death.
Legal Fees	These may be charged to determine actual owners and to contest wills, etc.
Forced Sales	If taxes are owing at your death, the IRS will often force the sale of property at a reduced price in order to collect taxes.
Federal Estate Tax	Can be as high as 55%.
State Inheritance Tax	Can climb as high as 11% depending on the state.

The last two items in this list, federal estate tax and state inheritance tax, consume the largest amount of your wealth at the time of your death if you have not planned a way to protect your assets from taxation. When we do not plan for the disbursement of our money during the Distribution stage, it will be subject to far more taxes than are necessary. Unfortunately, this stage is where most people lose the majority of their money. For example, after retirement most people worry about outliving their cash reserve, so they are extremely frugal and don't spend very much. When they die, a majority of their assets are then left to be distributed in a lump sum to their children. But this lump-sum distribution, if not handled properly, can be subject to excessive taxation. To illustrate this point, let's suppose that John and Mary lived very frugally during their 25 years of retirement. After death, their remaining assets totaled just over $300,000 and were slated to be disbursed to their children as a lump-sum cash distribution over a one-year period. But distributing their assets in this way caused the $300,000 to be taxed at a 50 percent tax rate, costing their children half of their parents' inheritance.

Warren Burger, former Chief Justice of the Supreme Court, is another example of what can happen to your assets during the Distribution stage if you do not plan to protect them from estate and inheritance taxes. Because he had only prepared a simple will, which lacked adequate detail, his $1.8 million estate was subject to thousands of dollars in unnecessary taxes. According to the online court and legal reporting cable network, Court TV, "the former Chief Justice of the Supreme Court left behind a self-written, 176-word will. He gave his entire estate to his two children. But he failed to give any power to his executors and made no provisions for estate taxes."[4]

Burger's lack of planning cost his heirs almost $600,000 in probate costs and estate taxes. The sad part is that almost the entire $600,000 could have been saved if Burger had prepared a simple trust, done some estate

---

LAST WILL AND TESTAMENT OF WARREN E. BURGER

I hereby make and declare the following to be my last will and testament.

1. My executors will first pay all claims against my estate;

2. The remainder of my estate will be distributed as follows: one-third to my daughter, Margaret Elizabeth Burger Rose and two-thirds to my son, Wade A. Burger;

3. I designate and appoint as executors of this will, Wade A. Burger and J. Michael Luttig.

IN WITNESS WHEREOF, I have hereunto set my hand to this my Last Will and Testament this 9th day of June, 1994.

/s/Warren E. Burger

```
We hereby certify that in our presence on the date writ-
ten above WARREN E. BURGER signed the foregoing instru-
ment and declared it to be his Last Will and Testament
and that at this request in his presence and in the
presence of each other we have signed our names below
as witnesses.

/s/Nathaniel E. Brady residing at 120 F St., NW,
Washington, DC

/s/Alice M. Khu residing at 3041 Meeting St., Falls
Church, VA
```

planning, and held annual reviews to be sure everything was in order. Below is an estimate of savings if Burger had prepared a Revocable Living Trust as compared to what his heirs actually received.

Even a chief justice of the Supreme Court, who should have known and understood the tax laws, did not prepare his estate to be properly distributed. He failed to implement Principle 8 by getting properly organized,

	Estimated Cost of Burger Estate	With a Revocable Living Trust	With Trust & Additional Estate Planning
Estimated Value of the Estate	$1,800,000	$1,800,000	$1,800,000
Estimated Federal Estate Tax (33%)	$396,000	$198,000	$0
Estimated Virginia Estate Tax	$78,000	$39,000	$0
Estimated Probate Costs (7%)	$126,000	$0	$0
Estimated Value After Costs	**$1,200,000**	**$1,563,000**	**$1,800,000**

and then completely missed the boat on Principle 9, which consequently made his heirs victim to the very system to which he was sworn to uphold. It ended up costing them $600,000!

You can see from the above chart that you can protect virtually 100 percent of your wealth during the Distribution stage if you will take the time to understand the tax laws governing estate disbursement and take action to protect those assets through living trusts, wills, etc.

Paul VanEkert: Lack of Planning

Case History

Paul VanEkert* is another example of what can happen if you don't take Principle 9 seriously: Paul was a 57-year-old rancher from Utah. In preparation for retirement, Paul decided to meet with an insurance planner to determine what he would owe in estate tax upon his death. The planner explained to Paul that his total risk would be $222,000 and that if he purchased a life insurance policy, that risk would be covered by the policy at his death. He was advised by a new practicing attorney in the area to hold off on the coverage until the policy could be further examined, so Paul declined the coverage and sent the insurance planner on his way. About nine months later Paul died suddenly without having taken care of the life insurance. His two boys, who had ranched with him and helped Paul successfully run the business, were forced to sell the ranch to cover outstanding debts and to meet the IRS's tax requirement that the $222,000 in estate taxes be paid within nine months of Paul's death. This forced a hasty sale of the ranch to a neighbor who came forward offering to buy the property at a greatly reduced price. The loss to Paul's family was tremendous, both financially and emotionally. In less than a year the boys lost not only their means of support, but the legacy which Paul had wanted to pass onto them. Today, his sons are working as hired hands for the new owner of the ranch. If Paul had taken the life insurance policy, his two sons would have kept the family ranch going and had a wonderful inheritance to pass on to their own children.

* Names changed to protect privacy.

Now let's summarize how much you can save in taxes if you take the time to understand and apply Principle 9.

Accumulation Stage: Taking advantage of the Schedule C tax system and looking for viable ways to write off business, travel, and other expenses can generally save you a minimum of $2,000 per year in taxes.

Conservation Stage: By organizing properly, using the right forecasting tools, and investing wisely, you will be able to cut taxes on the growth of your investments up to 50 percent.

Distribution Stage: By organizing your estate, preparing wills, protecting assets through living trusts and other tax-sheltered programs, you will be able to eliminate almost all inheritance and estate taxes in most cases, and at the very least pay only a fraction of the costs.

Although taxes can be the source of much fear and frustration, they need no longer tear through the fabric of your financial life and weaken your accumulated wealth. Besides the value of getting your spending and borrowing under control using Principles 1, 2, 3, and 4, when you know the rules about taxation (Principle 5), keep on top of the changes (Principle 6), and get organized so you can see exactly how you will be taxed (Principles 7 and 8), you will be that much closer to putting all the pieces of your financial puzzle together because you will have the benefit of Principle 9 working for you to help you retain more of your money. If you're still paying more taxes today than you need to, now is the time to change. Commit today to make Principle 9 a part of your life!

✓ CHALLENGE #9: Examining Your Tax Liability

Accumulation Stage: If you are a W-2 employee, consider what hobby or activity you are currently engaging in that could possibly be converted to a legitimate business venture. Then…

1. Come up with two ways you can take advantage of the tax deductions allowed on Schedule C. (As a reference, we have included a copy of the business write-off section of Schedule C on page 198; to access a free report listing the most common tax deductions allowed by law that businesses can take, visit www.moneymastery.com, or call (888) 292-1099.)

2. Refer to Part II for more information on how to legally structure a business, how to take tax deductions with confidence, and much more. If you are already self-employed, study Part II carefully to be sure you are conducting your business appropriately.

Conservation Stage: Assess your ability to protect as much of your investment and retirement savings programs from taxes as possible during this stage by using a forecasting tool to see how much of these will be subject to tax. Decide which programs may need to be converted to a better tax-saving plan.

Distribution Stage: Assess your ability to protect as much of your assets from inheritance and estate taxes as possible by setting a specific time to hold annual reviews, then evaluate the ways in which your property and money will be distributed at the time of your death. Determine whether you need to convert any of these assets into a tax-sheltered program such as a living trust.

Because understanding taxation is such an important part of money mastery, we have devoted not only this chapter, but six additional chapters in Part II to this important topic. This section will help you understand in even greater detail how to take advantage of all the "good" tax laws. We strongly encourage you to explore, through Part II's step-by-step approach, how to legally pay the least amount of taxes possible. It's easier than you think to get this important part of your financial life under control. Stop cheating yourself out of thousands of tax deduction dollars. After discovering the power of the 10th Money Mastery principle found in Chapter 10, turn to Part II and learn the secrets that will change the way you pay taxes forever!

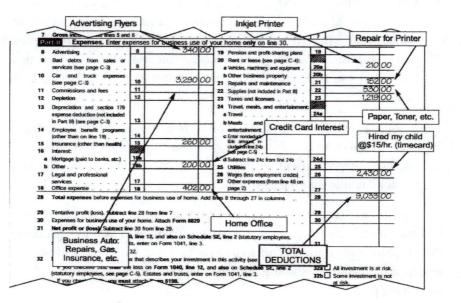

Put Money in Motion to Create More Money

W e begin this chapter by introducing a principle that in our experience will have more impact on your financial well being than all the other principles combined.

Principle 10: Money in Motion Creates More Money

How does money in motion produce additional wealth? Let's take a look at banks as a prime example of Principle 10. Suppose you deposit $1,000 in a bank. The bank pays you in turn say 4 percent interest on that amount. What does the bank then do with that $1,000? The illustration on page 200 illustrates how banks put money in motion, continually turning money over and over to make a profit.

The process begins when your bank puts additional money with your $1,000 and lends it out as part of a car loan and gets 10 percent interest on the loan; it will then make 6 percent profit (after paying you 4 percent interest) on that car loan, right? Now when the car dealer gets the loan proceeds, he puts that money into his bank. While the car dealer has the money on deposit until needed, that bank loans his money out on a home construction loan at a rate of 9 percent. Then, the contractor for that construction job puts the money in his bank and before he makes payroll or buys lumber, his bank has already loaned that money for a computer at 14 percent. When the computer dealer puts the loan proceeds into his bank, his bank turns around and loans it out on a boat for 10 percent. The boat dealer then deposits the loan proceeds in his bank, and that bank loans that money out on a Visa card at 18 percent.

Although this is a very simplified illustration of a highly complex system that is governed by the Federal Reserve Bank as well as a set of

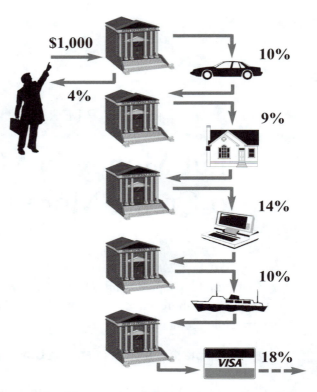

strict federal regulations and banking protocols, you can see from this example that $1,000 will typically multiply within the banking system eight to ten times — often this will occur very quickly, within hours or days. The banks benefit every time that money turns over, no matter what the rate — 18, 6, 10, 8, and even 4 percent. If you add up all the turns on that original $1,000 in a year, the banking system will have earned between 38 to 42 percent while you only earn 4. Who's winning this game? The point is, that if like the bank you can get your money to do more than one thing at a time, you can look forward to both safety for your money and higher rates of return. This idea is worth repeating:

> *If you can get your money to turn over, or in other words,*
> *do more than one thing at the same time, you can make*
> *a constant and higher rate of return on that money.*

In the prior bank example, we showed how these institutions literally turn money over and over again. In this next example, we'll demonstrate how more than just money can be put in motion to build income and wealth. Take for instance a large public company that sells shares of stock. Let's say this company builds roads and bridges and takes the money from the sold shares to buy roadgraders and other machinery. It then uses this equipment over and over again on many jobs, "turning" it many times to make a profit. The equipment only needed to be purchased once but is used many times over to create additional wealth. This company, rather than getting a set "rate of return" on their money like its shareholders, actually uses its equipment to turn over a greater and more continual profit.

"Okay," you might be thinking, "that's fine for banks and large public companies, but what about me?" Let's apply this concept of "money in motion" on a more personal level through the following account of one of our clients.

Michael Silva: Turning Product Over Again and Again

Case History

Michael Silva* owned and operated a small grocery store in New Mexico. His gross profit margin on all sales was 7 percent. The average number of days it took Michael to turn his entire inventory of groceries was 21 days. Assuming he had $100,000 in merchandise on the shelf, he made close to $7,000 every three weeks. When Michael learned from his Money Mastery coach the value of Principle 10, he took inventory every six months and decided to research how fast each item in his store turned over. His study revealed that Cheerios in the cereal section turned over three to four cases a day, and if he could keep that shelf stocked completely for the entire year, gross sales on Cheerios alone would total $57,000. The Cheerios were being ordered and stocked by an untrained employee who left the shelf bare at least half of the day every day. When people wanted to buy Cheerios and constantly found an empty shelf, they began to shop somewhere else. Michael knew he would have to make changes in the cereal isle.

A product that wasn't turning over quickly was hot chocolate mix since the warm weather in New Mexico discouraged its sale. For an entire year, the store only sold one case at a profit of about $28. By using Principle 2, Michael was able to track his inventory of hot chocolate more closely to compare it against what he actually sold and determined that he only needed to purchase one case per year. Tracking his inventory also revealed that he was losing one case of beer per day on average. He reported this to the police and they were able to stop the theft by apprehending the underage drinkers who were stealing from his store. Once he had a firm understanding of which products made him a profit and which were liabilities, he made necessary changes in advertising and product purchasing so he could turn his entire inventory over every seven days, thus applying Principle 10. This meant that every week (not just every three weeks) he was making 7 percent on his inventory, tripling his previous profits. And he was able to do this without increasing his utility usage, labor costs, or subjecting himself to any additional overhead expense required to maintain the store.

"The wonderful part of applying Principle 10 is that I was able to triple my profitability without any additional money out of my pocket and without taking any additional risk," said Michael. "Basically, I just became more aware of my ability to turn a profit and revised some of the processes in my store so that my money began working overtime for me. Up until I made those changes, my money really wasn't working very hard at all because I hadn't put any momentum behind it. I run inventory every six months now and my store is operating much more efficiently," said Michael.

*Names changed to protect privacy.

A Simple Idea

Although the idea of making your money do more than one thing at a time is actually quite simple and is one of the easiest and most risk-free ways of generating additional wealth, it is rarely understood. In our experience, it is very difficult for people to change the way they think about money especially when most are still living paycheck to paycheck. Their first tendency is to spend any extra money on consumable goods rather than think about how it could be used to make a profit. This mindset prevents people from ever creating a cash surplus and makes it virtually impossible to understand the power of Principle 10 or how to apply it. The importance of having a cash surplus can only be explained to a point, and then it must be experienced in order to fully comprehend it. Having a cash surplus not only allows you to purchase more of the consumable goods you may need and want right now, but also opens up wonderful opportunities to create additional long-lasting and far-reaching wealth. As the old saying goes…

You have to have money to make money.

The ability to create this cash surplus is only possible when each of the other nine principles are applied to your financial situation, coming together like a crescendo behind Principle 10. The application of all the principles builds momentum and creates opportunities to put your money to work in very exciting ways to create even more money. Applying each of the 10 principles at the same time has exponential power to transform your life, creating a multiplier affect on your financial resources. Systematically building from one Money Mastery Principle to the next and applying each principle on top of the other is like multiplying two times two times two times two — the end result is much greater than if those numbers are simply added together. That's because each principle builds on the power and potency of the one that came before.

$$2 \times 2 \times 2 \times 2 = 16$$

On the other hand, applying some of the principles part of the time is much like adding two plus two plus two plus two. You will see some results, but the overall effectiveness will be much less potent.

$$2 + 2 + 2 + 2 = 8$$

When you apply all of the principles all of the time by controlling your spending, eliminating debt, planning for the future, protecting your assets, and reducing your taxes, you automatically become more efficient with your time and resources, creating a surplus of both that can go to work to make additional wealth. Let's take a look at how this efficiency with time and money can work in every area of your financial life and how an abundance of time, wealth, and resources are only possible when all the pieces of your financial puzzle work together.

First of all, with your spending under control, you have eliminated the waste associated with impulse purchasing, which frees up more cash. And because you spend much less energy trying to figure out where your money is going every month, you have also freed up more time. Second, as you work to eliminate your debt, you are saving massive amounts of interest expense that can then be used to create more wealth, plus you're spending less energy working to pay for that debt, making you more efficient with your time. Third, increasing your savings and planning for the future is naturally creating more resources that will eventually make even more time available to you, which you can then use to think up new ways to make even more money. Fourth and finally, knowing the actual rules governing tax law saves you hundreds of hours you once wasted worrying about IRS audits and all the "unknowns" associated with tax filing, plus it is saving you thousands of dollars that you can now use to create more wealth.

Putting all the principles together creates opportunities to maximize your resources and your time to their fullest — this is what Principle 10's "money in motion" is all about.

You add motion to your money when you add
all the Principles to your life.

People who have learned to apply Principle 10 (and all the other principles as well) manage to get their money to do more than the average person can. It has been said that if given $1 million, the average person would misuse that money in less than 10 years and end up with the same sum of money he started with. But a financially principled person knows the power of the "multiplier affect," and rather than squandering or sitting on their resources has learned to put them in motion to continually turn a profit that will secure them a bright financial future.

In our coaching, we spend considerable time with clients teaching them how to examine where and how they should be spending their money by asking them to look at what will get them the best return. It is vital that people resist spending all their extra money on consumable and depreciating assets so that they can create a cash surplus and keep the momentum of their money going. We discourage borrowing too much money for homes, cars, and consumer goods because this forces the borrower to pay three times the value of the item, making it extremely difficult to set any additional money in motion. Can you see how not applying each of the other nine Money Mastery Principles makes it exceptionally difficult to make Principle 10 work for you? Following is an example that perfectly illustrates this point.

Mark and Stacey Kleinman: Applying Principle 10

Case History

Mark and Stacey Kleinman* were spending much more than they brought in each month. In addition, they were so deeply in debt that it took nearly half of their income just to pay their loan obligations. They had no idea how to create an additional side business in order to take advantage of Schedule C tax write-offs. This couple was also very disorganized and had no estate planning or wills prepared. Needless to say it was very difficult for their coach to explain the concept of Principle 10 to Mark and Stacey. But fortunately the Kleinmans saw the value of applying the other Money Mastery principles. First, they reviewed their spending habits for the previous 12 months and were shocked to see that they were literally upside down, spending over $300 more a month than they had. They cut their spending and started tracking their money using Principle 2 and immediately found they could save $71 a month on their auto insurance. They stopped eating out so often and saved another $120 per month. Mark and Stacey continued this process until they found the entire $300 they were over-spending each month. They began to discuss their finances with each other on a weekly basis and their conversations went from blaming to quiet decision-making. They got in control of their emotions and eventually in control of their spending.

The second financial improvement the Kleinmans made was to start contributing to their company's 401(k) plan. They could do this because once they got their spending under control, they found some additional money they could then contribute to Mark's employee-matching program, which they had never utilized before. They calculated that their monthly contribution to the plan would grow to $234,600 at retirement. Using Principle 3, the Kleinmans began setting money aside for this program.

Using Principle 4, the Kleinmans began powering down their debts. Mark and Stacey figured that they could pay off all their debts within seven years and save over $180,000 in interest expense. Money they were using to pay off debt could then be saved and used to create an additional $560,000 for their future. Applying Principles 5 and 6, Mark and Stacey got better informed about laws governing their retirement plans and how taxes would affect their money. Stacey began a small flower arranging business based on a 10-year hobby and began saving $2,300 a year in taxes through implementing Principle 9.

Once the Kleinmans got in control of all the other areas of their finances, they were finally prepared to take full advantage of Principle 10 by closely examining their assets, investments, and equipment to make sure these resources were creating money for them rather than just sitting idle. They determined that buying a truck to help Stacey make her deliveries was a depreciating cost that would not bring any additional value to the business. They then decided to lease a truck, and spend the money they would have used to purchase the vehicle on appreciating assets, which in their case was more floral arranging supplies and equipment. By applying the other nine Money Mastery Principles to their lives, Stacey and Mark now have an additional $1,289 per month.

*Names have been changed to protect privacy.

Like Stacey and Mark, you too are ready to take full advantage of Principle 10 because you have been taught how to apply each of the other nine principles. As we continue to explore ways that you can set your money in motion so that it can do more than one thing for you at a time, we invite you to consider the wisdom of the following Chinese proverb:

"When the student is ready, the teacher shall appear."

Having come this far, we are confident that you are ready — we know that you are prepared. The teacher — Principle 10 — is now before you. There are incredible opportunities to create more money all around you. The options are endless! Although there is no formula for making Principle 10 a success in your life, there are lots of options for applying it and we strongly encourage you to consider each of them. We will assist you in this effort by showcasing a number of ways that money, products, equipment, time, talent, real estate, and any number of resources can be utilized to create additional wealth.

Ideas: Turning a Profit Again and Again from a Single Notion

How many times have you had an idea pop in your head that you thought was an absolute stroke of brilliance? Have you ever considered that some of these ideas could be set in motion to create additional wealth? Mindy Potts* did. As a dental hygienist, she spent countless hours pouring molds of people's teeth and mouths. As she poured these molds, she thought about Principle 10 and decided it might be a fun idea to use plaster to make molds of a baby's hands and feet. From that idea she designed a keepsake product for parents that allowed them to make plaster molds of their children's hands and feet. In the beginning she sold over 40 of these kits a month. In time, retailers like Wal-Mart and Shopko began signing distribution agreements with her to sell her kits in their stores. Sales took off, and Mindy was asked to appear on a cable shopping network where she sold over $100,000 worth of product in less than eight minutes. Needless to say, Mindy no longer works as a dental hygienist and the "little idea" which she had one day while pouring molds in the dentist office has begun turning a profit for her in a way she could never have imagined. This one idea, which she had in one single moment, is now producing untold wealth for her over and over again, demonstrating the power of Principle 10 in a very exciting way.

Rent: Making Money from Existing Property

Charging someone to live or work within a space is an obvious way that people can make a profit from an existing asset. As part of applying

Principle 10, Joylyn and Steve Ashcraft* were advised by their Money Mastery coach to finish the basement of an office building they owned. Steve said he didn't have the money, but their coach advised the Ashcrafts to sublease the space to someone who did have the funds to finish the basement. Joylyn and Steve thought this was an excellent idea and were surprised that they hadn't thought of it themselves. The Ashcrafts then found a tenant who was willing to improve the basement by putting in floors, plumbing, window wells, and stairs if the Ashcrafts would give him a $2 credit towards his lease every month for every $1 he spent making improvements. The amount of money the tenant spent making improvement carried him for a full three years before he ever had to make a rent payment to the Ashcrafts. The tenant really enjoyed the arrangement because he didn't have to pay rent for over 36 months. The Ashcrafts were pleased because they didn't have to spend any money for the desired improvements to the basement and were still able to benefit because the property value of the office building went way up. Just after the three-year mark, Joylyn and Steve began receiving $380 a month in rent from the tenant that they are now saving as part of their retirement fund. The building is now worth $74,000 more than it was because the basement has been improved; it also brings in cash flow to the Ashcrafts because they can collect rent on it. All this was possible for Steve and Joylyn without costing them an extra dime. In this case, the Ashcrafts used their real estate property to get their money to do more than one thing at a time.

Skill: Getting Your Talent to Reward You Again and Again

We all have skills we use on a daily basis either to make us money or to entertain and delight others. But when was the last time you examined all your talents to determine which of them could be used to turn a profit for you? Maria Carlisle* certainly hadn't considered carefully her options when it came to her writing skills until her Money Mastery coach explained how she could make Principle 10 work for her. As a freelance writer, Maria charged an hourly wage for her advertising and marketing services. She was paid a good rate for each of these projects, but once they were completed, she never saw an additional penny generated from her work. As she began a project for one of her clients as a ghost writer for a book, she began to realize that once this large project was complete, she would never see any more benefit from the countless hours she was spending researching and writing the book. Maria began to wonder how she could turn her writing skill from a talent that only made her money once to something that made her money again and again. She concluded that she needed to structure her next book-writing project so that she could retain royalties each time the book was sold. This she did, and today she is receiving a 5 percent royalty fee on a book she co-authored. Instead of just getting an hourly one-time return on her invested time and skill, Maria is now getting her work to pay her over and over again. What's more, she is not required to pay any FICA (Social Security) tax on the royalty proceeds. Using her skills as a means to turn a profit, Maria is not only making an hourly wage for her work, but is getting her skill to do more than one thing for her at a time.

Leasing: Turning Need into a Continual Source of Profit

Talia West* loved the thought of getting into the wedding business. She leapt at the chance when she ran across a sale on eBay for 25 white bistro chairs at a really good price. She bought the chairs and began adding to her collection over the next several months, purchasing the plastic lawn chairs at end-of-season sales through garden centers and big-box retailers. After a year, Talia had 250 chairs that she stored in a shed in her back yard and began renting out for garden wedding receptions. She averaged four weddings the first summer she began leasing, recouping half of her investment.

After two summer wedding seasons, Talia had replaced the cost of purchasing the chairs and now turns a continual profit every summer of at least $4,000 between the months of May and September. There is very little cost to Talia for storing and maintaining the chairs, which means she gets to keep virtually everything she makes from her rental business. Buying the equipment once and leasing it over and over again has proved to be a lucrative source of income for Talia that helps her put her money in motion to make more money.

Real Estate: Buying Trust Deeds to Generate Additional Wealth

As people apply each of the Money Mastery Principles, in time they find themselves in control of their financial situation, with no debt and a surplus of funds they can use to make additional money. Guy Walters* was just such a person. Guy had no debt and a fairly good chunk of money to work with but really had no idea what to do with it. He was advised by his Money Mastery coach to buy trust deeds with the money as a way to turn a profit. This he did by purchasing the deed of bankrupt properties from banks at approximately $0.18 cents on the dollar. At one point he became interested in a defaulted triplex with a price tag of $140,000. Its actual appraised value was $170,000, but Guy offered the bank $50,000 to take the property off their hands. At first the bank balked at his offer, but knew that maintaining the property until it could be sold at a price closer to its actual value would not be cost effective. It did not want to be hassled with trying to find tenants and keeping up the grounds so it sold the trust deed to Guy. He then found suitable renters for each of the apartments and began renting each for $850 a month, generating over $30,000 in one year. Using this profit, he made improvements on the property and turned around and sold it for $180,000. You can see from Guy's case that the original $50,000 eventually made him an additional $130,000, which he then used to buy additional defaulted trust deeds to continue the process. Using his investment in real estate, Guy is applying Principle 10 in order to create additional wealth.

Knowledge: Generating Money Over and Over by Applying an Educational Background

Sue and Derek Copperfield* both had degrees in biology and were employees for the state where they lived. One managed industrial chemical dumping, and the other was responsible to monitor the water fowl along the Missouri River. The Copperfields had grown to love the Missouri River and wanted to live near it. They were able to secure an option to purchase a piece of land within the flood zone, but didn't know how to approach a lender to get enough money to be able to build a home on the site. Their dream was to create their own "farm over the water." While discussing these problems with their Money Mastery coach, the Copperfields were advised to apply Principle 7 by stepping back to look at their long-term big picture. Once they did this, they decided to verify the property's value so they could qualify for a loan by planting ginseng in the two to three feet of standing water found on the property. From their biology background, they knew that the property possessed the ideal conditions needed to grow ginseng. It would take 10 years to harvest a good crop, but Sue and Derek knew it could become very profitable for them. Once the ginseng started to produce, they could harvest the crop for decades to come. They estimated that they could have a net profit of about $20,000 per year after the initial 10 years of maturation occurred. In addition to the ginseng crop, this property had a large standing forest of straight hardwood trees. These too could be harvested and sold to produce a net profit of approximately $20,000 per year and allow for replanting to maintain the cash flow.

To make their dream of creating a "farm over the water" come true, the Copperfields tracked all their expenses using Principle 2 and were able to put together enough money to pay for a commercial appraisal. This appraisal verified the property's ability to produce an income of $40,000 a year. A local credit union then loaned Sue and Derek the money to build a new home on stilts with a big patio that extended out to their ginseng crop. They were also able to pour a gravel road to their home and build a bridge over a large canal. Using all the Money Mastery Principles, and especially by applying Principle 10, through their knowledge of biology Sue and Derek will be able to retire in 13 years at the age of 53. Money from the ginseng and the hardwood lumber will generate more money for them with less tax liability than if they were W-2 employees.

Technology: Creating "Multiple Impressions" from a Single Web Site

It goes without saying that the high-tech advancements made in the last 20 years have been phenomenal. Wonders like the Internet have opened up a world of opportunity for small business that were previously reserved for large international corporations with big budgets. Nathan Hall*, a real estate agent, is a perfect example of how taking advantage of this technology can turn a profit again and again. Prior to the broad adoption of the Internet, Nathan would spend countless hours preparing marketing fliers, letters, and other materials to help him sell a single residential property. He then decided that he could automate his processes by creating a Web site on which he could place several property listings and their individual amenities and benefits. By doing so, he eliminated the need to mail to each individual prospect a sales letter and flier announcing the available properties. Instead, he began marketing his site through Internet search engines and through linking his page to other co-op sites that helped him drive additional traffic to his Web page. This increased his exposure in the market. Taking advantage of the World Wide Web, Nathan is now able to compete with larger real estate firms because he gets some of the same kinds of exposure in the market as these big, multimillion dollar companies, without having to individually cold call each prospect. The Web makes it possible for him to prospect more than one person at the same time, reducing his out-of-pocket marketing expenses and decreasing the time and resources required to locate potential buyers. This has allowed Nathan to use his energy to locate additional properties he can list on his Web site, increasing his sales figures 49 percent and helping him turn a profit quicker and more often than he did before.

* Names changed to protect privacy.

Additional Leverage Ideas to Help Set Your Money in Motion

Following are several more ways in which you can get your existing money and financial resources to do more than one thing at a time for you.

1. Apply savings to debt. Once you have applied Principle 3 and begun saving at least 1 percent of your monthly income, with time you will build up a pretty fair amount of money in your Emergency and Emotional savings. Rather than "parking" that money in a passbook savings account that will make you very little interest, why not deposit the money in your HELOC (home equity line of credit)? This puts the saved interest expense in your pocket (which is usually always going to be more than what you'd earn in passbook savings) while still keeping that money available for those emergency and emotional events for which you may need it.

2. Turn a nonproducing (or low-producing) asset into a high-producing asset. Money that you have deposited into a 401(k) or IRA account, for example, is sitting there earning a modest amount of interest. While it's nice that you have put this money aside, it's probably not wise to put all your long-term savings into such "stagnant" programs. Investing some of your money into real estate or equipment that can be leased out is a better way to get your assets to produce more money for you.

3. Spread out your investments. Don't put all your investment funds into qualified plans such as IRAs because these plans will be taxed at a time in your life when you need these funds the most (i.e. retirement).

4. Increase your return on investment. While it's important for people with large debt loads and little savings to be quite conservative early on with their savings habits, as you get your spending and borrowing under control by applying all the Money Mastery Principles you will begin to see your wealth accumulate. When this occurs, it is foolish to leave your money in a low-return investment program such as passbook savings and certificates of deposit. Consider, instead what savings should be converted to higher yielding investment plans.

5. Examine ways you can make your current investments more valuable. Can you convert real estate space into rental income property? Do you need to study the market and trade investments where more lucrative prospects lie? Can you use the equity in your current real estate holdings to purchase additional properties to begin a "rolling" real estate investment?

6. Deposit money into treasury-only checking and savings. Check into depositing your money into a U.S. Treasury-only checking and savings account where your investment is safer and will yield significantly higher interest rates than standard passbook savings accounts.

7. Purchase real estate to produce positive cash flow. Invest in the vast variety of revenue-producing real estate opportunities including repossessions, lease with the option to sell, new building, property syndication, and a whole host of other options.

8. Establish a business line of credit. This is "good debt" that allows you to stock more inventory, buy more product, increase advertising in your business, etc.

9. Consolidate credit card debt and/or vehicle debt into a HELOC. This will allow you to lower interest rates and convert the loan into tax-deductible interest.

10. Hard money lending. Loan money to individuals or businesses on a secured basis for a short-term at high-interest rates and fees.

11. Leverage money through Forex trading. Become involved in foreign currency exchange.

While these suggestions should not be considered a comprehensive listing of all the ways Principle 10 can be applied to your life, we are confident that they have helped generate some new and different thinking in you. What skill, talent, property, equipment, or knowledge do you possess that could be used to create a "machine" that is continually working for you? In what ways can you better use the assets and financial resources you already have at your disposal to get a better return on investment? Rather than think in terms of using these existing resources to create more wealth, many people continue to fall back on the idea that they need to have a better job or invest in risky stock opportunities in order to create additional wealth. Many of our Money Mastery clients are able to generate 10 to 20 percent more money per month just by using what they already have available to them to turn a profit. In addition, they do this without the risk that other investments can bring to the game.

Applying Principle 10 is like putting work clothes on your money and sending it out as a hired hand to make you more cash. And the best thing about it is that this money works for you day and night, seven days a week,

365 days a year.

Remember, when you apply Principle 10 you are not working to make money, you are putting your money (and resources) to work for you!

Each of the "Money in Motion" examples we have highlighted in this chapter not only demonstrate the power of Principle 10, but also the importance of applying each of the other nine principles at the same time. It is not enough to apply Principles 2, 3, and 4 by getting spending and borrowing under control. And it isn't enough to casually apply Principle 7, for example, or Principle 9 here and there in an effort to maximize the money that comes available to you as you implement the other principles. It isn't enough to assume that all is well because you seem to be doing some things so much better than you once did. Being content with applying only part of the principles, part of the time is like owning a beautiful ocean island where time is spent on the beach with good food, sun, and the sound of the waves crashing on the shore. Things may seem fine, the surroundings are pleasant, and you appear to have everything under control. Would you ever want to leave such a situation? If you thought all was well, then probably not. You're comfortable where you are and making the effort to get out of your beach chair and do something different doesn't seem worth it.

But, what if at some point a geologist showed up in his stinky fishing boat and informed you that according to his calculations, your beautiful island is sitting on top of a volcano and is going to blow within three days to two weeks? To prove his point, he takes you to a part of the island where a fissure in the ground is spewing steam. Would you stay there and take your chances that all will remain well, or will you get on his stinky boat, the only boat within hundreds of miles, and leave? The answer is obvious.

Without the knowledge, consciousness, awareness, and wisdom that each of the Money Mastery Principles can bring to your life when applied systematically, you will not have the motivation to make change when it is necessary. You will be satisfied with what you know and not realize there may be danger lurking ahead or opportunities for building wealth that you may be missing! Without a system like Money Mastery, a person will never see how to change, and consequently will never realize any real momentum or power behind their cash flow. A systematic approach, like that which Money Mastery offers, brings all the principles together and makes it possible, as we have already noted, to multiply the affect of your actions over and over again to create additional wealth.

Remember, you add motion to your money when you add all the Principles to your life.

In order to keep that money in motion it is vital that you not take for granted any of the Money Mastery Principles. Following are just some of the ways that people sabotage their best efforts at applying all 10 principles all of the time:

1. Consume every bit of disposable income on depreciating items.
2. Lack reserve accounts when an emergency takes place or the market takes a downturn.
3. Don't know the rules when they sign a contract, thereby roping themselves into a costly mistake.
4. Pay three times what they need to in tax expense.
5. Lack the discipline to use extra money to pay off debt, instead using it for impulse purchases.
6. Lack discipline and financial organization, thereby making it impossible to streamline the processes that will affect taxes, retirement, assets, and property.
7. Lack vision for the future by failing to step back and look at the big picture.
8. Sit on their money and resources rather than making these work for them.

We're confident that you have begun to strip from your life these saboteurs. By now you are successfully controlling your spending using Principles 1, 2, and 3. You are eliminating your debt by applying Principle 4. And you are maximizing your assets using Principles 5, 6, 7, 8, and 9. Now you are ready to implement a total money management system by applying Principle 10. This principle has the ability to exponentially build wealth for you at a rate you never dreamed possible and to provide you with the resources that will allow you to have the time to live your life the way you want to live it. As we noted in the Introduction, the reason most of us work is not just to acquire more things, but so that we can create enough cash surplus to have the time to pursue our most cherished dreams and desires. Applying Principle 10, along with all the others, makes it possible to have the freedom to spend as much time as we want doing what we want.

Again we encourage you to examine all the possibilities for wealth creation that are available to you. The whole world is waiting and ready to be explored. Take the time today to look carefully at yourself, your mindset, your resources, and your attitude. If you will, we can promise that you will open yourself to a bright and prosperous future!

✓ CHALLENGE #10:
Get Your Dollar to Do More Than One Thing at a Time to Create a Cash Surplus

This week we challenge you to:

1. Ponder what talent, skill, idea, knowledge, property, equipment, or source of money can be put in motion in order to create more money.

2. Pick one of these available resources and determine a method by which you will use it to generate additional income.

3. Pick three other money-leveraging ideas from the list on page 212 and implement them.

4. Consider getting financial coaching in order to help you better understand how to leverage your money. A good one-on-one mentor can help you see your own individual strengths and weaknesses and how to put all the pieces of your financial puzzle together.

PART II

TAX STRATEGIES

CHAPTER 11

Why You Should Start
a Home-based Business

Having turned to Part II of this book, we're confident that you have learned to appreciate the importance of Money Mastery Principle 9 and are interested in learning more deeply about the subject of taxation and how it can dramatically impact the amount of money you make and keep. In this part of the book, we will discuss in greater detail some of the concepts we introduced in Chapter 9, explaining the rules* that govern how your money will be taxed and giving you practical applications that will help you take advantage of those rules. As you have already learned through Principle 5, knowing the rules brings power and control into your financial life like nothing else can, and when combined with the information found in this section, will help you save anywhere from $2,000 to $5,000 in tax deductions every year.

It goes without saying that taxes are a huge part of our lives and have a pervasive affect on everything we do. Almost all Americans pay a fortune in taxes over a lifetime, but most don't fully understand the true extent of their tax bill. In fact, when the average federal income tax bill of 39.2 percent is added to all the other "add-on" taxes such as FICA, state income

---

* The principles and strategies being treated herein are applicable to both U.S. and Canadian citizens; while there are minor differences the basic principles still apply to both countries. For more information on Canadian tax law and the Canada Customs and Revenue Agency (CCRA) contact Money Mastery: (888) 292-1099 or the Tax Reduction Institute at (800) 874-0829.

tax, sales tax, property tax, and so forth, the average American ends up paying between 42 and 55 percent of their earned income to the government.[1]

Part of what keeps us enslaved to this huge tax burden is that, as a nation, we have become entrenched in a "W-2" mentality where we believe that the only way to make a living is to work for someone else and have a set percentage of taxes extracted from our paycheck. But working within this W-2 system isn't helping most people get ahead. Today, many households need two or even three incomes just to survive. Sadly, even more than one spouse working outside the home does not produce any major positive effect on most people's bank accounts. Jane Bryant Quinn's article in *Woman's Day*,[2] which we profiled in Chapter 2, illustrates this point quite well. If you remember, Quinn assumed in her article that the husband in this family was earning $40,000 per year, and his wife, Lori, wasn't working. Every month the family was short on funds, so this prompted Lori to get an administrative job for an annual salary of $15,000. When Quinn examined the economics of working for this extra income, the results were startling! Remember that after all the non tax-deductible expenses that Lori incurred due to her new job, she ended up taking home a paltry $1,156 a year from her annual $15,000 salary! She could have netted that entire $15,000 had she earned it in a side business, an increase of almost 13 times her take-home pay as a W-2 employee. Notice that Lori would not be spending dramatically any more money than she would already be spending operating her own home-based business. She would still be eating out, going on trips, and driving her car the same as if she were a W-2 employee. But by having her own legitimate business, many of these ordinary and necessary expenses would be tax-deductible.

Launching Your Own Business Makes "Cents"

There are several reasons why more people are favoring self-employment over traditional W-2 jobs. First of all, your own home-based business gives you the opportunity to make more money! Statistics show that the majority of millionaires are not trust fund babies, but people who started their own businesses. This helped them control how much money they could make and exactly how they would spend their time. Being in business for yourself opens so many more opportunities for growth and prosperity for you than being a W-2 employee alone. In addition, your own business gives you the benefit of saving valuable tax dollars. This is the initial benefit you'll enjoy by starting a business. Did you know that 70 percent of all revenue for the federal government comes from W-2 employees and that corporations pay only a fraction of that? With your own business, you can dramatically reduce that number because you can deduct expenses that you would not otherwise be able to deduct on a personal level. Additional benefits of starting your own business include not having a commute (unless you have a really big home!), not having to deal with a boss, and not having to put up with corporate politics. Did you know that there are currently an estimated 30 million people working from their homes? This number is expected to more than triple to 97 million by the year 2015 and to keep on growing.[3] Working from home has become and will continue to be one of the greatest mass movements in U.S. history.

Here's why launching your own business makes so much "cents":

- As we noted in Chapter 9, using Schedule C (when filing 1040 tax forms) and the tax laws for the self-employed, you can deduct all kinds of expenses that are not allowed on Schedule A. With proper documentation, you can write off your house, spouse, and even your children (by hiring them and paying them a reasonable wage), business vacations, cars, and food with colleagues (more details to come in Chapters 13 -17).

- You can set up a pension retirement plan that makes any government plan seem paltry by comparison.

- You can glean more tax deductions, which is in a sense, like having Congress subsidize you while you are growing your business.

- If your business produces a tax loss in the first year or so, you can use that tax loss against any other form of income you have. It can be used against wages earned as a W-2 employee, dividends, pensions, or interest income.[4] You can also use the loss against your spouse's earning if you file a joint return.[5]

- If the tax loss exceeds all your income for the current year, no problem. You can carry back the loss two years and get a refund from the IRS for up to the last two years of income taxes paid, or you can carry the loss over 20 years. That's right, you can offset up to 20 years of income.[6]

As we noted in Chapter 9, it is imperative that you take advantage of all the tax laws that will save you the most money during the Accumulation Stage by thinking outside of the W-2 box. This idea is so important that it is the basis of our first tax-saving strategy.

Tax Strategy 1: If You Don't Have a Business, Start One!

If everyone in the U.S. employed full-time as a W-2 worker would start a legitimate part-time or full-time business and follow the tax deduction strategies we will outline in the next several chapters, each person could reduce his or her taxes anywhere from $2,000 to $5,000 each year.

When our clients begin to understand the power their own home-based business has for earning extra money and saving tax dollars, they are usually very excited about the prospect. They are also more than just a little nervous about launching out into new territory. We often hear people express both excitement and fear in the same breath:

"I've always wanted to work for myself, but I've never seen a way that I could actually do it."

"We've talked about starting our own business a number of times but I've always wondered when we would have the time to launch such a venture. We both work more than 50 hours a week."

"It seems like it would be very rewarding, but also very risky. Besides, I'm not an entrepreneur."

Have you ever had any of these kinds of conversations with yourself? We often hear objections like the following from people who are afraid to launch a new business.

I already work myself into the ground...when would I have time to start a business?

This is a common concern that many people express because they lack the proper perspective about what it means to really start a business. They falsely assume that people who succeed at working for themselves don't have a regular W-2 job. Actually, most people who start a successful venture are able to do so while still working their regular job. These people are flourishing because they don't take the prospect of striking out on their own too seriously and since it is not their only source of revenue, they don't make too many bad decisions due to financial stress. Successful small business people realize that the amount of time they spend on their business doesn't matter, and the size of their business doesn't matter. What matters is the intent behind a home-based business: to make more money each month, and to save tax dollars. They determine for themselves how much time and energy they want to devote to the venture.

What we have also found is that as a person works a side business, it can become so successful and so much more viable as a means of support that many people end up walking completely away from their W-2 job. Now whether this happens for you or not, it doesn't matter. The important thing is to have the proper perspective about what it really means to "start a business." If you think that this prospect has to be difficult, time-consuming, or exhausting, perhaps it's time to think again. It's a lot easier than most people think!

Michelle Kapos* decided to change her perspective about launching her own business when she realized that she wasn't completely happy with her job as a teacher at a public elementary school. She was, however, very happy with her efforts selling Mary Kay cosmetics and spent every Saturday conducting seminars, teaching classes, and giving facials. Each weekend, Michelle sold over $500 worth of cosmetics, $200 of which she kept as gross profit. Michelle decided she needed to consider her Mary Kay business as a viable home-based venture and use it to save more tax dollars. Using Schedule C, Michelle now deducts her car expenses for travel to and from consultations as well as entertainment and food expenses while she is hosting prospective clients. She saves $1,000 in taxes each year working only 16 hours extra every month on the weekends. She plans to retire from teaching at age 31 and become a full-time Mary Kay consultant. For now, she uses her Saturdays to make extra money and save tax dollars.

* Name changed to protect privacy.

I'm not an entrepreneur...what can I possibly do for a business?

This is the most common objection we hear. Unfortunately, many people view themselves as simply a "nine-to-fiver," with no idea of what they could do to make extra money in a home-based business. Our response to this objection is that you don't have to have the ambition of Bill Gates to become a successful business owner. All you need is a little imagination. The biggest obstacle to forming a small business venture that we see is a lack of vision. Without this vision it can be almost impossible to remove yourself from the predictable and "safe" haven of your W-2 job. You may go on indefinitely, stuck in a rut that affords no other choice besides collecting a paycheck from someone else. Imagination is so important. As Einstein once said,

"Imagination is more important than knowledge."

It has been our intent to infuse you with this imagination and vision for the future by introducing you to the 10 Money Mastery Principles. With an understanding of those principles, especially Principle 7, "Always Look At the Big Picture," you should now have a clear view of all that your financial life should be today and tomorrow. Having committed to changing your life by accepting this principle and all the others, you should now be ready to take action by starting a small business. It will be one of the best steps you can take towards eliminating ruts of predictable behavior — behavior that keeps you in a cycle that prevents financial growth, encourages excessive taxation, and does little to mitigate economic risk.

With a little imagination, you will begin to see just how many ways there are for you to make extra money in a side business. As we noted in Chapter 9, we tell our clients that there are many hobbies and activities that could be considered a legitimate business venture if they would consider them as such.

Remember Perry and Michelle Kamboris whom we profiled in Chapter 9? They realized that their knowledge and interest in their Husky dogs, along with their love of travel, could be turned into a business opportunity that could save them thousands of dollars in taxes each year. Since they were already heavily involved in the Huskies as a hobby, it seemed only logical to them to take advantage of that interest by turning it into a legitimate business and a viable tax write-off.

Hobbies and interests that our clients have transformed into home-based businesses also include teaching adult community education classes, public speaking, buying and selling real estate, leasing property, cutting hair, selling cosmetics, selling household cleaners, online trading, currency trading, and teaching piano or other musical lessons. These are only a few of the ideas that can be turned into a home-based business venture. There are literally hundreds of opportunities if you will take the time to explore them.

What do you like to do in your spare time? What products do you like to use that you would be more than happy to sell to others? What hobbies could you convert into a viable home-based business? Let your imagination run wild. The possibilities for financial growth and happiness are endless when you step outside the W-2 box.

Okay, I'm sold on the idea...but can I really succeed?

Many people are thrilled with the prospect of being more than just a W-2 employee, but they are also afraid of the risks. We like to point out that research consistently shows that the majority of home-based business ventures (because of their inherent lower risk and overhead) are successful. In fact, according to the Small Business Administration, the average home-based business succeeds in its first year and achieves an average income of $40,000 per year with many earning more, and this is not even counting all the tax benefits that you can earn once you are in business.[7]

We should note that the same benefits accrue to franchises. Franchises number in the thousands and cover a wide gamut of interests and products. If you are interested in finding out more about franchises, visit the Web.

The Risks of Not Starting a Business

One rental income

100% exposure

Although launching a business can seem like a gamble, the risks of remaining strictly a W-2 employee may actually be worse. How much of an economic and emotional impact did your last layoff have in your life? If you've ever lost a job you know how totally exposed and vulnerable it can make you feel.

Following is a good example of the way in which W-2 employment fully exposes a person to economic hazards.

Suppose Sally and Roger purchase a three-bedroom house to rent to a single family. They use the rental proceeds to pay for the mortgage on the house, but then the renter decides to move after six months. Until Sally and Roger can find another renter, they are 100 percent responsible for the payment of the mortgage. *Sally and Roger's exposure is now 100 percent.* Renting a single-unit dwelling is much like being a W-2 employee — if you lose your job your economic exposure is going to be 100 percent.

But, let's say that Sally and Roger, instead of buying a single-unit dwelling, purchase a multiple-unit building that has 10 apartments. If one renter decides to move, Sally and Roger can still count on the other nine rent checks to help cover their mortgage payment, mitigating their risk from 100 percent to only 10 percent

Having a side business is much like renting out multiple units within an

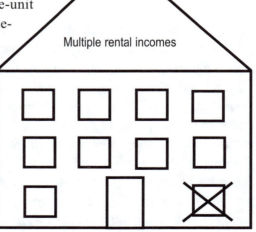

Multiple rental incomes

10% exposure

apartment building; it helps mitigate your risk should you ever lose your W-2 job because it provides a means of income on which you can fall back. In addition, the emotional cost of losing a job is also mitigated. That's because you are not emotionally invested in just one thing. With your own business you can spread out your emotional risk across other income-bearing interests. That way, if anything happens to your job, you can feel more confident and know that you have worth even if your employer doesn't think you do. Finally, there are some good tax laws that accrue to you when you are self-employed that can subsidize you while you are building up this business. These good tax laws do not apply to those people who are solely W-2 employees.

Success or failure? Only you can decide...

Success or failure in a business is rarely determined by the business itself, but rather by the business owner. Once you have put your imagination to work and caught the vision of what you'd like to do, keep in mind two things that will determine whether that new venture will succeed:

Action & Knowledge

These two things are the main reason why one person will succeed and another will fail at the exact same business. As we have already noted, a successful business can only get started by taking action. Some people want the benefits of having their own businesses, but they don't do anything to make it happen. Those who make a business work are constantly taking action in a consistent and regular manner.

But that isn't the only thing that will ensure success. There are plenty of people who are always working, always taking action, but may still fail at running a business. That's because they aren't taking the right actions. They must combine their work efforts with the correct knowledge in order to make a business succeed.

Combining action and knowledge together is like drilling for oil. If you set up a drilling rig in your backyard, it's going to fail at producing oil unless your backyard is in Texas or Alaska! Not only must you set up the rig, but you also have to know the right place to set it up if you're going to find oil.

How can you ensure that you take the right actions and know the right information so that your business will succeed?

Learn to duplicate the success of others.

Duplicating the strategy of others is much quicker and more effective than going to the school of hard knocks. This method of mimicking others' successes is also known as "modeling." Modeling is well illustrated by the way the McDonald's Corporation blazed a trail to success that many have since followed. In the early 1950s, McDonald's and other start-up companies discovered that through franchising they could grow many times faster than other firms that followed a conventional business model. For example, a company, instead of investing millions of dollars to build new stores, could let independent franchisers do it for them. It seemed like a great idea, but at first it wasn't successful on a consistent basis so the media constantly criticized it. News articles featured destitute families who had lost their life savings through franchising schemes. Virtually every state attorney general in the U.S. condemned the new marketing method — some Congressmen even tried to outlaw franchising entirely. Over the years however, Ray Kroc and his management team at McDonald's developed a turnkey franchise business team that made it possible for franchised McDonald's restaurants to succeed. This newfound success turned public perception of franchising around. Today, virtually every franchise business model, to some extent, is based on the business system created by McDonald's. Franchising has become one of the most respected ways of doing business in the world and literally thousands of franchises are available for almost any business that you can imagine

Akin to franchising are such opportunities as reputable multilevel marketing (MLM) companies and real estate buy/sell programs that provide a proven business model that thousands have followed successfully. Such network marketing opportunities and trading programs provide proven products or services, solid management personnel, and years of time-tested success. The step-by-step approach that such business models can offer is one way to break into business for yourself if you're a bit nervous about the prospect.

There are countless other ways in which to launch a business; getting familiar with the people and practices behind your particular business interest will go a long way towards making your new venture a success. If you take the time to explore your options, you'll find hundreds of opportunities to enjoy tax deductions you never even knew existed. Add to those tax savings the satisfaction of being your own boss, controlling your own schedule, and determining how much money you want to make, and you can't afford not to start a new business.

If you already have a business going, make sure you are enjoying the many financial advantages to which your smart choice entitles you by learning how to deduct as many taxes as possible through the information found in this part of the book. The tax advantage alone can, in many instances, make a side business venture the single best financial move you will ever make.

You will find many wealth-building tax tips contained in this book that are based on the actual experience of thousands of clients we have coached throughout the years. We encourage you to read on as we explain the details you will need to know to make your business a tax success. In the meantime, get on the road to launching your own business opportunity by taking the following challenge.

✓ **CHALLENGE #11:**
Determine What Hobby or Interest Could Be Converted into a Legitimate Business

1. This week, examine closely your daily activities, hobbies, interests, and where you most love spending your time. Is there something you do in your "spare time" that could be turned into a business venture? What about a particular skill you possess that others rely upon for which you could begin charging a fee? Brainstorm any and all ideas and then write them down. Discuss them with your spouse and children. Roll these ideas off your friends and neighbors. Imagine yourself doing the activity on a daily basis. Consider the logistics of how and where you would conduct the business. Settle on one or two ideas that you are serious about exploring. Check out individuals or companies that are already doing a similar type of business and see how they are doing. Are they making money or "starving on the vine?"

2. If you are already running your own business, this week we challenge you to throw out all your biases about tax planning and read on about how you can get all the deductions to which you are legally and ethically entitled. Remember Principle 5, "Know the Rules," and Principle 6, "The Rules Are Always Changing," and don't assume that your accountant knows everything about saving you valuable tax dollars. Remember, your accountant is only as good as the information you provide him or her.

The key to taking all the deductions you're entitled to in a business venture is to run your business with an honest expectation of profit and to have your expenses be ordinary, necessary and reasonable for that business.

By launching a home-based business and using the tax strategies outlined in this book, you can become more financially stable and make your life a whole lot less "taxing!"

CHAPTER 12

To Incorporate or Not

T ake action. Remember, it's one of two things a person must do if he or she expects to be successful at a new business venture. Now that you have taken that action by determining what kind of business on which you wish to embark, the next step is to make sure you have the proper knowledge you will need to start that venture off on the right track.

Tax Strategy 2: Consider How to Best Legally Structure Your New Business Venture

The information in this chapter, while certainly not comprehensive, outlines five basic ways a business can be legally structured and will help you determine whether you should incorporate your new business or not. Before becoming entrenched in the every day effort of running your business, the knowledge presented in this chapter will help you determine how to take the best advantage of all the available tax benefits. This information will also help you learn how to limit your liabilities as a business owner.

There are no hard and fast rules about the best way to structure a business, and naturally the decision will be based on your individual circumstances. But keep in mind, there are certain laws that regulate the way business may be conducted in the U.S.*, and as Money Mastery Principle 5 teaches, you must know these rules!

*The principles and strategies being treated herein are applicable to both U.S. and Canadian citizens (with the exception that Canada is limited to Partnerships, Sole Proprietorships, and C Corps). While there are minor differences, the basic principles still apply to both countries. For more information on Canadian tax law and the Canada Customs and Revenue Agency (CCRA) contact Money Mastery: (888) 292-1099 or the Tax Reduction Institute at (800) 874-0829.

Sole Proprietorship

A sole proprietorship is a business entity that is not incorporated and allows a person running that business to be taxed personally. Without question, this is the simplest way to structure your business. Here's why this business entity may be right for you:

Advantages

- Requires no federal or state unemployment taxes.
- No "double taxation," meaning that only the owner is taxed and not the business itself.
- No shareholder or board meetings to hold.
- No federal tax ID number to obtain from the IRS unless you have employees – this means you can use your own Social Security number for tax filing.
- No special tax filing forms required other than Schedule C with your 1040 form.

Sole proprietorships also have the advantage of being the best entity to use if any losses are incurred. If you have losses in your business, which is usually the case in the first year or two, these losses can be used against any form of income on your tax return such as wages, interest, dividends, pensions, rents, etc.[1] For example, Mike earns $50,000 in a regular W-2 job. If he starts a business that generates a tax loss of $10,000, he only pays federal and state income tax on $40,000 of his regular W-2 salary if he is structured as a sole proprietorship. In addition, if the losses he incurred exceeded his income, he can carry back all business losses two years, or carry forward business losses 20 years and offset the next 20 years of income.[2]

Moreover, sole proprietorships allow some fringe benefits such as:

- A 100 percent deduction for medical insurance premiums for the owner and his or her family when the owner pays the premiums directly out of his or her bank account.
- Business owner gets to keep all the profits.

- No expenses for incorporating.
- Simple structure so there's less paperwork and fewer tax filing forms.
- Lower cost to maintain business.
- Flexible; passing on ownership is fairly easy.
- Easy to promote business in some ways because clients and customers personally know the owner of the business and can expect his or her personal touch.

With all these advantages, you would think that a sole proprietorship is the best way to structure a home-based business. There are, however, some drawbacks that can be rather substantial.

Disadvantages

The biggest drawback to a sole proprietorship is that you are responsible for paying both employer and employee FICA tax for the business. This means that instead of just being responsible for your portion of Social Security tax as the "employee" in your company, because you are also the "employer" of your proprietorship, you're responsible to pay the FICA tax that employers are required to pay for their payroll employees. Essentially, a sole proprietor pays double FICA taxes. This can be quite costly.

Another disadvantage of being a sole proprietor is that as a business owner, you are personally liable for everything that happens within the business. A sole proprietorship does not protect the individual owner against liabilities, and although much of this risk can be mitigated with business risk insurance or personal liability insurance, we believe that any business that has substantial potential for liability should not be a sole proprietorship. Your decision should be based on how much exposure you want to take on personally.

Big Tip: *If you have any employees, you will have substantial liability because all employers are liable for the acts and conduct of their employees. Thus, if you have any employees, you should NOT be a sole proprietor.*

Pembrook Stevens: Freelance Writer

Case History

On the day that Pembrook Stevens* was laid off her third public relations job in ten years, she decided it was time to strike out on her own as a freelance writer. Because of the nature of her work, she wasn't too worried about limiting her liability and wanted to keep things simple so she conducted her business as a sole proprietor. This allowed her to take a percentage of her apartment rent as a tax deduction for office space. It also let her deduct car, utilities, phone, and many other expenses related to her business. She was also able to write off 100 percent of her medical insurance premiums, which were substantial since she was self-employed and had a difficult time obtaining reasonably priced individual coverage.

Pembrook, however, did pay more than her fair share in Social Security taxes. Because she was single, FICA taxes accounted for a large percentage of her tax burden each year. While she enjoyed the simplicity of a sole proprietorship, she also knew that incorporation might save her thousands of dollars in Social Security tax. Today, Pembrook is weighing each method for structuring a business and determining if remaining a sole proprietor is the best option for her. In fact, because of the high Social Security taxes she is paying, she may prefer to structure her business as an S Corporation, which will be discussed later in this chapter.

*Names have been changed to protect privacy.

Partnerships

A partnership is defined as a legal entity that involves two or more people who share profits in a venture. This structure is a little more complex than a sole proprietorship but is still less complicated and formal than incorporation. Paperwork for partnerships must be filed with your state government.

Advantages
• Requires no separate tax at the partnership level, meaning both partners

are taxed individually as sole proprietors (the tax is determined based on ownership levels).

- All income and losses pass through to the partners as if they earned them individually (thus a partnership is called a "pass-through" entity).
- Unlike sole proprietorships, losses are limited to the sum of the cash or property basis you contributed to the partnership and all loans that you guaranteed or made to the partnership.
- Different skills and abilities of each partner allow diversity and strong support for the entity.
- Partnerships can take advantage of almost all of the same tax benefits as that of a sole proprietor.

Disadvantages
- A partnership requires the filing of a separate partnership tax return.
- Because this business structure involves more people than a sole proprietorship, salaries are usually paid to either the partners or staff or both, so a federal tax ID number is required.
- Subject to federal and state employment tax on salaries.
- The biggest disadvantage to a partnership is that you are unlimitedly liable for partnership debts and for the acts of your partner (unless you form a limited partnership which protects each partner from personal liability). In fact, this liability can be such a major problem that we do not regularly recommend that our clients form a partnership with another individual (with the exception, perhaps, of husband and wife).

John Caldwell & Nathan Hamblin: Property Management Partnership

Case History

John Caldwell* and Nathan Hamblin* are a good example of a business partnership. The two men had complementary skills and desired to work together as a business team, forming a property management company called ITC Properties. Through this company, John and Nathan bought real estate, improved these properties, and then rented or sold them. The partnership required that both John and

Nathan be responsible individually for the property mortgages. But forming a partnership where they bought and sold property allowed the two men to save valuable tax dollars through deductions for real estate business. As a partnership, all income and property that came into the partnership was passed to both John and Nathan as if they had earned them individually, plus each had a different set of skills that helped them run the business. For example, John was skilled at showing and selling the properties while Nathan had experience in accounting and bookkeeping. Each contributed to the business in his own way.

The partnership also had some disadvantages because it required them to file a separate tax return, which was costly. In addition each of their salaries was subject to federal and state employment tax. They also had to deal with the inherent liability that comes with a partnership, each agreeing to be responsible for the acts of the other partner, putting themselves at some risk.

*Names have been changed to protect privacy.

Regular "C" Corporation

Corporations are legal entities that also require filing with state government. They are separate entities that call for their own tax return to be filed with the IRS (IRS Form 1120). A "C" corporation is taxed separately on all monies that are not paid out in expenses, bonuses, or salaries. Corporations are very formal beasts. In fact, based on the complexity and formalities involved, corporations can be very unwieldy so you should carefully consider each of the pros and cons of incorporating before making a move.

Advantages

*   The biggest advantage is that corporations limit liabilities. If you maintain the formalities, your liabilities are generally limited to the assets of the corporation with the exception of malpractice suites. (In malpractice, the owners may be unconditionally liable regardless of the way the business is structured.).

- Can deduct 100 percent of any disability insurance premium, which is a tax-free benefit to employees.
- Can accumulate (with planning) $50,000 per year for future business needs and have this amount taxed at the 15 percent rate. If you are in a 40 percent tax bracket, this represents a substantial 25 percent savings. We should note here that this is a major overlooked advantage of being a regular corporation.
- Can have many different classes of public or private stock, which adds value to the company and is great for estate planning and raising capital.
- Dividends are taxed at a maximum rate of 15 percent (just like long-term capital gains).

Tip: Because liability protection is so important in making the decision of whether to incorporate, we almost always recommend some form of corporation or LLC (limited liability company) if workers are employed. If you have employees, you MUST limit your liability through the legal protection allowed by incorporation laws. For example, if you are incorporated and one of your employees accidentally burns your restaurant to the ground through a grease fire, you will not be responsible to pay for the loss of the building personally unless you have assumed or guaranteed any indebtedness. Responsibility for the building is transferred to the business entity itself.

Disadvantages

- If funds are paid out again in dividends you could be "double taxed" on these dividends, meaning that the funds would be taxed first through the business entity and then taxed to you as a dividend. In fact, based on the complexity and formalities involved, double taxation is the biggest headache of incorporating. We should note however that this headache can be somewhat alleviated with proper year-end tax planning with your accountant.
- Must hold yearly stockholder meetings, even if you are the only stockholder, and yearly board of director meetings.
- Must have a separate business bank account; if you do not take this step and co-mingle your personal funds with business funds, you will automatically forfeit your legal protection against liability. (While it is

essential for all business entities, including sole proprietorships, to set up separate business bank accounts and distinguish between all business and personal funds, corporations are legally bound to do so.)

- Must obtain a federal tax ID number from both the IRS and the state.
- Some states impose strict taxes on corporations. For example, California currently requires that a corporation pay what the state's normal tax rate would be or $800, whichever is higher. Thus, if your corporation is located in, or does business in California and incurs a loss, you will wind up paying the state a minimum business tax of $800!
- If planning has been done poorly or incorrectly, the corporation will be subject to potentially nasty surprises such as having to pay taxes on accumulated earnings (also called "future income").
- Can be very expensive and costly to file taxes because of the amount of paperwork required.

Cautionary Note: *If you are a "personal service corporation" you will be taxed on any money left in the corporation at the end of the year at a flat 35 percent rate. A personal service corporation is a regular C Corporation whose principal activity is the performance of personal services by its employee-owners. They also involve certain occupations such as law, medicine, accounting, architecture, veterinary, dental, etc. If you are in these fields, you should consider very carefully whether to structure your business as a C Corporation or, at the very least, conduct yearly year-end tax planning in order to insure that most of the profits are removed from the corporation in the form of salaries or bonuses.*

Hot Tip: *Because many business owners don't keep up with the required formalities and don't perform the required year-end tax planning necessary to avoid double taxation, we rarely recommend structuring your new business as a regular C corporation. This should only be set up with careful advice from your lawyer and/or accountant.*

"S" Corporations

This type of corporation is a hybrid mix of sole proprietorships and regular C corporations. An "S" Corporation is made by first forming a C Corp and then filing a "Sub S" election. Here's why you may want to consider forming your business as an S Corp:

Advantages

One of the biggest advantages of an S Corp is that it can help you eliminate some of your Social Security taxes. For example, let's say Sam earns net after expenses $90,000 as a sole proprietor. He pays income tax on the $90,000 and pays 15.3 percent in Social Security taxes on that $90,000. This amounts to $13,700 alone! However, if he forms an S corporation and pays himself a reasonable salary of $55,000 a year and receives the rest in the form of a dividend, because dividends are not subject to Social Security tax, Sam will only pay Social Security on the salary and not on the remaining $35,000 dividend. He saves 15.3 percent on $35,000, which represents a $5,355 yearly savings! This method of saving Social Security taxes is not possible with any other business structure.

Additional advantages that S Corps enjoy:

- All income and losses flow through to the owners (just like a partnership), thus eliminating most of the double taxation problem.
- Limits liability just like a regular C corporation, so if you have employees, this is a good choice.
- Stockholders are taxed on the earnings of the corporation based on their ownership so you can split off income into lower tax brackets. For example, if there is only one owner of the corporation and the business brings in $100,000 annually, that owner will be taxed at the 50 percent tax bracket. But say he gives part ownership to each of his three children and his wife. Now there are five stockholders, each receiving a fifth of the $100,000 dividend or $20,000 each. His 17-year-old son can now be taxed on his share of the dividends at a much lower tax bracket because of his age.
- Allows taxes to be filed using IRS Form K-1, which reduces Schedule C into a much more generalized statement of business dealings, lessening tax exposure.

With all these advantages, you might think that an S Corp would be the ideal business entity, and for many people it is. However, just as with the other business structures, an S Corp also has its drawbacks:

Disadvantages

- No more than 100 individual stockholders are allowed.
- There are no provisions for several classes of stock like in a C Corp, thus greatly limiting estate planning and opportunities to raise capital. In addition, these private shares cannot be sold and the company cannot go public in order for shares to be bought and sold on the stock market.
- Subject to the same formalities as a regular corporation, meaning shareholder meetings must be held, even if there's only one individual, with the same paper work and meeting hassles.
- Must formally document all business activities for tax purposes.
- Cannot create a self-insured medical plan like you can with certain sole proprietorships and a regular C corporation. This kind of plan allows regular corporations to deduct 100 percent of health and disability insurance premiums; sole proprietors can also take this 100 percent deduction.

Greg and Betty Wallace: An "S" Corporation

Case History

While working as W-2 employees, Greg and Betty Wallace* decided to form a leasing and venture capital services company by structuring it as an S Corporation. This allowed the husband and wife team to limit their personal liability while also reducing their Social Security taxes. In fact, the Wallaces were able to reduce their FICA tax by 50 percent. In addition, they took advantage of lower taxes by splitting off income from the business by paying dividends to their children who were part owners of the company. The Wallaces did have to hold quarterly and annual stockholder meetings and keep minutes but the somewhat formal structure of their business, while not as complex as a C Corp, provided them with liability protection they could not get through a partnership or sole proprietorship. For the Wallaces, an S Corp was the best way to structure their business, especially with tremendous savings in FICA tax.

*Names have been changed to protect privacy.

Limited Liability Companies (LLC)

This is the newest method of structuring a business and is a fairly recent innovation within the last 10 years. An LLC is similar to a sole proprietorship, however it provides the same protection from liabilities as that of a C or S Corporation. In fact, this structure allows you to elect to be treated as a corporation without having to deal with the formalities of such. If there is only one owner, you can file and be taxed as a sole proprietor. If there are two or more owners, you will be taxed as a partnership.

Advantages
- Limits liability just like a regular corporation.
- One person can own the LLC, which eliminates the need to file a separate tax return.
- Other entities such as a C Corp, trust, or partnership can own an LLC.
- Does not require the formal meetings and documentation of a C or S Corporation.
- Tax filing and other paperwork are simple and inexpensive.
- Can claim all the same tax advantages of sole proprietors and partnerships.
- Don't have to hold shareholder meetings or keep meeting notes.
- Management control need not be proportional to ownership.

Disadvantages
- Does not provide a FICA tax-break like an S Corporation does (except in the case of hiring children — then their salary is not subject to FICA taxes if they are under age 18).
- The laws that govern an LLC are not uniformly written among the states.

Jackson Montgomery: Setting up an LLC

Case History

Jackson Montgomery* began Small Business Development, LLC as a means to help people learn how to set up a viable home-based business. As an accountant and financial advisor, Jackson felt he could assist people in learning some of the tricks to launching a successful side business venture. By structuring his own company as an LLC, Jackson mitigated his liability and also made certain tax-saving benefits available through his wife and children. He hired his wife and paid her a salary for helping with the business. In addition, he also made each of his children a 1 percent owner in the business and paid them a regular dividend, which helped cover their expenses. None of this dividend was subject to FICA tax since they were under 18 years of age. Through an LLC, Jackson can pay his kids a FICA-tax-free dividend as a part owner and help offset family expenses.

*Names changed to protect privacy.

One final thought on multiple ownerships within partnerships, LLCs or corporations. What happens if you and one other owner in your business do not get along? Bad relationships have resulted in some of the most expensive and protracted legal battles around. This kind of business contention is worse than a divorce. Thus, if you have a partnership or have structured your business as a corporation or an LLC and have multiple owners, we strongly advise that you establish a buy-sell agreement at the launch of your business. This agreement provides a formula for buying out another's interest in the partnership or company due to incompatibility, death, or disability. This will eliminate a lot of problems and you'll be glad you did it. Think of "buy-sell" arrangements as a sort of business pre-nuptial agreement.

As we have already noted, the way you formally structure your business can protect you from liabilities and save you thousands of tax dollars depending on your personal circumstances. While we have outlined the basics with regards to each of these entities, it is imperative that you take the time to learn more of the rules behind each of these business structures so that you can choose the one that is right for you.

Note: We strongly recommend that you seek out the professional help of your accountant or attorney in order to sort out the issues with each of the five business entities we have outlined in this chapter.

✓CHALLENGE #12:
Determine How You Will Legally Structure Your Business

This week we challenge you to take the time necessary to learn more about each of the ways you can legally structure your business. To do this, we recommend the following:

1. Read *Lower Your Taxes: BIG TIME* by Sandy Botkin for detailed information on the benefits of various corporate entities.
2. Search the Web for more information on corporations, sole proprietorships, partnerships, and LLCs.
3. Refer to your local library for more specific information.
4. Contact your state's division of corporations and commercial code or department of commerce.
5. As noted above, seek the advice of professionals such as accountants and lawyers. Keep in mind that just because these people are professionals does not mean they are infallible. It is your responsibility to know as many rules as possible. Learn enough so that when you do seek out their advice, you'll know whether it's sound or not. Remember Principles 5 and 6.
6. Request a free Money Mastery report comparing each of the five legal entities outlined in this chapter and their pros and cons by calling (888) 292-1099 and asking for "Legal Entities Comparison Report."
7. Be sure to separate the business from yourself. Co-mingling personal and business money creates problems: 1) it dilutes tax deductions; 2) it prevents you from seeing the forest from the trees; 3) it prevents you from seeing when you are profitable or not; and 4) it creates problems when IRS audits come along. To help you separate yourself from your business, be sure to do the following:

   a) Set up a separate checking account for your business and dedicate separate debit and credit cards for the business.
   b) Register your business name with the proper controlling authorities. We recommend using a name other than your own

as the name of your business to limit personal liability exposure in case of loss or lawsuit.

c) Obtain a business license from your city.

d) Set up a separate accounting system for your business. Be sure to create a balance sheet, cash flow statement and profit and loss statement for your business. (Be sure not to co-mingle your personal funds with your business funds.) Consult with your financial coach or accountant if you need more help.

Once you have investigated each business entity, determine which structure is right for you. Then read on....

The following chapters will help you learn what you need to know to set up your home office so that you can take advantage of as many tax saving strategies as possible.

CHAPTER 13

You're in Business, So Act Like It!

D o things right the first time.

Such advice is sound, especially when it comes to setting up a new home-based business. In the last chapter we outlined how to start things off on the right foot by selecting the best way to legally structure your new venture. Now you are ready to begin "setting up shop" and it will be imperative that you do this right the first time, too. In this chapter we have outlined some very important rules that will help you conduct your new venture — rules that will help you see that if you're going to be in business, you must act like it!

As we have already emphasized in the last two chapters, running a business is a good way to make more money and the best way to take advantage of all the tax deductions available to you during the Accumulation years. Why? If your business produces a loss, you can generally deduct that loss against any form of income you have such as interest, dividends, rents, retirement income, and wages. In fact, you can even use those losses against your spouse's income, if you file jointly. These are only some of the wonderful tax-saving advantages of being in a home-based business.

Naturally, the IRS knows about all these wonderful benefits, but it's counting on you not to know them for yourself. While it may appear that the IRS doesn't want you to take advantage of the home-based business strategy and is constantly scheming for new ways to keep you in the dark about all the "good" tax code, it is actually rather indifferent about what the average taxpayer does and does not know about tax law. It just assumes that most people don't know the law and will not take the time to become informed about it, and figures that if you are not going to learn the tax laws then it will take advantage of your ignorance by accepting whatever you are willing to pay into the federal coffers, even if it is in excess of what's actually required by law. The IRS and Congress assume that this ignorance about tax law will also cause you to deduct expenses to which you are not entitled, which takes money out of the federal coffers. Of course they want to avoid such losses. That's why if you don't know the law about how to run your business as a legitimate venture, the IRS feels perfectly justified in declaring that you are "playing" at being in business and not actually running one. If the IRS can demonstrate to its satisfaction (and the courts' if it should get that far) that you are only engaged in a hobby (or simply "monkeying around") then no business losses can be taken by you.[1]

Activities that are deemed hobbies, or not engaged in for profit, do not qualify for business losses above the income from the hobby.

You must demonstrate a clear, honest expectation of profit with a bone fide business purpose, and business expenses must be ordinary, necessary, reasonable, and directly related to the business. That means if you only make $200 in a year from your business, for example, your deduction will be limited to $200. Even worse, there is no carryover of those excess deductions, you just lose them if they are declared to be a hobby by the IRS.[2] Thus, reclassifying your activities as a hobby rather than a business is the IRS's favorite weapon. Therefore it is vital that you apply the following tax strategy.

Tax Strategy 3: Run Your Business Like a Business, and Not Like a Hobby

Fortunately, Congress has given all taxpayers a way to be absolutely sure that their activities will be treated like business operations and not like a hobby. If your activity shows a profit for three or more consecutive years out of five, it will be presumed by the IRS that you are engaged in a viable business.[3] For those business owners engaged in activities such as horse racing, dog racing, dog breeding, car racing, dog and horse training, etc., then that activity should show a profit two out of seven years.[4]

What if you don't show a profit for three years out of the five, or if your first years are a loss? As long as you are running your venture like a real business endeavor and not as a hobby, the law cannot pronounce limits on your losses, even if the IRS tries to declare your business a hobby without waiting the three years for you to establish an operating history.[5]

That's why it's so important that you know the rules about how to run your business like a real business. There are numerous standards that the courts use to ascertain whether you are actually running a business, and helping you understand them is what this chapter is all about.

The Rules of the Game

Rule #1: Show Business Intent. You must show that you entered your business activity with the intent to make a profit. As we have already noted, it doesn't have to be a big profit, it can actually be quite small, but it does have to be some kind of profit. A majority of court cases on this subject indicate that you are required to have an honest profit objective when you undertake the venture. Thus, if you have a sincere purpose in the venture, including eventually reaping an overall profit, it will be assumed that you have a profit motive.

Tip: Document business intent by creating a business plan, obtaining a business license, and setting up separate checking accounts and accounting systems for your business. Another way to document your intent is to get contracts with vendors or get a letter from your sponsor (for MLM networking opportunities) stating why you are entering into the business and emphasizing your desire to make a long-term profit or career out of the home-based venture (more information on this later in the chapter).

Rule #2: Be Businesslike. The idea of a "business" begins in the mind. You must understand that a business is not you and you are not a business — they are two separate and distinct entities that need to operate as such.

> *Remember, the business is a separate legal entity*
> *by definition of tax and business laws.*

That means you need to conduct your business in a businesslike fashion. This may sound very simple, but it's probably the single most important factor in the IRS's determination of your intent. Is the manner in which you conduct your activity in accord with good business practices? Regardless of whether you make a profit, the IRS essentially wants to see that you are serious about running your business.

What steps should you take to run your activity in a businesslike fashion?

1) **Keep accurate and complete tax records.** This is very important. In fact, you really have no choice but to do so if you're going to be in business for yourself. This will help your accountant so that he or she can help you save the most tax dollars and so that you can protect your business activities from an audit. It is our goal to help you see that keeping sound supporting documentation is the best way to keep the IRS off your back, and to help you save more tax dollars than you ever imagined. To do this, you must create new tax habits that will help you keep accurate records.

These new tax habits are not unlike the new spending and savings habits you created when you first began learning the 10 Money Mastery Principles. Therefore, keeping a detailed, accurate tax diary should not be very hard for you to do, especially now that you have embraced Money Mastery Principle 2. Using this principle, you have made a habit of keeping track of how you spend money. Using this same principle, we encourage you to keep track of how your business is conducted and how your day is spent while running that business.

2) **Create a separate bank account for your business.** A number of recent cases have indicated that the courts expect you to keep separate books and bank accounts for your business.[6] Don't co-mingle your personal funds with your business accounts, not even if you are a sole proprietor. Co-mingling personal and business money creates problems:

- It dilutes tax deductions.

More Reasons Why Documentation is So Important

- All the numbers included in your tax return are your responsibility. You create the numbers, not your accountant. You are required to have adequate support for your tax return. When you sign your return, you attest to its accuracy under penalty of perjury. And the only way to be sure this information is accurate is to keep good records.

- The IRS states in its official publications that you must maintain records that support accurate tax returns. Also, these records must be made at or near the time of the expense so that you will be sure to have accurate recall. Such records must be permanent and complete. Failure to meet the adequate documentation standards of the Internal Revenue Code can result in disallowance of your valid deductions.[7]

- Documentation is also important because the IRS thinks you might cheat on your taxes, and accordingly you are assumed guilty until you prove yourself innocent. The burden of support for your deductions is on you. IRS examiners are not required to help you keep records. You have total responsibility for proving your deductions.

- Finally, accurate records are important because failure to keep them results in very stiff penalties if you are audited.

Important Note: For more information on the best way to keep accurate records, refer to Appendix H.

- It prevents you from recognizing when you are profitable.
- It creates problems if IRS audits come along.

Be sure to set up a separate checking account for your business[8] and dedicate separate debit and credit cards for it as well.

3) **Be sure to control your own money.** Do not transfer the authority to sign checks over to family members, for instance, or other employees. Sign your own checks. Use purchase order systems where applicable.

Rule #3: Create a Business Plan. It is very important that you take this step.[9] Most courts have looked favorably on taxpayers who had a business plan showing projected income and expenses for their activities. The key, obviously, is that you want to show on your plan when you expect to start producing an overall business profit. You don't want that plan to show a profit ten years down the road, with a loss every year subsequent to that. You want to demonstrate to the IRS that you expect to make a profit as quickly as possible. The numbers should have some reasonable basis in reality as well. In other words, you should have a rationale supporting each number, i.e., an expert informed you about the number, or you referenced it through other substantiating material. You should document how you estimated each of your figures.

If your business requires inventories, obviously you should have enough inventory on hand to meet your profit objectives. Not every business will have inventory, but if yours does, you should be aware of this when creating your business plan.

Business plans should generally project your business profitability from five to ten years — ten years is safer. The business plan should include not only a projection of income and expenses, but also your plans for marketing the business. A marketing plan will answer this one simple question: What do I intend to do to make money? (For more information on resources for creating a business plan, consult your local bookstore, or search the Web.)

Rule #4: Register your Business Name. Go through the proper controlling authorities to have your new business recorded on the books governing the area in which you live.

Rule #5: Obtain a Business License. File the proper paperwork with the city in which you live to obtain a license. If you are ever audited, this will show the IRS that you are intent on running a bona fide business venture.

Rule #6: Remember that Your Own Statements May Testify Against You. In determining whether you are involved in business activities or just a hobby, the IRS listens to what you say. In fact, they are very happy to listen to your statements and then use your own words against you.[10]

Suppose you say to someone, "Well, I'm only in this business to escape taxes." Or, "I just want someplace to dump some expenses." Or, "I'm only in this to get a discount on some decent golf clubs." If the IRS gets wind of statements like these, it will claim, and rightly so, that you are not in business to make a profit and you will not be treated as a business entity. One couple we know that distributed Amway products wasn't aware of how their statements could be used against them. In tax court, the IRS attorney asked them if they would continue business even if they never made a profit, to which the couple answered yes. This showed the judge that these people were in their "business" more for social reasons than to make a profit. He disallowed all losses for this couple's Amway business. Again, we can't emphasize enough that you must watch what you say! Your own words can be used against you in a court of law.

Rule #7: Run Your Business the Way Similar Profitable Businesses Are Run. You should try to show that your activity is being carried on in a similar manner to other profitable business ventures.[11] If you conduct your activity the way other successful people in the same business do, you will be able to argue vigorously that you are conducting your activity like a business with the expectation of making money. If you want to be a millionaire, hang around millionaires, or as they say:

"If you want to fly like an eagle, don't hang around with turkeys."

In addition, if you follow the path of a coach, mentor, or other financial expert, your chance of becoming successful is further enhanced. Adopt marketing efforts similar to those that are successful.[12] Remember our discussion about successful modeling we outlined in Chapter 11? For more information on running your business like other profitable ventures, refer to the list on page 254.

Rule #8: Understand That Your Prior Business Experience Can Help or Hurt You. If you have no prior business experience in a particular line of work, the IRS may decide that you are taking a big chance, and therefore find it questionable that you ever had a profit motive.[13]

The courts have long held that this strike against you can be overcome by making sure that you extensively study your line of business.

1) **Advertise Your Business.** Keep copies of the advertising flyers, promotional pieces, and press releases you use to promote your business.

2) **Create Business Cards.** Your business cards should indicate in what type of business you are engaged, your address, and telephone number.

3) **Maintain a Business Telephone Listing.**

4) **Use Promotional Materials.** Keep copies of brochures, press releases, etc.

5) **Use a Variety of Marketing Strategies.**[15] Don't just put one ad in one paper. Also, if you are in a multilevel operation, don't just listen to what your upline tells you to do if you are not making money. Consult with people such as financial coaches or entrepreneurs who have been successful at marketing a business.

6) **Generate Yearly Financial Statements.** This seems to be an important factor for judges. Businesses generate yearly financial statements so that the owners can control expenses and help them achieve profitability.

Investigate the business you are going into before you launch it.[14] Do a feasibility study; see how profitable the type of business you want to launch can be. Listen to training tapes, take seminars, and attend training meetings. You can never get enough training, and it will serve to improve your bottom line at the same time it helps to satisfy the IRS that you are really taking the business seriously. Document all your training, lectures, and outside reading using your daily tax diary. This is very important. Every time you receive training or go to a seminar, document it.

Thoroughly investigate your business venture before jumping into it:

- Get a credit report on the sponsoring company (for network marketing).
- Check out the competition to see what they are doing.
- See how much money other distributors or business owners are making in the same business.
- If you can, review some financial reports related to your industry or business venture.

The more thorough your investigation, the better the chance that the IRS is going to believe you are in business to do business.

Rule #9: Devote Regular Time to Your Business. Although you don't have to devote your full time and attention to your business, it is very important that you devote some time in a regular manner to your activity. Businesses are conducted in a regular and systematic manner, hobbies are not.

Nobody says that a home-based business must be a full-time duty, but the more time and effort you put in it, the better. At least one case on the books has shown that an average of as little as one hour per day was substantial enough to prove a profit motive.[16] One hour a day, four to five days a week is better than putting in eight hours every two weeks.[17]

Now you might be asking how the IRS would know whether you actually put in one hour every day. How do they know you are actually seeing people in your business and visiting prospects and doing marketing? They look at your tax diary, that's how. A good diary is irreplaceable because it can go a long way towards proving that you are running a business, not engaging in a hobby. For more information on keeping an accurate tax diary, refer to Appendix H.

Rule #10: Keep a History of Income, Losses, and Steps You Have Taken to Improve the Bottom Line. Maintaining this kind of history is a very important step. In any business, expenses can certainly exceed income.[18] Businesses do have losses, and the hobby loss provisions aren't based on the assumption that no decent business person ever had a loss. However, real business people do everything necessary (and legal) to turn those losses into profits.[19]

You should watch out for expenses that are unreasonable. Expenses should be in proportion to your income. For example, a case involving an Amway distributor showed that his accounting fees alone had exceeded his entire gross income from his business. Because of this, the court held that the distributor's activities constituted a hobby.[20] Marketing expenses are an exception to the principle of proportionality since they can be very costly in the early stages of a company's existence.

This concept of using excessive and unreasonable expenses as a way of assessing the lack of a business profit motive has been applied to a lot of cases. For example, a person who has a travel business and tries to deduct all her family trips, despite very little gross income, is going to have a tough time proving that these trips had a profit motive. This is especially true if each trip cost more than the gross income of the business venture itself!

Your main objective should be to show that you are really trying to make a profit or turn your losses around. You want to show that you do have a reason for spending a large sum of money in one area. The best way to do this is to document, document, document! Document all marketing activities and all reasons for trips, noting the business intent and the necessity for taking the trip in order to make money. Again, refer to Appendix H for important information on documenting your business activities.

Note: Recent IRS cases indicate that there needs to be some gross income in order to be considered a business. If you are in a business that shows no gross income at all, the IRS is likely to see this as evidence that you are not in business and that you are conducting a hobby instead.

Rule #11: Keep In Mind that Income From Other Sources Can Affect an IRS Ruling. The IRS also looks at the amount of income you have from other sources.[21] This may not seem fair — if you make $200,000 and you go into a side business, you are more suspect than someone making $20,000 — but that's the way it is. The greater your income from other sources the less likely the loss from your other activity will be deemed a loss. This situation, however, does not mean all is lost. There are a lot of people who make hundreds of thousands of dollars and still claim losses from their side businesses. But certainly this situation requires that you dot your i's and cross your t's more carefully.

Rule #12: Be Alert If You Are Involved in Inherently "Suspicious" Activities. There are certain activities that seem to be inherently more suspicious than others to the IRS.[22] These are business ventures that may have more potential for significant personal pleasure. Following are some examples:

- Antique Collecting
- Stamp Collecting
- Travel & Tourism
- Writing

- Ministerial Duties
- Music Recording and Production
- Raising Show Horses
- Training and Showing Dogs
- Automobile Racing
- Network Marketing Businesses

If you are involved in one of these activities, you need to pay close attention to all the other rules we have outlined in this chapter.

For more information on how to set up and run a business, refer to Appendix D for checklists and resources.

While the rules that determine whether you are running a business or engaging in a hobby may make starting a business seem like a lot of work, we can assure you that learning these rules will make running your business a lot easier and will bring peace of mind. It will also prepare you to take full advantage of the tax savings we will explain in upcoming chapters. Only by committing yourself to get organized as Money Mastery Principle 8 teaches, will you ever be ready to launch a business that will run smoothly and efficiently for you, even in the early stages. As you form new "tax habits" it will become easier and more automatic to do the things we have discussed in this chapter. Plan to start your new business venture on the right foot by doing things right the first time.

✓ CHALLENGE #13:
Review the "Business vs. Hobby Checklist" and Obtain a Good Tax Diary

1. This week, review the following checklist to ensure that your venture will be conducted as a business and not a hobby:

✓ Try to have a profit in at least three out of five consecutive years, or two out of seven years if you are involved in animal breeding or racing, or automobile racing.

✓ Document your business intent by creating a business plan or obtaining contracts from your vendors.

✓ Obtain a business license from your city.

✓ Conduct your business in a businesslike manner.

✓ Document all business activities using a tax diary or daily planner.

✓ Keep business and financial records separate from personal finances.

✓ Open a separate bank account for your business.

✓ If your business requires inventory, make sure you have enough to justify your business plan goals.

✓ Use advertising, business telephone listings, and marketing materials as appropriate for your business, and change your advertising and marketing strategies from year-to-year if you are not making money.

✓ Investigate your business activity; document efforts.

✓ Obtain training continually; seek out expert advice; document efforts.

✓ Work your business regularly and document your activities daily.

✓ Keep a history of your business by keeping minutes and copies of contracts and resolutions on file, and show how you took steps to improve your bottom line.

✓ Refer to Appendix D of this book for more information on how to properly set up a business.

✓ Create yearly income and financial statements.

2. This week, be sure to obtain a good tax diary for recording your daily activities. (Refer to Appendix A for information about various tax diary products.)

CHAPTER 14

Your Home Office:
A Tax-saving Resource

K now the rules. We have emphasized again and again how important it is to heed this advice. So many people suffer when they take for granted the power of this Money Mastery principle. It can be applied in several areas of your life to bring peace, control, and stability. And when it comes to taxation, it's especially critical that the rules of the tax game are known and understood. In Chapter 13, we outlined some very important rules that will help distinguish your new venture as a business, and not simply as a hobby. You are now ready to learn some rules about the way to physically set up an office so you can be sure to run your business in a way that will ensure you the most tax savings. While these rules are generally relevant for all types of business, they are especially applicable if you are structured as a Sole Proprietorship or LLC. If you are structured as a C or S Corp, consult with your financial coach and/or accountant for more information pertaining to tax-saving strategies related to home office deductions for such entities.

Without question, a home office can be a valuable resource for tax deductions. Unfortunately, many people don't understand the wealth of tax savings they can get from a home office because they've heard a few myths about the limitations placed on a home office. These need clearing up:

Myth #1: I can't claim a home office deduction because my house isn't zoned commercially. The truth is the IRS does not care at all about the zoning laws in your area. You can live in a commercial, rural, residential, or agricultural zone and it won't make a bit of difference to the IRS.

Myth #2: I can't claim a home office because I don't have a back entrance in my home. The fact is the IRS is not concerned about how many entrances you have in your house.

Myth #3: My accountant said that the home office deduction isn't worth the trouble. Here's what the numbers say, and these numbers are based on a $220,000 home: The value of an office in such a home is about $2,500 a year in cash, which if you invest that at 6 percent, makes the actual value of a home office (over a five-year period) worth almost $15,000 every five years! In our opinion, paying yourself $15,000 every five years because you operate your business in your home sounds pretty worth the trouble, don't you think? (See Appendix G for a more detailed explanation of these figures.)

Myth #4: My accountant says that the home office deduction is limited to my income so if I don't make enough profit in my business, it isn't worth taking it. This is partly true. Your home office deduction is, indeed, limited to the net income from your business after taking all your other business deductions. Consequently, if you are not working your business, or if you are not making any kind of substantial income, you do not get an immediate benefit.

However, no "immediate benefit" is not the same as no benefit at all. If your deduction exceeds your net income from your business, you can carry it over into future income years indefinitely. So, as you make more money, you can offset those nice increases in income with carry-over deductions.

As you can see, a home office can be a very legitimate tax deduction.

Tax Strategy 4: If You Are Eligible for a Home Office Tax Deduction, Take It!

Here's how to assess whether you can apply Tax Strategy #4: The law states that a home office deduction is available only to the extent that a portion of the dwelling unit* is used as a home office exclusively and on a regular basis.[1] That means that your home office must be:

1. Your principal place of business; and/or
2. The place of business where you meet and greet customers, patients, or clients in the normal course of your business; and/or
3. Used for a second business you have; and/or
4. Used to display sample products or as storage space for inventory.

In addition, if you are using an office in your home to do work as a regular W-2 employee, then the home office deduction is allowed only if the exclusive use of the office is for the convenience of your employer.[2] Thus, your employer must require you to take work home, and not provide you with an office at work.

Let's examine each of the criteria we have outlined above in more detail:

Criteria #1: Principal Place of Business. What constitutes a principal place of business? A famous case called the "Doc Solomon" decision explains.[3] Dr. Solomon was an anesthesiologist. He worked in three different hospitals in Fairfax, Virginia for 30 to 35 hours a week. In his condominium he converted one of his bedrooms into an office where he worked another 10 to 15 hours a week. He did his billing and medical logs from home, read x-ray film from home, and, even more interesting, he had no other office. The hospitals for which he worked would not provide him with one.

Naturally, Dr. Solomon felt justified in claiming the home office deduction on his tax returns. His argument was, "My home has to be my principal place of business because I don't have another office." Dr. Solomon was audited and the IRS took him to court because they disagreed with his reasoning. A tax court heard the case and said, "Dr. Solomon, you are right." The IRS didn't like that answer so they took the case to an

---

*A separate structure, not attached to the dwelling unit, also qualifies if it is used in connection with your trade or business. This means if you convert your garage or another outbuilding for use as a workshop, for example, it could qualify for the home office deduction. Other examples include a florist's greenhouse or an artist's studio.

appellate court. The appellate court said, "Dr. Solomon, you are right." Of course, the IRS didn't like that either, so they went all the way to the Supreme Court. And as you know, that's where the buck always stops. The Supreme Court said: "Dr. Solomon, you are wrong. We have two tests we use to determine whether a home property is a principal place of business for a home office."

Test #1: "Where do you do your most important functions?" To that, Dr. Solomon's response was, "My most important function is done at home. That is where I do my billing."

"No," said the Supreme Court, "that is not your most important function, Dr. Solomon. You are a doctor of anesthesiology, so your most important function is done where you deliver your anesthesia — in a hospital. You don't do that out of your home. Now let's look at another way to qualify using test number two."

Test #2: "Do you use your home office for more than 50 percent of your at-work time? Take the total amount of hours you work in a week, Dr. Solomon," said the Supreme Court, "and divide by two. Does that yield more than 50 percent of your hours physically spent in your home?"

In Dr. Solomon's case, he spent 15 hours a week at home and 35 hours a week in the hospital, so he obviously didn't qualify. He was not entitled to the home office deduction under either rationale.

You will be happy to know, however, that there is now an exception to the "Doc Solomon" decision, especially as it applies to Test #1. Remember Money Mastery Principle 6, "The Rules Are Always Changing?" Due to tremendous complaints about the effect of this case on small business, Congress passed a special exception that took effect in 1999. This exception provides two new rules that help small businesses escape the clutches of the Solomon decision: [4]

New Rule #1: *Your office at home is used to conduct the administrative or management activities of your business; AND*

New Rule #2: *There is no other office where you conduct substantial and administrative activities for your business.*

That means, in terms of Test #1, the new rules allow that your primary function does not necessarily have to take place in your home office as long as your office at home is used to conduct the administrative or management activities of your business and you have no other office where you can conduct such activities. Thus, if you keep your logs, do your paperwork, listen to sales tapes, make business calls, create business materials, etc., out of a set place in your home, you will be legally eligible for the home office deduction.

But what about Test #2? Do the new laws Congress passed help overcome the difficulties of this test? Well, not directly, but the way this test is worded can be a bit misleading. Note that what test #2 is actually saying is "Do you perform any significant administrative services in another office for that business?" If you don't, you qualify for the exception. Let's look at some examples:

- John and Mary have W-2 jobs but they also have a part-time network marketing business. They have no other office for this business. They do all paperwork and greet all clients in their home. Their home qualifies as a principal place of business under either the Soloman ruling or the exception.

- David and Cari are real estate agents. Although their broker provides them an office, they rarely use it other than to drop off contracts and attend sales meetings. All calls, mailings, and real estate research is done at home. Their home qualifies as a principal office since they don't perform significant services out of the other office.

If you keep good records and work the 50 percent required time in your home in order to operate your business, you will have no problem taking the home office tax deduction. Moreover, even if you don't meet the 50 percent test, if you meet the exception to Soloman, that is, you conduct your significant administrative activities for your business at home and don't have another office where you can conduct those administrative activities, then your home constitutes a "principal office" for purposes of the home office deduction.

Criteria #2: Meet-and-Greet Test. If you don't use your home office 50 percent of the time for your home-based business, and don't meet the exception to the Soloman decision, you can still qualify for the home office deduction. An exception allows you to claim the deduction when you use your home office as a place where you meet and greet your clients (be they customers, patients, distributors, etc.) as a regular and ongoing part of your business.[5] Such use must be substantial and integral to conducting your business.[6]

During an audit, the IRS will look very closely at your actual physical meeting with clientele or customers. Telephone contacts do not count, no matter how lengthy or how frequent.[7] Meeting and dealing with clients in your home office is what counts. Now-and-then meetings do not qualify.[8] The law requires that:

- Meetings occur in a planned way
- Such meetings are ordinary (or regular)
- Such meetings are an essential part of the way you conduct business.

Be sure to keep track of all your hours for these meetings. Every time you work, you should note in your tax diary what you are doing. When you see clients, you should note this in your diary.

Criteria #3: Home Office Deduction for a Second Business. You might be able to qualify for a home office deduction in yet another way. If you happen to have a second side business, you can claim a deduction for that as well. The deduction does not have to relate to your primary business.

Criteria #4: Display or Inventory Storage. If you use space in your home to display or store products that you sell on a wholesale or retail basis, you can add the square footage of this space to the space you claim for the home office deduction. One of the requirements, however, is that your residence be the sole fixed location for your business.[9] In order to help you meet this criteria, our recommendation is to take photographs of the location in your home where you store inventory or display product samples. This is vital. By doing so, the IRS will have proof that you are using the space in this manner and cannot question you.

If you can meet any of the above four criteria you will have no problem proving that you use your home to conduct business and can take the home office deduction. Once you decide to take it, you should be aware of a few rules that can help you substantiate your claim.

Exclusive Use

You must use a room, or portion of a room, exclusively and regularly in one of several business functions in order to take a home office deduction. When the IRS says "exclusively," it is not kidding. This means that no personal or other non-qualifying work activities may occur in your home office area. If you watch TV in the designated home office area, unless it's solely for videotape training purposes, remove the television.[10] Remove those cookbooks from the shelves in your home office work space, and remove the games and other family fun activities out of the area. To qualify for the home office deduction, you don't have to use an entire room as your workspace. If you want to use part of a room for business, you can do that. However, there should be some physical separation of the business area from the personal area.[11] If you keep your desk, chair, and filing cabinet in your living room, for instance (which is the way many home-based businesses start out), then the square footage those items occupy qualifies for the home office; the rest of the room's square footage does not. You are not allowed to co-mingle your business and personal furniture. We often hear people wondering if the IRS will really send someone over to their house to see if they are using an exclusive portion of a room for business. Yes, they will. Fortunately, if they plan to send anyone by your house, they will give between four and 12 weeks advance notice. Even with a notice, however, the IRS still manages to nail the unsuspecting taxpayer.

Here's an example of just how sneaky IRS agents can be. When Sandy was working as an attorney with the IRS, one of his agent colleagues audited a person claiming the home office deduction. Everything appeared to be in order in this taxpayer's home office. But then the agent ran a directory of the taxpayer's hard drive and discovered a game called "King's Quest" on it. Naturally, a person can have games loaded on their office computer; they just can't play them in their home office. The problem was that the taxpayer played the game and then saved it onto his hard drive in the same year that he was claiming the home office deduction. Even though he may have played the game only once during the year, by keeping the computer in the area he claimed for his home office, this taxpayer lost his deduction.

In another instance involving an audit, an IRS agent visited the home of the taxpayer and noticed a sofa bed in the home office area. Of course it was perfectly acceptable for this taxpayer to have a sofa bed in his office, as long as nobody slept on it! The IRS agent knew what would happen if he just flat out asked the taxpayer if anybody every slept on the sofa bed — of course his answer would be "No!" Instead, after completing the audit, the agent sat on the sofa and said, "Gee, you know, I'm thinking of buying something like this for my parents to use when they come to visit me. My dad has a bad back. Do you have any experience with this? About somebody who might have hurt his back?" Obviously, the taxpayer was taken off guard and said, "Yeah, my brother and dad come to visit me and they don't have any problem. My mom doesn't have any problem." The agent then nailed him because he now had proof that the individual used the sofa bed in his home office for personal reasons and disallowed the deduction.

So how can you absolutely, with confidence, prove a home office deduction? Follow these tips and you will be totally secure:

1) Photograph Your Office. A photo can be a very important piece of documentation. Take pictures of the bookshelves, the file cabinets, the desk, and the general workspace. Make sure you have all your personal items out of the area before you do so. You don't want the IRS to see *Crossword Puzzle Secrets* in the photograph. Date the photos, but don't send them to the IRS. Simply hold onto them in case you ever do get audited. They will come in very handy. Photographs establish exclusivity.

2) Prepare a Floor Plan. Keep blueprints of your home to prove the amount of space occupied by the home office. If blueprints are not available, make a drawing of your home showing the relationship of the home office's square footage to the total square footage of the home.

Using a floor plan with the actual square footage of your home you can easily calculate how much square footage you can deduct for a home office. You can also maximize this space using different computing methods. (For a sample floor plan and more information on these maximizing methods, refer to Appendix C.)

3) Prominently Display Home Office Address. Put your address and telephone number on business cards and stationery.[12] The IRS takes the position that if people don't know you're alive and kicking somewhere, you can't take a home office deduction.

4) Use a Guest Log. If you physically meet and greet clients at home on a regular basis, you can absolutely prove your home office exists using a guest log. Every time clients come to your home, have them write down their name, address, and occupation.

5) Document Use of Your Office in Your Tax Diary. This is where a tax diary can pay for itself a hundredfold. Use your tax diary to record what activities you performed in your home office such as, "Studied for my network business from 8:00 to 9:00," or "Made calls from 9:00 to 12:00, HO (home office)." This work activity log in your diary does not need to be an elaborate document; simply keep some notes about what you did during the day. If you ever get audited, you may have to answer questions about work or phone calls or training sessions that occurred two or three years prior.

When you make long distance calls, are you required to write down every person's name that you call in your tax diary? Generally not. But you should log it somewhere as a business-related call. During an audit, the IRS would ask, "Is this particular activity business or personal?" If you have not kept a log of your daily business activities, how will you ever know? You might look at your phone bill from three years previous and not be able to discern between calls made for business and calls made for pleasure. Don't forget, if the IRS audits you, they will not be doing so the same year you made those calls.

Remember, keep a good tax diary and organize all records.

Furnishings and Equipment

A home office deduction relates only to the real estate and utilities for the office, and not for the furnishings and equipment used in it. However, such furniture and equipment can be depreciated. The rule is: Furniture, whether you qualify for a home office deduction or not, is depreciable only to the extent that you use it for business.[13]

For example, say you work at home and 80 percent of the time you use a desk for business. Even though you don't claim a home office, 80 percent of that desk becomes depreciable. If you sit on chairs, use desk lamps, computer equipment, file cabinets or bookshelves, these can also be depreciated if they are used to conduct business.

How do you depreciate furniture and equipment so you can deduct it? First, you must keep good tax records, as we have already emphasized. By doing so, within a 90-day period, you can determine what percentage of your time is spent in business and personal use and then use that time to help figure what percentage of the desk, chair, carpeting, lighting, equipment, etc., that you can depreciate. Second, determine the depreciation amount allowed for the item. This amount is the lower amount of the original cost, or today's market value.[14] So let's say you have an antique desk you bought three years ago. It cost you $500 and today it's worth $550.

The amount you can write off for that desk is the lower of the two figures. This depreciation rule assumes you work your business regularly, emphasizing once again how important it is to give your business, even if it's part-time, consistent efforts.[15]

What qualifies as a write-off for a home office? Anything you use in business other than an automobile. Examples include:

- Photocopy machines
- Computers
- Printers
- FAX machines
- Office furnishings including rugs, lighting, desks, chairs, bookcases
- Software

If you choose to depreciate such items, then you have to keep the item in your business for seven years or you must recapture some of that depreciation.

For example, a person buys a rug and a photocopier for his home-based business for a total of $4,200. He can either depreciate that amount over seven years or he can elect to write off the entire amount in the year he purchased the items. Writing off the entire cost in the year it is purchased is usually the best course, but again, that deduction is limited to the income from the home-based business. If you don't have a lot of income, you will have to carry over the deduction. If you work your business as hard as you should, you will have the advantage of more income, and more income brings increased tax benefits as we have just outlined.

As of 2006, you can elect to expense up to $108,000 worth of business equipment per year.[16] What happens if you want to purchase more than $108,000 worth of equipment and furnishings in a year? Anything you purchase over that amount must be depreciated instead. Let's say you buy $150,000 worth of equipment for your business. You can elect to write-off $108,000 of it and the remaining $42,000 you can depreciate. You can also choose to wait. You can buy only $108,000 worth of equipment in the current year, and in January of the next year, buy the additional $42,000 worth of items that you need. In this way, you can elect to write off $108,000 in the current year, and $42,000 as part of next year's purchases, avoiding any depreciation. Waiting may be a better way of saving tax dollars than purchasing all $150,000 worth of equipment in one year.

Be sure to consult with your accountant about all the rules for depreciating furnishings and equipment for your home office.

Other Things To Consider About the Home Office Deduction

If you are eligible for a home office deduction, you have to claim it. You cannot simply decide not to deduct it if you do meet the eligibility requirements we have outlined above. Why is this? If the IRS discovers that you are eligible, they will insist that you have to reduce the basis of your home by the amount of depreciation allowable anyway, so you might as well take it.[17]

If you rent, you can take the claim by deducting a portion of your rent as it equates to the square footage of the home office. For example, if you pay $750 per month in rent on a 1,000 square-foot apartment, and your home office occupies 250 square feet of that space, you can deduct one-fourth of your rent (or $187.50 per month; $2,250 per year) for your home office. As you can see, you don't need to own your home in order to claim the home office deductions. It is available to renters too.

Another thing to consider is that the home office deduction is limited to the net income from the business activity you conducted at home.[18] Consequently, if you have any expenses above and beyond the net income, you will not be able to deduct those home office expenses. That doesn't mean you shouldn't take the home office deduction because any expenses disallowed solely because they exceed your business income can be carried forward until you have sufficient income from your business conducted from home.[19]

✓CHALLENGE #14:
Determine Whether You Can Take the Home Office Deduction

This week, review the four criteria for claiming a home office as outlined in this chapter to determine if you meet any of them, then be sure to do the following:

1. Determine the exact amount of square footage your home office area will occupy in your home. Use blueprints or floor plans as necessary. (See Appendix C for more information on calculating floor space.)

2. Be sure to keep the office free of personal belongings. If you have already established a work area, remove such things as TVs, computer games, personal books, board games, etc.

3. Take photographs of your office area and date them.

4. Purchase a guest book if you plan to meet clients in your home.

5. Have business cards and letterhead printed with your address and business phone on them.

6. Begin to log your personal and business time so that you can determine your "business percentage" time for the purpose of depreciating furnishings and equipment.

CHAPTER 15

Deduct Meals, Entertainment, and Auto With Confidence

By now you're beginning to see that if you want to get serious about reducing your tax bill, you must become better informed about the way the tax system really works and what you can do to best take advantage of it. At this point, it should be clear that you can't be meek about reducing your tax burden. Those who sit back and accept what is put before them regarding their tax obligations will end up paying far more than is actually required by law.

It may be true that "the meek shall inherit the earth," but in today's world, the meek are also more likely to overpay their taxes!

If you want to get serious about reducing Excessive Taxation, you must be assertive in learning and applying the guidelines outlined in this book. If you have followed these guidelines, you have now decided upon and launched a new business venture, legally structured it in a way that is most appropriate for your circumstances, and set up your business and home office work space so that you can confidently claim as many tax deductions as possible.

Now it's time to get even bolder. In this chapter we will help you learn how to write off business activities you engage in on a regular basis — and we'll teach you to do this with confidence.

Tax Strategy 5: Put Extra Cash in Your Pocket by Properly Deducting Meals, Entertainment and Auto Expenses

Unfortunately, this tax strategy is one that many people fail to benefit from because they aren't aware of all the opportunities of which they can take advantage. Several of our clients, after learning about the power of this tax-saving strategy, realize that they've lost thousands of dollars in tax deductions over the years because they didn't fully understand it. That's because they never learned what you're about to learn from any other source, and their accountant certainly never sat down and explained it to them.

Before we begin our explanation, we should note up front that the whole topic of expense deductions is a touchy one with Congress and the IRS. But with a good business accounting system, a tax diary, and our advice about the importance of documentation ringing in your ears, you're armed and ready to keep the IRS off your back forever. If you follow the recommendations made in this chapter, you can bullet-proof your tax return while taking full advantage of the "good laws" designed to give a tax break to the self-employed. Guaranteed!

Rules for Deducting Meals

One of the most important activities in which small business people engage is meeting potential customers or clients for lunch, or taking them out for an evening of entertainment as a means to secure more business. Why not take full advantage of the tax write-offs allowed by law for such things?

Following are the questions we are most frequently asked regarding this tax deduction:

- What are the substantiation requirements for my meal deductions?
- If I buy someone else's meal what can I deduct?
- Can I deduct a meal expense if I'm not present at the meal?
- When can I deduct my spouse's (or significant other's) meal costs?
- If I go "Dutch Treat" with someone, can I deduct anything?

Let's address each of these questions beginning with how meal deductions can be substantiated.

The Five Substantiation Requirements:[1]

1) The cost of the meal.
2) The date you ate the meal.
3) Where the meal was eaten.
4) The purpose for which the meal was eaten, i.e., why did you take the person out to eat?
5) With whom was the meal consumed, i.e., what is their business relationship to you?

Every time you entertain, you should be in the habit of writing down these five requirements in your tax diary: cost, date, location, purpose, and business relationship. If you keep track of these elements "in a timely fashion" (another IRS rule we will discuss in this chapter) you will never have to worry about taking this deduction again. We should note, however, that if you don't track them, no matter what other support you may have for your meal expense it will not be allowed as a deduction.

Let's consider each of these substantiation requirements:

Cost. As always we recommend you record this item in your accounting system and/or tax diary — this is what the IRS means by "timely basis." You cannot come back later and hope to remember how much the item cost. You must do it on the day the event occurred.

Note: If the cost of the meal was not more than $74.99 you do not need to keep any documentary evidence such as a receipt, a voucher, or a credit card charge copy.[2] However, we recommend keeping all receipts because they act as a triggering mechanism to help you practice good accounting and documentation. Keeping all receipts will help simplify your life because collecting them disciplines you to do the same thing every time and helps you remember to record all activities on a timely basis.

Date. Record the date when the meal took place. If you keep track in a tax diary or daily planner, the date on the diary page is adequate support.

Description. Give the nature of the meal you are claiming and the location where it took place. Some people assume this means they must describe the meal they ate — "hog jowl and grits" — but this is not so. The name of the eating establishment is sufficient. If the meal is $75 or over you are required to keep a receipt; naturally it will include this information.

Business Purpose. Of the five elements, this is the most important. You must record why you took someone out to eat. Be specific.[3] Note in your diary that you talked about skin care needs, for example, or legal or tax reduction needs, or whatever activity fits the business you are in. Be brief, but be specific. Perhaps you discussed referrals with the person you took to lunch, or maybe the opportunity to launch a new venture. If you were to record such purposes as "good will" or "prospect" don't expect them to be accepted because they aren't specific enough. If you simply write down the word "customer," it is not specific enough.

Consider the following examples of specific business purpose documentation:

- Pre-qualified buyer
- Pre-qualified seller
- Talked about inviting Charlie to the business ("recruiting discussion")
- Asked for referrals ("referral discussion")
- Talked about nutritional needs
- Talked about skin care needs
- Talked about weight loss needs
- Talked about legal needs.

Business Relationship. Record the name and occupation in your tax diary of the person you took to lunch/dinner. Naturally, the IRS will not call these people to verify that they ate lunch with you, but it does want to know who they are and what their business is in relation to you.

The illustration on page 275 from a typical tax diary is a good example of how each of the five substantiation requirements should be recorded.

Notice how simple it is, yet specific where it needs to be. The date (not referenced in this graphic) appears at the top of the diary page. Each of the other four elements are properly recorded, including the cost of valet service. A good tax diary, which will usually include fields for noting each of the substantiation requirements, provides the trigger you need to record these elements within 24 hours of the meal. How does the IRS know if you record it in a "timely fashion?" It asks you. That's why you must get into the habit of recording these items each and every time you entertain clients. If you leave out any one of the five, your deductions will be disallowed and you will be hit with a 75 percent civil fraud penalty[4] should you ever be audited. There's no kidding around here.

ENTERTAINMENT					
WHO?	S. JONES				
WHERE?	PALM				
WHY?	OBTAIN REFFERALS				
BREAKFAST		HOME		OTHER	
LUNCH	20 00	GOLF/ETC.		COATS & VALET	4 00
DINNER		COCKTAILS			
TOTAL	——	TOTAL	——	TOTAL	24 00

(ACTIVITY 1)

Following is a personal example in Sandy Botkin's own words about the value of recording these five elements in a good tax diary:

"On the eve of going to work for the IRS, I was a tax shelter syndicator with $11,000 of entertainment expenditures. All new employees of the IRS must be audited. The IRS agent assigned to audit me looked at my records and saw that I followed the five substantiating requirements throughout my diary. I was allowed every single dime of that $11,000 entertainment claim — every single dime. Moreover, the whole entertainment audit only took four minutes because my documentation was so good!"

From this you can see how important it is to document everything. The key is to have a triggering mechanism that prompts you to make daily notations in your diary. A good tax organizer will help you keep receipts in a neat and orderly fashion and help you remember to write down the details of the meeting that the receipt documents.

But I don't have time to record all that stuff....

This is a complaint we sometimes hear, much like the one we hear about tracking the spending of money. As we noted in Chapter 2, many people believe they don't have the time for keeping records. This idea has cost, and will continue to cost such people loads of money. In the same light, this attitude also robs people of valuable tax dollars as well because without keeping track on a daily basis of their activities, they cannot boldly and confidently deduct every expense to which they are legally entitled. How long does it actually take to write down each of the five substantiating elements? No longer than 10 seconds. That means that it should take you no more than about 10 minutes per week to potentially save thousands of dollars in taxes. If you were to save at least $10,000 annually putting in a maximum of 500 minutes per year by properly documenting your deductions, this would produce tax-free earnings of $20 per minute or a tax-free $1,200 per hour!

On a per minute basis, nothing is more cost-effective than keeping proper records for the IRS.

It's your choice. You can give 30, 40, or even 50 percent of what you earn to the government in overly inflated tax payments, or you can take the time to document your activities and save yourself thousands of dollars. It's up to you. Make your life easier beginning today by doing the following:

1. Gather all receipts.
2. Record the five substantiating requirements in your tax diary or on the receipt.
3. Post the receipt to your tax diary or accounting system.

The Rules Governing How Much of a Meal You Can Actually Deduct

Any meal that you purchase for someone else is deductible by 50 percent for your cost and 50 percent of your guest's cost,[5] including the tip. What about drinks? These too are 50 percent deductible. Now doesn't that sound great?! Isn't it wonderful to know just how good the tax laws really are when you understand how to take advantage of them?

What else do you need to be aware of when taking this 50 percent meal deduction?

1) You must talk business during the meal in order to claim the deduction. The IRS requires a substantial business discussion. This means that your primary purpose for the entertainment is to conduct business and you have a clear and specific business conversation.

2) You cannot take the same people out too frequently. Entertaining the same person every day is not acceptable. Once a week is the most the IRS will generally allow.

3) Meals must take place in surroundings conducive to a business discussion.[6] In order for a location to have "conducive surroundings" it must meet two tests:

Test #1: There is a long, hard surface between you and your business associate where you can get a contract signed. For example, you could meet in a bar where there are at least three hard surfaces where you could sign a contract: a table, a bar stool, or the floor.

Test #2: There is no floorshow. This means no tailgate parties, orchestra, or any other distracting events.[7]

What do you need to do in these dinner and lunch meetings to be sure you are actually conducting business?

Usually when a prospect or client meets you for lunch they will ask, "How's business?" Your reply should always be: "Business is unbelievable, but I never have enough customers [prospects, referrals, etc.]." By making such a statement, you have discussed business. By saying you "never have enough . . ." you are also indicating that you are seeking more business from the person with whom you are eating the meal. Specifically discussing any prospects, referrals, or possible projects that may come up in the course of the conversation will further help you meet the IRS requirement to conduct a substantial business discussion. After the meal, you should document this discussion in your tax diary. By doing so, you will never have to worry about an IRS audit again.

Rules for Deducting Spouse (or Significant Other) Meal Costs

Sometimes people ask: "My spouse works with me in my business; can I ever take her out alone to eat and talk about business? And if I do, shouldn't I be allowed to deduct her meal costs, just as I would with any other business client?" The answer to this question is absolutely not. You can never take your spouse alone to dinner and write it off because the IRS has a rule known as the "closely connected" spouse rule.[8] A rule called the "closely connected significant friend" also exits. The IRS is a big, romantic teddy bear at heart — it believes that if you go out to dinner with your spouse or significant other, you will have far too many other warm and cozy things to talk about to ever get around to talking about business!

Is there any way that you can ever take your spouse out to dinner and deduct the expense? Yes...whenever you entertain another couple for the purpose of discussing business, you may bring your spouse.[9] Bringing a spouse or friend along allows them to entertain the spouse or friend of the contact with whom you wish to conduct business, making it easier for you to have a one-on-one business conversation with that contact.

Rules for Deducting "Dutch Treat" Meals

What if you go out with your client and the two of you split the bill? This falls under what the IRS calls the "Dutch Treat Rule." Both you and your client will be permitted to take a deduction. Here's how it works:

You and your client (we'll call him George) split the bill for lunch and your share is $24 (it was a nice lunch). Under the Dutch Treat Rule, you must subtract your average cost of eating a meal at home (refer to Appendix E for the formula for calculating this average at-home meal cost) or in a fast food restaurant, which in this case we'll say is $4, from the cost of the business lunch you had with George.[10] The difference is $20. The amount you can write off is 50 percent of that, or $10. Now $10 may not seem like much to you — but if you do this twice a week, for instance, that's $20; if you do it 50 weeks a year, the amount you can deduct adds up to $1,000 per year. Many small business owners miss out on some valuable tax savings because they do not know that taking a percentage of your Dutch Treat meal is allowable.

There are some internal IRS policies related to this rule of which you need to be aware that are not documented anywhere else:

1) You are limited to two Dutch Treat lunches in a week, or a total of 100 Dutch Treat lunches in a year.
2) However, you are also allowed 100 Dutch Treat breakfasts, and 100 Dutch Treat dinners.

In the course of a year, you could write off a percentage of 300 Dutch Treat meals, literally "eating" away your taxes!

Other Meal Deduction Rules to Consider

What If You're Not Present at the Meal? People often ask if they can deduct a meal that they buy for someone else when they are not physically present at the lunch or dinner gathering. You might say to one of your prospects, "Here's a gift certificate to this restaurant," or "Try this great little place I discovered and send me the bill." Marketing professionals may spend hundreds of dollars a year treating others to such meals. Unfortunately, not one penny of it is deductible if you are not physically present during the meal.[11] It is specifically provided for in the Internal Revenue Code that gifts of entertainment for food are not allowed when you are not present.[12] This is considered cheating by the IRS and auditors will get you for it. Actually, in this case, the IRS's position is quite reasonable. That's because it allows business deductions for meals assuming that business will be discussed during the course of those meals.

Rather than giving away gift certificates, you should be giving away certificates for entertainment that do not include a meal such as theater seats, baseball and football games, concert tickets, etc. This will save you the most tax money. That's because these kind of entertainment expenses can be deducted up to 50 percent of the face value of the entertainment or ticket, and you do not have to be present in order to take advantage of the write-off.[13] You could also treat such donations as business gifts and take a 100 percent deduction for them as long as they don't exceed $25. Congress has allowed that entertainment tickets may be classified either as entertainment or as a business gift.[14] Someone who gives away a ballet ticket or theater ticket to a potential client can deduct 50 percent of the cost of the ticket so long as they record in their tax diary the reason for giving the client the ticket. Be sure to record the name of the donee, the date of the gift, and a notation about the reason for giving it, such as "referrals."

Business Club Dues and Lunches. Dues for such clubs and civic organizations are almost fully deductible.[15] You may also deduct dues paid to professional societies.[16] Trade association dues are deductible if the association's purpose is to further the business interest of its members.[17] Thus dues paid to the "MLMIA" or "HomeBusiness Alliance," for instance, would be deductible.

Business lunches held at a specific business organization are 50 percent deductible. Note that meals incurred and paid for while talking business at the club are also deductible but may fall under the Dutch Treat rule in this case. We should add that country club and health club dues are not deductible.[18] At one point, these dues were permissible, but today, under the guise of "tax simplification," Congress has eliminated them.

Sales Seminars and Presentations at Home. Based on a tax court memorandum decision[19] and also a private-letter ruling, all food and refreshments served to prospects at home during a sales seminar or sales presentation are 100 percent deductible! Isn't that great? You must, as we have said before, document your activities on the day of the sales presentation.

Okay, now that we have spelled out all the exciting deductions for meals and the rules governing how those deductions can be taken, let's move on to entertainment deductions.

Rules for Deducting Entertainment

Entertainment is a four-syllable word that is often used in place of a simple one-syllable word: fun. We think you'll like what we're going to explain about how to deduct entertainment expenses for your business, or in other words, all your fun. What this means is that if you go to the theater or play a round of golf or go to a football game, you can deduct some of the cost of that activity, making what you do twice as much fun!

Based on IRS regulation, you may deduct up to 50 percent of your fun if you talk business in a business setting.[20] Of course the IRS will never believe that you talked business while you were watching "Hamlet" or while you played a round of golf.[21] So if you want to write off the golf game, the play, or any kind of fun, the rule according to the IRS is: You must talk business either preceding the fun or following the fun at any time during the same 24-hour day as the "fun" occurred.[22]

Suppose you are going to a football game with Jack, a potential customer, and you are buying his ticket. As you drive to the football game (preferably in Jack's car), you talk about his real estate needs and then you go to the game. Does this meet the IRS requirement for talking business within the same 24-hour period? You bet. Now why do we suggest having Jack drive to the game? Because the IRS does not allow you to deduct mileage for entertainment, so Jack might as well pay for that!

Here's another example: Let's say you call Janet and talk about some of the latest skin care products available. Then, three hours later you pick up Janet and go to a movie. Is that talking business within the same 24-hour period? Absolutely! Suppose you go out to lunch with Mike and talk business over lunch. Then you say, "You know, it's such a beautiful day, what do you say we go play golf?" And Mike says, "Show me how to play and I'll play!" Is that talking business within the same 24-hour period? Of course.

Similar to anything else related to taxes, however, it is your burden to prove that you actually did talk business in the same 24-hour day as you had fun. That's why a good tax organizing system and tax diary are so important. In the illustration below, you can see an ideally documented diary day.

Notice how this particular type of tax diary triggers you to document each substantiating factor required by law including the cost, date, location, purpose, and business relationship. In this example, you can see that $381

ACTIVITY 2					
WHO?	J&S ROCK				
WHERE?	PALM AND KENNEDY CENTER				
WHY?	JOHNSON REFFERAL AT DINNER FOLLOWED BY THEATRE				
BREAKFAST		HOME		OTHER	
LUNCH		GOLF/ETC.		THEATRE	120 00
DINNER	235 00	COCKTAILS	15 00	PARK, ETC.	11 00
TOTAL	—	TOTAL	—	TOTAL	381 00

has been totaled for food and theater tickets. The three most important words in the whole English language are noted on this example. Now most people think the three most important words are "I love you." Those are good words, but as far as the IRS is concerned, the three words that matter the most in this case and that appear on this example are: "followed by theater." By documenting the fun that came after the business meeting, this taxpayer will be able to deduct a portion of his entertainment expense.

What About Season Tickets...Can I Write Them Off?

The answer is yes, you can write off 50 percent of the cost of your season tickets for such things as theater, ballet, sporting events, and opera because the IRS says every event stands by itself.[23] Suppose you talk to Debbie, a friend, about your vitamin supplement products and then you take Debbie to the ballet using one of your season tickets. If you properly document the meeting and the entertainment following that business discussion, then you can deduct 50 percent of the cost of your ticket and her ticket.

Note: You can only deduct the face value of the ticket. Scalpers' profits are not deductible.[24]

What About Business Gifts, and When Can I Deduct Them?

Everybody gives business gifts. If you ever give a birthday gift to a prospect or that prospect's children, or wedding gifts, anniversary gifts, or baby shower presents, then you can deduct 100 percent of the cost of that gift.[25] That's the good news. The bad news is that the limit you can spend on the gift you wish to write off at 100 percent is $25 per person per year; husband and wife are treated as one person.[26] There is one exception to the $25 limit. If you give a person tickets to one of your season ticket events, then this gift is 50 percent deductible, regardless of its cost.

This $25 limit on gifts only applies to individuals. If you buy a gift for a business where there is no single person designated to receive or benefit from that gift, then there is no limit to the amount you can spend and write off at 100 percent.[27] For example, if you are giving a gift of candy or flowers to an electronics manufacturing company from which you are trying to obtain a public relations consulting contract, for instance, and you don't designate a specific individual in your gift card, that gift will be 100 percent deductible, no matter how much you spend on it.

Taking Advantage of the #1 Overlooked Business Entertainment Deduction

Most people don't know that they can take home entertainment as a business deduction if done properly. Here's how it works:

You invite a couple of your friends (i.e., prospects, customers, clients, referrals) over for a small dinner party at your home. What's usually the first thing that friends and neighbors always ask someone who is self-employed or engaged in running a home-based business? "How's business?" And of course you should say, "Business is unbelievable, but I never have enough contacts [referrals, prospects, projects, etc.]." Even if the party lasts four hours and you never talk business again, that 10-second conversation entitles you to write off 50 percent of the cost of that party! That's right, 50 percent. No time requirement exists which forces you to spend a certain amount of time discussing business; however, the rule is you must document what you did discuss. In addition, if you spend less than $75 to serve a light dinner to a couple of guests, then you do not need a receipt for your food and beverage.

Note: Your primary purpose for the entertainment party must be for business reasons. You can't combine personal reasons such as a birthday party, wedding etc. and make it deductible.

If you hold large dinner parties at your home, talking business to all 20 of your guests on an individual basis could become quite tiresome. There is a better way to meet the IRS's requirement.[28] The following case study shows you how.

Sharon Ladd: Hosting a Tax-deductible Dinner Party

Case History

At her eight-year anniversary of being in business for herself, Sharon Ladd* sent out a letter to all her prospects in Houston saying that she planned to celebrate the business anniversary. She invited these people to her house for a party. "I am celebrating eight years in the home-based direct sales marketing business; please come to my anniversary party," she said in the letter. Using such wording established a business-intent for the party, meeting the IRS requirement that she talk business. At the party, where she hosted over 20 people, Sharon didn't once talk business with any of her guests. Instead, she served a giant Texas-sized buffet and above each food platter she displayed photographs of what she did in her home-based business. Sharon also included products, testimonials, and prices, which as people took the food they could not help but notice. She then had her husband take pictures of everyone looking at the displays as they took their food. Doing so proved without doubt that Sharon was holding a business party where business was being discussed. How could anyone argue that Sharon had not held a business party? Of course Sharon was subtly doing business by inviting guests to a celebration party for her business and by exposing them to the products and services she sold. But the nice thing about this style of doing it was that she didn't have to talk to each individual person at the party about her business, and she didn't have to hit any of her guests over the head with a strong sales pitch. Sharon spent over $300 for that party. Was she required by the IRS to get a referral from the event? No. In fact she could have spent $3,000 and not received one referral. The IRS doesn't presume that it's the tax-payer's fault when a party is a "failure." It just accepts that not all marketing works!

* Names changed to protect privacy.

Exceptions to the Entertainment Deduction Rules

If you employ non-relatives in your business venture, there are exceptions of which you need to be aware. Consult with your accountant on these exceptions.

Maximize Your Business Automobile Deductions

Anyone who operates a small business venture knows that their car is one of the most vital tools they use to help run their business. It's also one that can cause potential tax problems if you are not aware of the laws surrounding it. Without question, claims for automobile expenses are the most frequently audited — the number one deduction that the IRS checks out. But, if you know what you're doing, your car can put thousands of saved tax dollars in your pocket.

Let's begin by explaining the two ways in which the IRS allows you to figure your car expenses:

1. "Actual" method
2. "IRS" method

The Actual method is just what it sounds like — you total up every penny you spend for your car including repairs, maintenance, gas, oil, windshield wiper fluid, insurance, wash and wax jobs, etc. The sum is your actual expense.

The IRS method can be used in lieu of all that figuring. Instead, this method gives a mileage allowance whereby you figure the automobile deductions you can take. In 2006, that allowance was $44.5 cents per business mile (which includes $17.0 cents in depreciation) with no limit to how many miles you can travel in a year.[29] Naturally, this allowance can change from year to year depending on inflation, so keep this in mind.

How do you decide which of the two methods will work best for you?

Suppose in 2006 you put 20,000 business miles on your four-year-old car that cost you $20,000; you could then claim $44.5 cents a mile times your 20,000 business miles; your deduction would equal $8,900. Not bad. For the owner of an average-priced vehicle, the IRS method may offer the most tax savings. The bottom line in determining whether to use the Actual or IRS method depends on the value of the car — the cheaper the car, the better it is to use the IRS method. That's because the more expensive the car, the less value the $44.5 cents per mile will have. The IRS tends to allow $.04 less than what it actually takes to operate a typical mid-size car (according to the American Automobile Association [AAA][30]). If you own a Mercedes, Porsche, Jaguar, Audi, Lexus, Cadillac, or large sports utility vehicle such as a Chevrolet Suburban or Ford Explorer, you should probably use the Actual method. That's because these cars cost more to run and maintain, so the low $44.5 cent mileage allowance really isn't going to provide much of a tax savings.

Figuring Deductible "Business Miles"

Regardless of which method you use, IRS or Actual, you will still need to keep track of all your "business miles." The IRS says that whenever you go from your home to a "temporary business stop" or in other words to a place that you don't go regularly, all that mileage is considered "business mileage."[31] Examples of a temporary business stop include:

- A client or prospect's home or place of business
- A down-line distributor if you are in a network marketing business
- A presentation you are giving
- To deliver a distributor's kit or deliver a product
- A seminar
- To visit an accountant or lawyer
- To pick up supplies
- Taking a prospect to lunch
- Anywhere you don't go regularly, or don't go every day.

The IRS breaks down these temporary business stops into four types of trips:

Type 1: Home is your principal office. All temporary business stops from your home constitute business mileage.[32] Thus, going from home to a meeting, seminar, or to the bank (for business purposes), or to visit a customer or client would constitute business mileage.

Type 2: Your home is not your principal office, but you travel outside of the geographic area of your normal work. In this case, all round-trip mileage would constitute business.[33] For example, Sheridan normally lives and works in Salt Lake City. If she has a meeting in Provo, a city 45 miles south of Salt Lake, she may deduct all round-trip mileage to Provo because she traveled outside of her normal geographic work area.

Type 3: Your home is not your principal office, but you are on a temporary job assignment or job site that is expected to last less than one year. Should you be temporarily assigned to a new job site or office where the job or the engagement is expected to last less then one year, you may deduct all round-trip mileage.[34] The key to taking this mileage as a business expense is that you expect to be there less than one year. If your engagement takes longer than that all mileage incurred after the one-year period would constitute non-deductible personal commuting.[35]

Type 4: Your home is not your principal office and you make some business stops outside your normal business location. This is where most of the confusion arises, and this is where the law becomes murky. It is our understanding that the IRS would mandate that your first "business stop" be deemed personal and your last business stop back home be deemed personal. All stops in between would be for business. Can the mileage between those stops be counted (other than the first and last stop) as business mileage? Yes. Those miles are counted as business whether you traveled one block away from your home or office or 100 blocks. You can see from this that working your business regularly will increase the chances that you will need to make a temporary business stop and you can then deduct those miles for business.

Example: Marc makes some business stops on the way to his office. He sees some clients and makes some presentations. His first stop would be deemed personal and all other stops on the way to the office, including his mileage from the last stop to the office, would constitute business mileage.

Tip: If your home is not your principal place of business, arrange your first business stop and your last temporary business stop as close to your home as possible so you can take the most mileage for all those stops in between. And try to avoid just driving straight from home to your downtown office — work your business on the way by making those necessary business stops and write off most of the mileage as business!

The flowchart on page 288 summarizes these temporary business stops. How does the IRS know that you went to a temporary business stop on your way to your office or on the way home? Simple — the auditor looks in your tax diary. If you do not have a downtown office, your diary is very critical. That's because you have to show that you are really spending at least a few hours per week working out of your home. Then, every

Flow Chart of Business Mileage

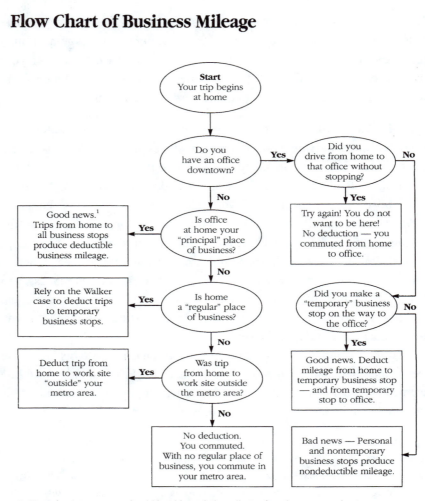

Start
Your trip begins
at home

Do you have an office downtown? — **Yes** → Did you drive from home to that office without stopping? — **No**

No ↓

Is office at home your "principal" place of business? — **Yes** → Good news.[1] Trips from home to all business stops produce deductible business mileage.

Yes (from "Did you drive...") → Try again! You do not want to be here! No deduction — you commuted from home to office.

No ↓

Is home a "regular" place of business? — **Yes** → Rely on the Walker case to deduct trips to temporary business stops.

Did you make a "temporary" business stop on the way to the office? — **No**

Yes (from "Did you make a temporary...") → Good news. Deduct mileage from home to temporary business stop — and from temporary stop to office.

No ↓

Was trip from home to work site outside the metro area? — **Yes** → Deduct trip from home to work site "outside" your metro area.

No ↓

No deduction. You commuted. With no regular place of business, you commute in your metro area.

Bad news — Personal and nontemporary business stops produce nondeductible mileage.

1. Home business owners should be able to deduct all trips from home to any business stop. Rev. Rul. 90-23, 1990-11 I.R.B. 4.
Rev. Rul. 90-23, 1990-11 I.R.B. 4.

time you go to a business stop you can count that mileage as business. But you must document this!

Now if you try to tell the IRS that you had zero commuting miles 365 days out of the year, don't plan on the auditor buying it. The IRS will not believe that you don't ever commute, even if you work out of your home office. It reasons that you more than likely will make some personal stops such as taking the kids to dance lessons or stopping in at the store for groceries. For this reason, you should show at least one day a week of commuting or some personal stops within your week.

Properly Documenting Business Miles

To document business miles, you must have a good tax diary as we have already stressed repeatedly. Second, you must be able to answer through that diary the following five questions:

Question #1: Do you have objective evidence of your automobile mileage? If you can say yes, you will be allowed all the deductions you want. If you say yes but really don't have a log, the IRS can hit you with a 75 percent civil fraud penalty. Be aware of how important it is to document mileage properly.

Question #2: Is your evidence in writing? As far as the IRS is concerned, putting it in writing proves the pudding. Keeping it on a hard disc such as a Personal Digital Assistant (PDA) would not be good enough unless you print it out.

Question #3: What is your total mileage for the car for the year? How can you know what this figure is? By placing the beginning and ending year's odometer readings in your diary, for each car you use for business.

Question #4: What is your business mileage for each car? Your diary or log must include this information if you want to tame the IRS's not-so-benevolent interest in you should you be audited.

Question #5: What is your commuting mileage? Remember, commuting is going to your office if you have an office away from your home. If you work part-time in a home-based business, whenever you go from your home to your primary job, that is considered commuting. You must account for your "other personal miles" as well. These miles are anything but commuting and include such things as the grocery store, cleaners, church or synagogue, driving kids around, etc.

The third thing you must do to properly document business miles is to write down your mileage at the time you incur it, or close to the time. If you use the "Actual" method for claiming expenses, you must keep receipts for everything.[36] If you use the "IRS" method, you will not need to keep gas receipts, but you will still need to keep a mileage log so you can multiply the miles driven for business by the current car allowance.

Methods for Keeping a Car Log

Perfect Daily Log: With this method, you keep track of your mileage every day and for every stop for the entire year. For example, if your home is not your principal place of business your log might read: "To office 5 miles, personal; to Kelley's office 14 miles, business; to lunch with Wilson 21 miles, business; to the printer 14 miles, business; back to my office 11 miles, business; home 5 miles, personal." This type of daily log is called a "perfect one-day log." People who can manage this kind of nitpicking precision every day all year long deserve a round of applause and a few sessions of therapy to relieve them of their obsessive-compulsive tendencies!

90-day Rule: This method works just about as well as the daily log, but you only have to keep track of your mileage every day, both business and personal for 90 consecutive days.[37] Pick any three months to track but be warned: This method only works if you are regularly working your business. If you are the type that only works six months a year it obviously won't work. That's because this rule assumes you have the same number of appointments each and every month and put about the same number of hours in your business from week to week and month to month (with the exception of vacations and holidays). Once again, regularly working your business can have its advantages — in this case it relieves you of the burden of keeping records every single day.

One-Week-a-Month Method: Using this method you can calculate your average mileage much as you would using the 90-day method. Simply keep track of one week in January, for instance, one week in February, one week in March, and so forth until you have tallied mileage for one week out of every month of the year.[38]

No-hassle Approach: There is an easier method yet. We call it the "No-hassle Approach." With this method, you keep track of your personal and commuting mileage only. Before traveling anywhere, note your beginning odometer reading, then keep track of your personal and commuting mileage. Let's say it's three miles from your home to your office. Note this figure in your tax diary, then write down all your business stops and include information about the stop. You will not need to note the mileage for these trips. Then when you return home, note your ending odometer reading and subtract your personal mileage from that figure. This number is the business mileage you can deduct. For example, let's say that in three months you drove 8,000 miles of which 2,000 were personal and commuting miles. The remaining 6,000 are business miles and can be written off.

If you fail to keep consistent records using one of these four methods, theoretically, the IRS will not allow you to guess or use an improper method referred to as the "finger in the wind approach." Claiming that, "I used my car 60 percent for business" won't work unless you have the tax diary supporting this. The key is to keep track of all your appointments. If you do, you can use those as a basis for calculating your business miles. If you just guess the IRS will disallow every dime of deduction and hit you with a nondeductible 75 percent civil fraud penalty.

Remember, it is imperative that you keep good records.

Use Two Cars for Business to Increase Tax Deductions

If you have more than one car you can deduct more than 100 percent of your automobile expense (provided you have the right documentation).[39] This can be done by swapping some of the miles around for each car by using them both for business. For example, an individual who used his car for 22,000 business miles out of 24,000 total miles would have used the car 92 percent of the mileage for business purposes. This person, whose spouse also had a car, could increase the deduction for expenses from 92 percent to 141 percent simply by putting some of those 22,000 business miles on the other car. The chart on page 292 illustrates this idea. In this case, by using two cars for business, the total business mileage percentage for Car 1 and Car 2 when totaled together increased the taxpayer's business

| | | Two Cars | |
Business/Personal Use	One Car	Car 1	Car 2
Total Mileage for Business	22,000	18,000	4,000
Total Mileage for Year	24,000	20,000	7,800
Business Percentage Usage	**92%**	**90%**	**51%**

mileage from 92 percent to 141 percent, providing him with $2,085 in extra tax deductions.

Cautionary Note: If you are using two cars in the same business, you may have to keep track of your mileage using the Perfect Daily Log approach. The reason for this is that you are not using the same car equally throughout the year, so the three-month or 90-day method will not be accurate enough.

Depreciate Your Car Using the Fastest Rates to Maximize Annual Deductions

You can maximize annual automobile deductions by depreciating your car. If you use the IRS method of calculating car expenses, $17.0 cents is built into the $44.5 cents per mile allowance (in 2006) for depreciation. Thus, on all business miles driven you are allowed $17.0 cents per mile for depreciation. So if you put 20,000 miles on your car for business you can multiply $17.0 cents by 20,000, which gives you $3,400 whereby you can reduce your basis for gain or loss.

There are three basic depreciation methods for business automobiles:

1) **Accelerated Depreciation:** Allows you more deductions up front in the first couple of years.
2) **Straight-line Method:** Allows you to take a set amount of depreciation each year.
3) **Luxury Limits:** Today's tax law further complicates matters by placing "luxury car" limits on depreciation.[40]

We recommend consulting with your accountant for details on these methods and for information on special depreciating rules for heavy vehicles weighing more than 6,000 pounds and for sports utility vehicles

(SUVs). For more information on how to deduct the cost of expensive cars, refer to Appendix F.

Note: If you purchase a sports utility vehicle (SUV) that carries passengers and has a truck chassis with a gross vehicle weight of 6,000 pounds or more, you can elect to deduct up to $25,000 of the business use of that vehicle and can depreciate the business use over six years, with the year of purchase counting as one of the six years. In addition, starting in 2006, hybrid cars that work on both gas and electricity, get special tax credits that can be used to offset your taxes on a dollar for dollar basis. Each model gets differing amounts of these credits; thus, you need to check with the automobile dealer to see what the IRS has approved for that model. Unfortunately, Congress only allows credits for the first 60,000 models produced of each hybrid car. Thus, you will also need to check with the dealer to see if your model still qualifies for these credits. What this means to you is that if you are thinking of buying a hybrid car, you need to do it as quickly as possible before that model reaches its 60,000 quota.

Should You Lease or Buy a New Car?

Many small business owners have begun to lease their business automobiles as a means to save money on car expenses. But does leasing offer you any real tax-saving advantages over purchasing a brand new car? Not really. It can, however, offer some other serious cash flow advantages over buying a new car that make it worth considering.

Advantages
- You can deduct a percentage of the lease payment as it relates to the number of business miles driven.[41]
- Sales tax is paid as you make the lease payment, spreading it out over the duration of the lease; you are not required to pay a huge lump sum in sales tax that you would have to pay if purchasing a new car — this improves cash flow for your business.
- Eliminates the worry associated with car repairs and reliability issues.
- You don't have to go through the hassle of shopping for a new car and obtaining a loan every few years — if your credit rating could use some improvement, qualifying for a lease is generally easier than qualifying for a loan because the lessor owns the car and assumes the risk of ownership, limiting your financial exposure.

- Allows you to drive a newer model car all the time.
- Doesn't normally require a large down payment, freeing up more cash for use in your business.
- Monthly payments are generally lower than if you purchase a new car (almost half as much for some luxury models) so again, you have more cash on hand every month to help you advance your business.
- Eliminates hassles of selling a car when you're ready for a new one — you just turn it back in. We should caution, however, that this is only true for a "closed-end" lease. An "open-end" lease, on the other hand, obligates you to purchase the car when the lease expires. While most leases are closed-ended, we strongly caution you to check the lease type before signing. We NEVER recommend leasing a car and then purchasing it at the end of the lease agreement, so be sure to obtain a "closed-end" lease.

Disadvantages

- If you go over the annual mileage allowance you purchased in your lease you are required to pay a mileage overcharge, which is usually 10 cents to 15 cents per mile. While you can purchase any number of miles per year, keep in mind that the lease payment increases as the mileage allowance goes up. Most leases include a 12,000 to 15,000 annual mileage allowance, so if you anticipate exceeding this amount you should purchase more miles as part of the contract because it is less expensive to do so upfront.
- Tax-saving depreciation calculations do not apply to leased vehicles.
- Sales tax is included in your lease payment, so in effect you are always paying sales tax as long as you drive the leased vehicle. This expense is greatly reduced if you buy a reliable used car and drive it for several years because you pay a moderate sales tax (as opposed to stiff new car sales tax) up front and do not have the expense again for a long time.
- Generally costs more overall than purchasing a new car of equivalent value because if you lease and then buy the car, you will pay far more than if you just buy a new car outright. For that reason, we never recommend leasing a car and then buying it.

Other considerations to help you determine whether to lease or buy:

- If your income does not vary from year to year, leasing might be a bit better than buying a new car.
- If it is very important for you to drive a new vehicle in your business (if you are in sales or real estate for example) then leasing may suit you.
- If you don't like to own cars for more than four years, leasing has some benefits.
- If you hate auto repairs and dislike leaving your car at the shop, leasing has an advantage because it is a fixed cost that reduces your exposure and the economic risk of owning a car.

Buying a Used Car

In general, it's usually better to lease a car only if you're going to drive it for less than four years. Unless you fit most of the descriptions above, we do not advise leasing a car as a tax-saving strategy. Instead, we recommend buying a reliable used car that you keep for at least four years and drive into the ground. By so doing, you will get the maximum amount of tax write-offs. If you don't need to drive a brand new car, buying a used car can be a great tax-saving strategy. We should note, based on computer projections, that buying a used car and keeping it ten years is the best financial strategy for utilizing vehicles in your business.

First of all, a used car costs much less to purchase and doesn't usually require a large down payment, freeing up cash you may need for your business. Second, because used cars cost much less than a new car they tend to get paid off more quickly, again ultimately freeing up more cash. Third, once the car is paid off you are not pouring money into a car payment or lease payment. Fourth, car repair expenses are tax-deductible to the extent they relate to the business mileage driven. Fifth, you can obtain some tax savings from depreciating the car. Sixth, your insurance costs may be lower because if the car is old enough, it may no longer require comprehensive coverage and you can choose to carry only liability insurance on the car, freeing up more cash for your business.

In the end, deciding whether to lease or buy depends entirely on your situation. We have found this decision to be highly emotionally charged (Money Mastery Principle 1) and there is no set hard-and-fast rule as to which is better. You should make your decision only after you have examined all the rules of leasing (Money Mastery Principle 5), looked at your overall financial picture (Money Master Principle 7), and have considered the volume of money that will be involved in either scenario. Remember Principle 10 and the velocity of money: you can only make more money in your business as you put your existing money into motion. You cannot put this money to work for you if it is tied up in an expensive new car payment or in a leased car that really doesn't offer any value to your business.

Choose carefully the best option. Overall, we feel the best approach in terms of tax savings is to buy a reliable car and keep it as long as possible, preferably at least ten years.

Claim Taxes and Interest on Car Purchases

If you purchase your business cars, which we recommend, here is another way you can increase the amount of deductions you can take for a business automobile. If you've purchased a new car that you use for a certain percentage of business, you can claim the taxes on the car and the interest on the loan you secured to get the car.[42] If you are in business, interest and taxes are deductible regardless of whether you use the IRS method or the Actual method. If you have not claimed these deductions, be sure your accountant files amended tax returns for up to the last three years to get deductions on the taxes and interest you have paid previously.

Depreciate Maintenance Equipment and Supply Costs

If you maintain your own car, you can deduct the cost of maintenance equipment and supplies in proportion to the car's business usage as part of the expense to your business of owning the automobile.[43] Identify everything you use on your cars and make a list of these items including battery chargers, cables, tire pumps, buffers, gas cans, hoses, tools, repair manuals, etc. Then see if you have receipts to verify the cost of the items. If you do not (which is likely), pile all the equipment and supplies together and take a photograph; this will stand as documentation if needed.[44]

Sell Cars that Produce Deductible Losses, but Trade Cars that Produce Taxable Profits

There comes a point when a car is no longer useful to a business and it's time to get rid of it. To avoid unnecessary taxation on the capital gains and ordinary income on some depreciation taken from the sale of a car, you may want to consider trading it in instead to defer gain over the life of the new auto you purchase. Consult with your accountant to determine whether you should trade or sell your used car to get the most tax savings.

As you can see from everything we have outlined in this chapter, there are many ways to deduct your meals, entertainment, and car expenses. Simply follow the guidelines we have outlined exactly as noted and be sure to document your activities daily. By following this advice, you can put thousands of extra dollars in your pocket each year. Plus, you'll never have to worry about an IRS audit again!

✓CHALLENGE #15:
Review the Checklist Regarding Deductions for Meals, Entertainment, and Automobile Expenses

1. This week, review the following checklist to ensure that all of your meals and entertainment are being properly expensed:

✓ Pick a "trigger" that will help you remember to write down each of the substantiation requirements for meals and entertainment on the day the meal or event took place. Be sure to obtain a tax diary to track such information if you have not done so already. (Refer to Appendix A for more information on tax diaries.)

✓ Eat in a location conducive to business, i.e. where a contract can be signed. Remember, no floorshows.

✓ Remember, you cannot deduct meal expenses when you don't attend the gathering or when you take your spouse out alone. Your spouse may be included as long as business prospects are present.

✓ Deduct Dutch Treat meals; document personal meal costs to support your Dutch Treat deduction.

✓ Talk business either before or after entertaining a prospect or client and document in the same 24-hour period.

✓ Deduct home entertainment by talking business with guests at small dinner parties.

2. Get the most out of your automobile by reviewing the following automobile deduction checklist:

✓ Figure your car expenses using either the "Actual" method or the "IRS" method.

✓ Figure your business mileage by keeping a daily log, a 90-day log, a weekly log, or through the "no hassle" method.

✓ Determine whether you should use two cars in your business.

✓ Decide, based on your particular business situation, whether you should lease or buy a car.

CHAPTER 16

Make All Your Travel
Tax Deductible

In the last chapter we outlined, in detail, how to deduct all meals, entertainment, and automobile expenses incurred in your business so that you can take these deductions with confidence. If you want to get even more serious about reducing Excessive Taxation, it's time to learn all the good tax law pertaining to travel. By learning these rules, you can deduct some or even all of your travel expenses regardless of where you go in the world. Armed with this valuable knowledge you will know how to appropriately plan all your trips so that you can mix business with pleasure while still writing off the maximum amount of travel expenses allowed by law.

Tax Strategy 6: Mix Business with Pleasure by Making All Your Travel Tax-deductible

If you operate a business you have the opportunity to write off all kinds of trips that would not be possible if you were nothing more than a W-2 employee. That's because the tax laws governing travel deductions are fairly liberal (believe it or not!) for the self-employed.

Let's begin by defining what kind of travel is tax-deductible. First of all, the IRS says travel must be "business travel" in order to claim it. Business travel occurs whenever you travel away from home, overnight, or for a period of time sufficient to require sleep.[1] "Aha!" you might be thinking, "I've been out of town on vacation in the last few years and had to sleep overnight, I bet all of that vacation would have been tax deductible." Well, no, it wouldn't be unless you conducted some business while on that trip. "Yes, but what about the time I went to Hawaii and while I was there I passed out my business cards?" Can you write off such a trip since you seemed to conduct "business" while there? The answer is probably not, because in addition to sleeping overnight somewhere, you also have to have a "primary intent to do business" before you go on the trip in order to claim the expense.[2]

Suppose in order to do more business you need to travel from Washington D.C. to New York where you must give a seminar during the day; let's further suppose that you then traveled home in the evening of the same day. Does that constitute business travel? No, because you didn't sleep overnight anywhere. What if you travel 70 miles down the road from your office to a nearby city to give an early-morning lecture and you sleep over in a hotel in that city the night before to be sure you make it to the lecture on time? Is that considered business travel? You bet. The IRS has no minimum mileage requirement for travel as long as your intent to do business was present before you made the trip and you slept overnight. You can travel 10 miles or 10,000 miles, it doesn't matter as long as you sleep overnight in a bed other than your own.

How can you show "business intent" before you travel? The following example of a woman we'll call Loni spells it out.

Loni is a public relations consultant who just happens to love Las Vegas. When she found there was a tradeshow in Las Vegas where she could meet some potentially important editors to discuss one of her client's consumer electronics products, she decided it would be a perfect opportunity for her to take in some of the new attractions she had been dying to see. Before the tradeshow, Loni contacted by e-mail 10 different editors she wanted to speak with at the show and set appointments to meet them in her client's booth. She conducted press briefings with these editors on the first two days of the show, and on the remaining three days, spent her time having fun on the town.

Was Loni able to write off the trip to Las Vegas? You bet. That's because she met all of the business travel criteria.

- She was away from home overnight.
- She contacted, in writing, people with whom she wanted to conduct business before her trip.

Tip: *Keep a copy of letters or e-mails showing that you had some business intent before making the trip.*

Now, even though Loni was able to write off this trip because it was considered business travel, she still had certain IRS requirements to meet that dictated what expenses she could claim and what percentage of those expenses could be deducted. Let's take a look at the way travel is categorized for the purpose of making expense claims. Expenses are deducted in one of two ways, depending on what type of expense is incurred while traveling:

1) **On-the-road expenses:** Any and all costs necessary to sustain life while traveling for the purpose of doing business, except for transportation expenses.[3]

2) **Transportation expenses:** Expenses you incur traveling to and from your destination.[4]

On-the-Road Expenses

You can deduct 100 percent of the cost of lodging, laundry, hairstyling and haircuts, dry cleaning, shoeshines, and even manicures[5] while on your business trip! So if you get your nails done while you are at a convention, for example, you can deduct 100 percent of that little trip to the salon!

Now what about food? Food is only 50 percent deductible.[6] You might also assume, since we have already noted in the previous chapter that you cannot deduct meal expenses when you eat alone, that you should not be able to take even 50 percent of your meal expenses when you travel. Actually, there is an exception to the "eating alone" rule that does not require you to discuss business with a prospect or client while eating on the road, allowing you to deduct 50 percent of your meal costs.[7]

What about transportation? Cost to travel to and from your destination are not considered "on-the-road" expenses by the IRS, and as we have already noted, are governed by another set of rules that we will detail later in this chapter.

"On-the-Road" Travel Deductions Rule

You do not need a receipt for travel expenses under $75 per expense.[8] There are two exceptions to this rule:

1. You must have a receipt for all lodging, regardless of the cost.

2. You should also try to have receipts for all transportation (this is not transportation for getting to or from your destination, but transportation once you have arrived such as rental cars, bus fares, train fares, and taxi fares). While not absolutely necessary, we recommend getting receipts for these expenses when you can. If you spend $100 on a cab that takes you from the airport to your hotel, must you have a receipt for that cost? Yes, because it's transportation and it cost more than $75. After arriving at your destination, let's suppose you eat a nice buffet breakfast and spend $10 for it. Do you have to have a receipt for that meal expense? No, because you ate it while on business travel and it cost under $75.

When it's time to go home, you check out of your hotel and get the bill, which is $1,200. After you pay the bill (the hotel supplied free resuscitation), you are sure to take the receipt for that lodging expense because you will need it in order to substantiate your very nice tax deduction for that hotel bill.

The "receipt" rules are fairly simple: Remember to keep receipts for lodging and local transportation. Otherwise, you probably won't need a receipt for almost anything else you purchase on your trip because it's unlikely that any expense will exceed $75. And remember to write down all on-the-road expenses in your tax diary!

Rule for What Constitutes a Business Travel Day

The IRS considers each day you are on the road traveling as a "business day." That means that you don't have to wait until you get to the seminar or that business meeting before you can deduct 50 percent of your food and 100 percent of your other on-the-road expenses. You can begin deducting them the minute you get onto the road. Let's use Loni again as an example.

Loni decides to travel to Las Vegas by car from her home in Evanston, Wyoming. She gets in the car on Thursday afternoon at about 3:00 p.m. and begins driving towards Las Vegas; it will take her approximately eight hours to get there if she drives straight through. She stops about 6:00 p.m. to eat at a nice little roadside restaurant and pays $10 for the meal. She doesn't keep a receipt for her dinner but does write it in her tax diary. Even though she hasn't reached the trade show yet, her time on the road can still technically be considered a business day because she's making efforts to get to a place where she will conduct the actual business meetings; thus, all of her life-sustaining expenses are deductible.

Now, let's suppose instead that Loni decides to leave for the trade show in Las Vegas about five days early so that she can stop in Salt Lake City along the way to ski and have fun with friends. The IRS has a rule that says she should try to travel at least 300 miles every day if she wants to count each of those traveling days as business days.[9] To figure whether you are within the bounds of this rule, take the number of miles you are driving to your destination and divide by 300. Round up for fractions. In Loni's case the total travel miles (if she took a more direct route and did not stop in Salt Lake City) from Evanston to Las Vegas are 650 miles. She would take that 650 miles and divide by 300, which gives her a little over two days to get to Las Vegas if she wants to write off the expenses she incurs while on the road. Does she have time to stop in Salt Lake and ski? Maybe, but it would have to be a very quick trip.

Rule for Deducting Spouse, Significant Friend, or Children's Travel Expenses

To understand how this rule works, let's suppose that Loni wants to take her husband with her to the trade show in Las Vegas. She certainly doesn't feel like traveling 650 miles alone. And besides, she has hired her husband, Kurt, to handle all her office and computer equipment, so she wants him to browse around the trade show and get new ideas for the best ways to update her home office. Because he's going to be at the trade show conducting his own business and he is her employee,[10] Loni can deduct all of Kurt's traveling expenses as well.

Now Loni decides that taking her three kids to Las Vegas would be fun, too, so she packs up the whole family in the car. What can she deduct of the costs she will incur to take her entire family to the show? She can deduct anything she would have spent had she gone alone.[11]

Loni's Deductions If She Takes Her Entire Family

Gas: Yes, she would have used fuel to drive either way. However, the rules that govern this deduction are covered under the "Transportation" category; refer to this section of the chapter for more information on how much of this fuel cost can be deducted.

Tolls: Yes, she can take these no matter who travels with her.

Lodging: Yes, if she has to stay in a room then that hotel room is deductible, but only the portion that the hotel or motel charges for a single occupant.

Food: Yes, but only 50 percent of her own meal costs; not those of her three growing children.

Other: Yes, anything she might have to purchase for herself, but not for those in her family. For example, let's say Loni wanted to get her hair done in Las Vegas at the hotel beauty salon. Could she deduct the cost of that haircut and style? Yes, at 100 percent. Now let's assume she also wanted to have her daughter come with her to get a trim. Could she deduct the cost of her daughter's haircut. No, because this is not an expense she would incur on her business travel if she were alone.

Suppose Loni wanted to get some dry cleaning done while she was at the trade show. Could she take this laundry to the hotel cleaners and then write off the expense? You bet. Remember, the IRS rule says that you can deduct any and all expenses (except for food) that you would incur while on the road at 100 percent. The IRS has ruled that not only can you deduct the costs of laundry or dry cleaning for the clothes that get soiled while you are on business, but the first dry cleaning bill you incur after you get back home is also 100 percent deductible![12] How's that for a good tax law?!

Rule for Deducting Cruise Travel

You may have heard that under some conditions, you can deduct a cruise as a business expense (if you attend a cruise ship convention, for example). It is possible to deduct some of the expenses for such travel, but the rules governing cruise write-offs are constantly changing. We recommend that you consult with your accountant or with the Tax Reduction Institute (TRI) for more information on how to meet the requirements for taking these deductions (TRI contact information can be found in Appendix A).

Transportation Expenses

As we mentioned earlier, transportation costs to and from your destination are governed by rules separate from On-the-Road Expenses. Transportation costs include the expenses you incur traveling to and from your destination. These costs include gasoline, airfare, train fare, etc. In order to deduct these expenses you must take one of three kinds of business trips,[13] each one being governed by a separate set of rules:

1) Foreign Business Trips
2) U.S. Business Trips
3) Convention Trips

The flowchart on page 306 summarizes the transportation rules for each of these three kinds of business trips and tells you what percentage, if any, of the transportation costs are deductible.

Rules that Govern Transportation Deductions for Foreign Business Trips

Suppose you want to take a business trip to Montreal, Canada because you speak French and know that you can find prospective business there. But while there you also want to have some fun. So, you decide to spend one day doing business and the other five days having fun. Now, using the flowchart, let's see how much of the transportation costs for that six-day trip to Montreal will be tax deductible.

Flowchart of Transportation Deductions

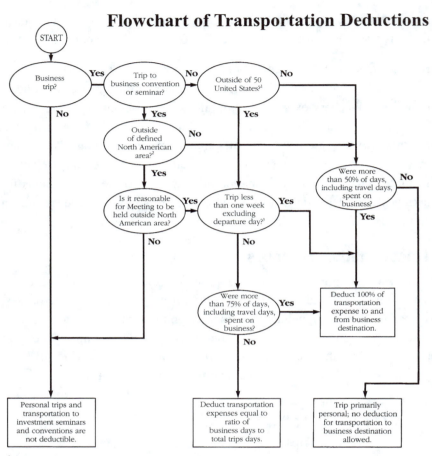

[1] Includes the District of Columbia but excludes U.S. possessions and territories.
[2] Trip outside Canada, Mexico, Jamaica, Barbados, Grenada, the U.S., its possessions, the Trust Territory of the Pacific, the Marshall Islands, the Federated States of Micronesia, Costa Rica, Dominica, Dominican Republic, Guyana, Honduras, Saint Lucia, Trinidad, Tobago and Palau. See Rev. Rul. 87-95, 1987-2 C.B. 79 and Rev. Rul. 94-56, 1994-36 IRB.
[3] Assuming one deductible business day during the trip; Reg. § 1.274-4(c).

From "Start":

1. Is this a business trip? Yes (follow the arrow to the next question).
2. Is this a trip to a business convention or seminar? No.
3. Is Montreal outside of the 50 United States? Yes.
4. Is the trip to be less than one week excluding the day of departure? Yes (because you will be gone 6 days total).

   Follow the arrows to the appropriate box and you will see that the transportation expense to and from your business destination to Montreal is 100 percent tax deductible! Isn't that great? Aren't you glad to know that you can spend just one day doing business in Montreal and spend another five days enjoying yourself while deducting all of the transportation costs to and from Montreal? This is known as the exciting "one-week loophole." Remember...

If you are on a foreign business trip and you return in less than one week, you can deduct 100 percent of your transportation regardless of the number of days worked.

Okay, let's consider a different scenario. Let's say you don't want to come back in less than one week. Instead, you want to conduct your business in Montreal on one day and then go to Prince Edward Island for the remaining nine days and have fun. How much of your transportation costs can you deduct? Using the flowchart you will see that this trip is:

1) A business trip
2) Is not a convention or seminar
3) Is outside the 50 United States
4) Takes more than one week

Now following the arrows, answer the next question:

5) Were less than 75 percent of the days spent on business, including travel days?

How do you answer this? Well, for starters, don't forget when calculating time spent on actual business that you may count the days traveling to and from your destination as "business days." So, in this case, it takes you one day to travel to Montreal and one day to travel back home, plus one day actually conducting business. So you have really spent three days doing business and seven days having fun. Do three days constitute more than 75 percent of your 10-day trip? No. Following the arrow on the flowchart you will notice that the transportation costs that you can deduct in this case are equal to the ratio of business days to total trip days. So, if your business days are three out of a total of 10 trip days, the amount of transportation you can deduct is only 30 percent. That's two-thirds less expenses you can deduct because you didn't make it home in less than one week. Therefore, the tax-saving tip you should remember about foreign business trips is:

Come back in less than a week or conduct business
75 percent of the time you are on the foreign trip so you can
deduct 100 percent of your transportation costs.

Rules for Deducting Transportation Expenses for a Business Convention or Seminar

To understand these rules, let's use Loni again as an example. Remember Loni was traveling to Las Vegas to attend a tradeshow (convention). She planned to work the tradeshow for two days and play the other three days of the convention. Loni took one day to travel the 650 miles from Evanston, Wyoming to Las Vegas and one day to travel back. Those two travel days can also be considered business days, so Loni spent four days on business and three days playing, for a total of seven days.

Using the flowchart, follow the arrows to the appropriate box to determine how much of Loni's transportation costs to the Las Vegas convention can be deducted:

1) Is it a business trip? Yes.
2) Is it a trip to a business convention or seminar? Yes.
3) Is Las Vegas outside the defined North American area? No.
4) Were more than 50 percent of trip days, including travel days, spent on business? Yes (four days is more than 50 percent of seven days).

SO

Loni's gasoline and other car transportation expenses to and from the Las Vegas tradeshow are 100 percent deductible.

The tax-saving tip to remember about travel for conventions or seminars is:

Spend more than 50 percent of your days on business
and you can deduct 100 percent of your transportation costs.

Rules for Deducting Transportation Costs for Trips in the United States

Let's say you settle on San Francisco as a place to conduct some business in order to promote your business. You love San Francisco, especially the great food. While there, you will talk to distributors and meet with potential clients you have set appointments with in writing before you leave on the trip. You will leave on Thursday and conduct some meetings on Friday and Monday. Based on this information, how much of your transportation costs to San Francisco are tax deductible?

Using the flowchart follow the appropriate arrows. You will discover that because you spend more than 50 percent of your trip days on business (don't forget that travel days are counted as business days), you can deduct 100 percent of your transportation costs to and from San Francisco.

The tax-saving tip to remember for U.S. travel is:

Spend more than 50 percent of your days on business and you can write off 100 percent of your transportation costs.

You can see that the flowchart on page 306 can be very helpful in planning any trip. It summarizes about 38 pages of IRS regulations and rulings into one very easy-to-use chart. Using this tool, you can make sure to plan your trips to mix business with pleasure while writing off the maximum amount of travel expenses allowed by law.

In addition, from the examples we have used, knowing how many days of a trip are considered business days is very important since the number of business days will dictate how much of your transportation costs can be written off. Let's discuss in further detail the rules that determine what can be considered a business day.

Rules for Determining What Constitutes a Business Day

Many people ask how much time they have to work in a day in order for it to be considered a "business day." The answer: Not much. There is no prescribed work time requirement. If you can get everything done in one minute, that will make the entire 24 hours within that day count as business. The IRS says that if you are there for a bona fide business reason, there is no time limit.[14] The key is, you must meet with others for a specific business purpose in order to count the day.

The rule for seminars or conventions is a bit different. You must spend a majority of your work day attending meetings.[15] Remember that you must spend 50 percent of your travel days on business if you want to deduct 100 percent of your transportation costs, so that means you would need to attend meetings a little more than half of a federal eight-hour work day, or four hours and one minute (this includes lunch). This is called the "Four-Hour-and-One-Minute" rule.

Rules Governing What Days of the Week Can Be Considered Business Days

Weekdays: Obviously any business you conduct on a weekday is going to count.

Travel Days: As we have already mentioned, the days you take traveling to your destination (regardless of the day of the week the travel falls on) are considered business days. But let's suppose, for example, that you want to take a ship to your business meeting in Hawaii because you're a nervous flier. "I'll take a plane to Los Angeles if I have to but I don't want to fly over the ocean. I'll take a cruise ship to Hawaii for $1,400 and then when the meeting is over I'll take the same boat and cruise back." If you do so, you will add several extra travel days to your total trip time that would not be required if you flew. Can you do this and still count those travel days? The IRS has said that you can take any means of transportation you want — boat, plane, car, train, etc., but the route has to be reasonably direct.[16] That means if you want to go to Hawaii by cruise liner, you can't go up the West coast to Alaska to get there. You must take a ship that is on a fairly straight course to your destination.

Note: Cruise ship travel is an odd bird with regard to transportation tax law and is figured differently than any other kind of travel. Congress views such travel as luxury transportation and for the purpose of figuring the tax deductions for it, has assigned the highest federal per diem rate multiplied by two. Consult with your accountant for more information on how to deduct this type of travel.

Weekend Days: The IRS says that if you meet two rules, you can count Saturdays and Sundays anywhere in the world as business days and write them off.[17]

Rule #1: You stay over Saturday and Sunday between business days.

Rule #2: It must be cheaper for you to stay over (no matter where you are in the world) than it would be for you to fly home and back again for the Monday meeting.

Let's examine this "weekend" opportunity more closely to see how it works. Suppose you have meetings planned in Anchorage on Friday and another meeting on Monday. Both Friday and Monday are then considered business days. The Saturday and Sunday of the weekend are sandwiched in between those two business days so you can write off all of your on-the-road expenses for Saturday and Sunday[18] and you can count them as business days for the purpose of calculating your overall transportation deductions.[19]

Here's another example: One of our clients, we'll call Shannon, who lives in Buffalo, New York wondered how she could write off her trips to Honolulu where she vacations frequently. After learning about these tax-saving travel strategies, Shannon contacted some distributors in a home-based business similar to hers to find out when there would be seminars taking place in Hawaii. She found a seminar that took place on a Friday in Honolulu. She left Buffalo on the earliest possible flight on Thursday at 6 a.m. and arrived in Honolulu at 6 p.m. She spent the rest of the day playing golf. Of course, based on the travel day rules we have already outlined, Shannon could count Thursday as a business day because she spent it getting to her business destination (even though she got in nine holes of golf before the sun went down!).

On Friday, Shannon went to the seminar. This day, naturally, counted as a business day. Saturday she spent on the beach, and Sunday she spent playing 18 holes of golf. Monday she had set up interviews with a potential distributor (in writing before she left on her trip) to get more information about a new product she planned to sell. After the meeting, she played more golf with some of these business contacts. Because she had sandwiched a stay over on Saturday and Sunday between business meetings on Friday and Monday, both weekend days counted as business days. Tuesday, Shannon spent the whole day on the beach until 6 p.m. She then took a late flight back to Buffalo. Tuesday was also considered a business day because she traveled home from her business destination. In six days, Shannon got in a lot of golf and sun and was able to legitimately deduct 100 percent of her transportation costs to do it. Remember...

If you sandwich Saturday and Sunday between business days, you can add them to the total number of business days you can use to calculate your total transportation deductions.

To summarize the rules that govern Transportation Expenses, remember to plan your trip according to the type of business meeting you will attend, where it will take place in the world, and make sure to take advantage of any and all days that can be considered "business days."

Other Rules to Consider for Travel Expense Deductions

We should note that you can deduct travel expenses to maintain out-of-town rental properties or seek a new employment opportunity. Consult with your accountant for the rules governing these travel expenses if they apply to you.

Bullet-proofing Your Documentation for All Business Travel

We have already discussed the kinds of receipts you need to keep in order to prove your on-the-road expenses. In addition to these, you need to have the appropriate documentation before, during, and after your trip for all travel expenses including food, lodging, transportation to and from your destination, etc. Keeping copies of letters or e-mails you sent to potential business contacts is one way to document the intent to do business before taking a trip. Another way is to keep copies of reservations or seminar applications or tickets, I.D. badges, or other proof that you attended an event. To further prove that you actually attended a seminar, conference, or business meeting, keep workbooks and notes and date them. Keep all such records for at least three years after the meeting, and guard your tax diary carefully. We recommend carrying no more than two months documentation around with you in your diary. If you use a PDA (personal digital assistant) to keep track of expenses, it is vital that you back up the information on the PDA every week to a hard drive or storage back-up device.

What should you be writing down about your business travel in your tax diary:

• Amounts spent daily on food, lodging, taxi fare, haircuts, laundry, etc.
• Dates of departure and dates of return
• Destinations to which you traveled
• Your purpose for making the trip.

Remember, the IRS will not allow you to make approximations.[20] What do you think happens to those deductions you forget to write down? They are lost forever because you can't go back and try to reconstruct a paper trail later.

Having the information you need to write off any and all expenses related to travel is extremely exciting. Now you have the knowledge required to plan your next business trip around a destination to which you would like to travel, mixing business with pleasure and taking the maximum deductions allowed by law at the same time. By following the guidelines included in this chapter and documenting all of your travel activities, you can save thousands of extra dollars every year and have fun at the same time!

✓ CHALLENGE #16:
Review Checklist Regarding Deductions for Travel

1. This week, get the most out of your travel by reviewing the following checklist to be sure your next trip is planned appropriately.

✓ Show business intent before making the trip by contacting, in writing, the people with whom you plan to meet.

✓ Record the departure and return dates of your trip in your tax diary; keep anything pertaining to the business you conducted while on your trip to substantiate your travel deduction including name tags, seminar tickets, seminar presentation materials, registration fee receipts, business contracts, etc.

✓ While traveling, be sure to write down all your on-the-road expenses in your tax diary so you can deduct 100 percent of these costs. In addition, be sure to record your food costs and the date you incurred them in your diary so you can deduct these at 50 percent.

✓ Make sure to get a receipt for all lodging and try to collect receipts for all transportation expenses incurred on location including taxi, bus, and subway fares.

✓ Keep receipts for any on-the-road or food expenses $75 or more.

2. Using the flowchart found in this chapter and the tax-saving strategies we have covered, plan your next vacation so that you can deduct 100 percent of your transportation costs.

✓ Make weekends deductible by sandwiching Saturdays and Sundays between business meetings on Friday and Monday.

✓ Mix business with pleasure by planning meetings around playtime in a destination of your choice.

✓ Locate seminars, conventions, or courses related to your line of work that are being held in a city to which you would like to travel and plan a trip around them.

✓ Hire your spouse so that you can deduct his or her expenses when they travel with you on business.

CHAPTER 17

Income Shifting:
Tax Secret of the Wealthy

B y applying each of the previous six tax-saving strategies, you are now in a position to apply a tactic that can drastically reduce your tax load. Since the inception of income tax, people have been developing methods of shifting income within family groups in order to reduce Excessive Taxation. The concept is simple: spreading income over several people, especially among those in lower tax brackets, is much cheaper when it comes to paying taxes than having one person pay tax on all the income. Thus, income shifting is a technique wealthy people often use to protect valuable assets from over-taxation. But income shifting is not just for the rich — anyone can take advantage of various aspects of this tax-saving strategy — married people, single people, single individuals with children, it doesn't matter.

Tax Strategy 7: Shift Part of Your Income to Family Members by Hiring and Leasing from Them

Each of the income-shifting opportunities we will outline in this chapter have the potential to put from $500 to $3,000 in saved tax dollars in your pocket — some even more.

Let's look at some income shifting methods.

Hire Your Spouse In Your Business

If you are a sole proprietor, partnership, C Corp, or LLC, and you employ your spouse in your business for legitimate business services, their wages can be deductible. Remember that all wages you pay your "employee" spouse are subject to Social Security tax (FICA)[1] — taxes that can eat into your business profits. The best way to avoid all those extra taxes is to pay your spouse a minimum wage (easily verified as a sufficiently "small" wage by the IRS) and then give him or her as many tax-free fringe benefits as possible.

In order to take advantage of the tax-free benefits we will outline in this chapter, the hiring of your spouse must be legitimate and "bona fide."[2] Don't be tempted to just call your spouse an "employee" without evidence of actual work performed — have your spouse sign a formal employment contract.

Set Up a "Medical Reimbursement Plan" to Pay for All Other Expenses Not Covered by Insurance

A Medical Reimbursement Plan is a written arrangement whereby the employer (you) hires an employee (spouse) and reimburses that employee and any of his or her family members (your children) for medical expenses not covered by medical insurance.

Some of the healthcare needs that you and your family might have that are not covered by a standard medical insurance policy include:

- Eyeglasses
- Hearing aids
- Contacts
- Insurance deductibles
- Co-pays
- Dental
- Orthodontics
- Preventive care
- Routine physicals
- Well baby care

- Chiropractic care
- Acupuncture
- Other non-traditional forms of medicine
- Prescription drugs
- Pre-existing conditions your policy declines to cover
- Over-the-counter medication that alleviates illness
- Medically required cosmetic surgery

These expenses can be written off using a self-insured medical reimbursement plan. This type of plan is probably one of the best tax loopholes ever created. The IRS has ruled that amounts reimbursed under an accident and health plan covering all bona fide employees, including the owner's husband or wife and family, are not included in the employee/husband or wife's gross income and are therefore deductible by the owner as business expenses.[3] You get a deduction and your spouse gets that reimbursement money tax-free. This money does not have to be included in the 1099 form or the W-2 statement. It is absolutely and completely tax-free! Now doesn't that sound nice?

How to Set Up a Medical Reimbursement Plan

The plan works the same whether you are married or single with children.

Step 1: Hire your spouse (or a child) part-time. Keep in mind that this will only work if you are a sole proprietorship, partnership, LLC or C Corp, not an S Corp.

Step 2: Draw up formal paperwork for both a medical plan and a reimbursement plan. This can be done through a good attorney for about $500 or you can do it yourself by referring to the toll free number and kit materials available in Appendix A of this book. Such medical reimbursement packages will include properly drawn-up employment contracts, independent contractor agreements, and a legal self-insured medical reimbursement plan. If you use such packages, you may still want to have your lawyer tailor it to your needs.

Step 3: Make your spouse or child the primary insured on a written medical plan.

Step 4: Have your spouse or child elect family coverage. This means that you, your spouse, and your kids will be covered.

Step 5: Reasonably set the number of planned benefits. According to the IRS, the total possible planned pay-outs plus the salary should be limited to the hours and type of work performed.

Step 6: Reimburse your spouse and family members for medical expenses not covered by insurance.

Note: IRS Regulation 1.105-5 states that a medical reimbursement plan for a sole proprietorship, partnership, or LLC can have as few as one employee. Thus, if your only employee is your spouse, you can still qualify for a medical reimbursement plan.

Establish a "Supper Money" Allowance for Hardworking Employees

Another wonderful income-shifting benefit you can offer family members that can help reduce your taxes is "supper money" funds. Such funds are what you agree to pay an employee when overtime work is required. Under this allowance, you get a deduction and the employee, that is, your spouse, gets that money tax-free.[4]

First of all, you should be aware that you cannot pay supper money to yourself. But if you are a sole proprietor and you hire your kids and/or spouse and they put in a 10-hour day, you can pay them supper money.

Nothing in the IRS code dictates the amount you can pay in supper money. But the chief counsel of the IRS has said that their internal policy is no more than $20 a day, two days a month for every employee who works overtime. Thus, occasional supper money can be paid to any employee who works over 10 hours and one minute a day (except you). That can mean tax-free money of up to $40 a month for your spouse and/or children.

Set Up a SIMPLE IRA

Another way to shift income to family members is by adopting a SIM-

PLE IRA. Without question, setting up a 401(k) or some other type of profit-sharing plan is an excellent tax-deferring strategy for the small business owner.

Established in 1997 by Congress in an effort to eliminate some of the cumbersome requirements of a qualified pension plan, the SIMPLE IRA is a written arrangement that provides you and your employees with an easy way to make contributions towards retirement. Under such a plan, any employee may choose between making any salary deduction contributions or receiving a salary. Here's what you need to know about setting up a SIMPLE IRA:

- Unlike a qualified pension plan, if you are a sole proprietor, you can participate in a SIMPLE plan.

- If you do set up such a plan, you must make matching contributions on behalf of each employee if they contribute to the plan.[5]

- As the employer, you must make matching contributions to your employees' contributions up to 3 percent of compensation each year, or as little as a 1 percent match for two out of five years.[6]

- An employee (which in most cases with small business owners is a spouse) earning at least $5,000 can contribute a percentage of his or her salary, or you can contribute a percentage of your net income up to $10,000 per year (in 2006). In addition, you as the sole proprietor can match your own contribution of up to 3 percent of your net income. For example, let's say you net $100,000 a year from your home-based business. You can contribute to a SIMPLE IRA as much as $10,000.[7] Plus your business can match your contribution — up to another 3 percent[8] of $100,000, which equals $3,000 on top of that.

SIMPLE IRAs Have Important Advantages

- If you have any employees, you will not have to worry about covering them if they do not contribute to the plan. If, however, they choose to contribute, you must match any of their contributions up to 3 percent of their wages.

- There are no administrative costs or filing requirements with SIMPLE plans. Most qualified plans can cost anywhere from $1,000 to $5,000 per year to administer. But SIMPLE IRAs cost you nothing. The funds you contribute go directly to the employee's own IRA without requiring you to do any complex filing with the IRS.

While qualified plans have their own advantages, if you are a small business owner, you should check out SIMPLE IRAs, reviewing your options with your accountant where necessary to determine where the maximum benefits can be achieved for you.

How to Set Up a SIMPLE IRA:

1. Obtain IRS model Form #5305 (5305-SIMPLE) from the IRS Web site: www.irs.gov.
2. Print and fill out a copy of this form.
3. Do not send back to the IRS; simply keep on file in case you need a record of it.

Hire Your Dependent Children Age Seven to 17

If you are a sole proprietor with children or grandchildren who will be going away to college or getting married someday, this part of the chapter is for you.

Suppose you have a 12-year-old daughter named Nicole. If you pay for Nicole's college education, the tuition might cost you $12,000 a year or more. Or, if you pay for her wedding at some point, that bill could easily run you $25,000. Although college educations and weddings are not tax deductible, if you run a business you can deduct the equivalent of such.[9]

Here's how:

First, you hire Nicole to work with you in your business (to provide legitimate business services).You pay her a wage[10], which is tax-deductible because wages are one of the expenses of your business, and she then puts that money away in a college savings account. At 18, Nicole takes that money and uses it for her own college education. Essentially, you have paid for her education after taking a tax deduction for it. If she decides to get married instead, she could use the money to pay for the wedding, allowing you to pay for it with tax-reduced funds.

The beauty of hiring Nicole is that if you are not incorporated, wages paid by parents to children under age 18 are exempt from Social Security taxes. If she is under 21, she would be exempt from federal unemployment taxes as well.[11]

Now, what if Nicole is quite a bit younger than 12? The IRS says you may hire Nicole as long as she is at least seven. Why does the IRS fix the age at seven? This law is based on what's known as the "Eller Case."[12] A man named Dr. Eller hired some of his children to work in his business. One of those kids was just seven years old. When Dr. Eller filed his taxes, the IRS audited him, stating that they didn't think it was possible for Dr. Eller to legitimately use any seven-year-old child in his business. The case went to trial. The tax court ruled that as long as the child did some sort of physical labor and Dr. Eller documented it, then he could hire the child.

Let's suppose you hire Nicole to work in your business at age nine; the older she gets, the more you can pay her. So you raise her wages from age 10 through 18. By age 18 when it's time for Nicole to go away to college, all those wages plus the interest they have collected over the years totals $30,000. She then says to you, "Dad, thanks a lot. I don't think I want to go to school, I want to buy a Porsche instead." Can she do that? Absolutely, when she turns 18 the money legally became hers. So what can you do to avoid such a catastrophe?

Employ a technique we like to call "Find the Money If You Can!" This technique can be accomplished by hiring Nicole in your business and letting her know about only some of the money she is earning which she can put away and use as she likes. The majority of the money you then take and put in a savings account without telling her where it is. If she makes the decision to go to school, you then simply liquidate the account and give her the money for tuition. If, on the other hand, she wants to buy a Porsche, you can say to her, "Okay honey, find the money if you can!" This is a very powerful technique and we suggest you implement it.

The IRS and Congress have said that you may hire your children and the first $5,150 (in 2006) you pay them in wages is tax-free.[13] Why is this? Let's say you are going to pay Nicole $5,150 in wages for 2006; you can then deduct that $5,150, as long as you can justify it for the hours and work performed. In addition, Nicole will be exempt from Social Security taxes and federal unemployment tax if you are a sole proprietorship. Wages for Nicole are reported on her W-2 as $5,150, but she then gets to deduct that entire $5,150 on her tax return as the standard deduction for that year. The result? You get a tax deduction and she gets the money tax-free. You can also claim your children as an exemption if they bank the money and use it for college later on. Isn't that great?

Tax Tip: If your kids will eventually be going to college, set up a Roth IRA for their wages and put away up to 100 percent of their wages with a limit of $4,000 per year (in 2006). The money is not tax-deductible, but is tax-free when used for their education.

Now you may be thinking, "Yeah, I'd like to hire my children, but what about child labor laws?" Parents who hire their own children are exempt from any state child labor laws. In addition to the tax-saving benefits of paying your children wages, hiring your kids to help you work your business can teach them resourcefulness, the value of work, and can start them on the road to better financial management at a young age.

What if you don't want your children anywhere near your business? Hire them to do their daily chores such as making their bed, washing the dishes, and taking out the trash instead. These wages cannot be claimed as a business expense since these chores have nothing to do with your business. However, if their total wages are under $5,150 (in 2006), they will be tax-free because they can deduct the entire amount on their tax returns. If you pay them $4,000 to do chores, they should be eligible to put that full $4,000 into a Roth IRA, which will be tax-free when used for college.

Hiring Older Children

If your kids are between 18 and 21, you can still get some benefit from hiring them because their wages, although not exempt from Social Security, are exempt from federal unemployment tax[14] and the wages would be fully deductible at your tax bracket, which is presumably higher than that of your child.

Setting Your Child's Wages

Unlike your spouse, you want to pay your children under 18 as much as possible because there's no FICA tax on such wages. But, the salary or wage you pay must be "reasonable" in order for you to take them as deductions. This means that the amount you pay for services must be similar to amounts paid for similar services by similar businesses under similar circumstances.[15]

So let's say you hire Nicole to do some filing and bookkeeping in your business at a salary of $100,000 a year. Is this reasonable? Hardly. A reasonable wage is what you would pay an outside agency to do the same thing. When setting the wages or salary, be sure to allow for the experience (or inexperience) and ability of your child. Also, consider the 10 factors the IRS uses to examine whether wages are reasonable:[16]

1. Duties performed
2. Volume of work
3. Type and amount of responsibility
4. Complexity of work
5. Amount of time required for work
6. General cost of living in the area
7. Ability and achievements of the child
8. Comparison of amount of salary with amount of business income
9. Your pay policy regarding all employees (if there are others)
10. Pay history of the child

The IRS does not care whom you hire in your business, except when it comes to your children. Then you need to be a little more careful about the way this takes place. The IRS will not audit you simply because you employ your children (hundreds of thousands of people do it each year), but if you ever get audited for any other reason, you must be ready to prove that your children really did work for you and at a reasonable wage. How do you prove it?

How to Properly Document and Pay Your Spouse or Children's Wages

1. Have all relatives working for you fill out a weekly timesheet. To get

your deductions for wages, you must prove what work was actually performed.[17] Each day your spouse or child works, the timesheet should show:

- Date
- Description of tasks performed
- Hours worked.

2. Always pay your spouse and children by check. Follow this advice meticulously — don't be tempted by any of this "under the table" non-sense. One of the biggest mistakes business owners make is paying their family members in cash. They think, "Oh well, here is some cash Tommy, go have fun, you've earned it this week." Bad mistake. Never, ever, ever pay by cash.

Always pay your spouse and children by check.

By doing so, you will establish an audit trail from you to your child to your child's bank account.

3. Fill out and file the right forms. When hiring anyone, even spouse and children, you will need to complete the proper paperwork before you can take full advantage of the income-shifting tax deductions we have outlined in this chapter.

4. Obtain a Federal I.D. Number. Use IRS Form SS4 to do this (available on the IRS Web site: www.irs.gov).

5. Obtain employee wage reporting forms. You will need IRS Form W-2, W-4+W-2.[18] These forms are for reporting tax withholding. If you pay your spouse or child $600 or more, you must give your employees a copy of IRS Form W-2 and file it along with IRS form W-3 with both the IRS and the Social Security Administration.

6. Obtain IRS Form 940.[19] This form is related to Social Security unemployment tax payments. Although you are not liable for unemployment taxes on wages paid to your child, you must file IRS Form 940

at the end of the year. If your child is under age 21, is your dependent, and your only employee, you simply enter your child's wages as "exempt" from unemployment tax and return the form to the IRS.

7. Obtain IRS Form 941.[20] Use this form quarterly to report withheld income taxes and deposits (available online: www.irs.gov). You can also have a service prepare all the forms for a monthly fee. In addition to filling out the proper forms, be sure to document your children and spouse's work activities in your tax diary.

   Moreover, complete an employment contract between you and your spouse and/or children. This contract should pay them on an hourly basis and note what fringe benefits will be available such as the self-insured medical reimbursement plan. We should note that an employment contract is included in the Tax Strategies System provided by the Tax Reduction Institute; refer to Appendix A for more information on how to obtain it.

Finally, remember that in order to hire your children, they will need to have a Social Security number.[21]

Note: In order to avoid all this paperwork hassle, use a payroll service. Payroll services will do all the IRS and state forms and send all the checks to the right places for you. They will even direct deposit the checks in your kids' account if you want.

Make Your Child a Part-owner and Pay Them a Guaranteed Wage

If your company is organized as a Limited Liability Company (LLC), an S Corp, C Corp, or Partnership you can make your child a 1 percent owner of your company and pay them a guaranteed wage without having to prove that they have performed any work for your company. The child would then be taxed on this wage at his or her lower tax bracket. Of course wise parents will not only pay their children this wage, but will teach their children the value of work by having them perform labor for the company for which they are then compensated. This income-shifting method reduces tax burdens while eliminating the requirements that sole proprietors must meet to prove that a child actually worked for the company.

Other Ways to Save Taxes Through Shifting Income to Family Members

What if you have a child who is not old enough to work or you have a college-aged son or daughter away at school who is never home long enough to work in your business? How can you hire such children? There are three additional ways to shift income to family members, even if you can't hire them or don't want to:

1. Gift to Push Taxes
2. Gift With Lease-Back
3. Sale of assets and lease-back

Gift to Push Taxes

This technique is one of the most effective methods used to shift income to other family members. In fact, this technique is so powerful that if everyone in the country knew about it, we could reduce the taxes paid into the U.S. Treasury by over $2 trillion dollars! The bad news is that 99.99 percent of the people who should be using this technique don't even know about it!

Gift To Push Taxes allows you to give away to lower tax-bracketed relatives (like your children or grandchildren) property that has gone up in value. They subsequently sell the property and become taxed on the gain at their lower tax bracket.

Suppose John makes a tremendous amount of money in his business, we'll say in excess of $ 1 million a year. John also just happens to be an online stock trader. On top of all this, he also pays $20,000 a year for each of his three kids to attend college. John (who is normally a very smart person) is doing a very dumb thing. Instead of paying all that money in tuition, as an individual in an extremely high tax bracket (50 percent) he should be giving each of his kids stock. They can then sell the stock and use it for their college tuition. Naturally they will be taxed on the gain, but only at a 15 percent tax bracket. By doing so, John would save 35 percent in taxes by letting the kids pay the taxes on the stock and use the gain to pay their own tuition. Such gifts can be given to relatives in the form of stocks, bonds, valuable collectibles, real estate, and so forth.

What's more, there are no income tax consequences for making such a gift.[22] There are, however, some gift-tax implications. If you are single, you can give away up to $12,000 per person (in 2006) per year gift-tax free.[23] If you are married, you can give away $24,000 per person per year gift-tax free.[24] In addition, you can give away up to $1,000,000 as a lifetime exemption from gift tax and the recipients of your gift will receive the same basis[25] and the same holding period as you did when you first purchased it. For example, if you paid $20 a share for some stock and today it's worth $45 a share, when you give it to your child, it's basis is $20. When they sell it, they pay taxes on the $25 gain.

Can you see how powerful this is? What happens if you have real estate worth $100,000, or stocks that have gone up substantially in value? When you consider that the stock market alone has gone up in total about $4 trillion over the last eight years, not counting all the appreciation that has resulted from collectibles and real estate, this technique has the potential for massive tax savings.

Because it is such a good technique, Congress tried to kill it with something called the "Kiddie Tax." Children under 18 can only earn up to $1,700 of investment income and have it taxed at their lower bracket.[26] Anything over $1,700 (in 2006) is taxed at the higher bracket of the parent. With that new limitation in place, the Gift Push Tax technique works best with children over 14 or investment income up to $1,700.

Note: Because Kiddie Tax makes investment earnings taxed at the parent's rate, it becomes even more important to put money in accounts for kids that will be tax-free, such as municipal bonds. Another terrific approach is to contribute money to a prepaid tuition or Section 529 plan. This allows you to contribute funds for your kids' education with all the appreciation and interest tax-free if used for qualified higher education expenses. For more information on this, read Lower Your Taxes: Big Time (Sandy Botkin).

Gift With Lease-back

This technique is one of the most powerful financial planning methods ever created. It provides a way of writing off all your business equipment twice. For example, if you have a car that will eventually fully depreciate, you can give that car away to your kids, and then lease it back from them. By doing so, you have put your kids in the leasing business — you are now deducting the lease payments you are giving your kids. In other words, you get to deduct that car twice.

What about computer equipment that becomes obsolete very quickly? After you fully depreciate a computer, can you give it away and lease it back from your kids? Sure. Now you are deducting the computer twice.

How about copy machines, fax machines, desks, filing cabinets, book-shelves, cell phones, and phone systems? You can use this technique with just about any property you use solely for business. Any equipment you use in rental property such as refrigerators, stoves, washers, etc., can also be used as gifts with leaseback.

Equipment can be leased under a three-year contract for 40 percent of what the equipment is worth. So let's say your computer and its software are worth $1,800 this year if you were to sell them. You could give the computer to your kids and then lease it back from them for $720 a year, or 40 percent of its value under a three-year lease. Every three years you can revalue the equipment.

What about cars? The IRS has actually published leasing tables to help you figure the lease payments. You can get these tables from IRS Publication 463, which tells you how much you can lease a vehicle. This technique is a perfect way to deduct more than once, items that you need today but maybe won't need five or ten years from now.

"But," you might be asking, "how does a 2-year-old grandchild own a computer? Or how does my 16-year-old daughter, a minor, own a car?" The answer is, they can't, so in order to use this technique properly, you will need to set up a trust. The trust, rather than your daughter, owns the car. You then lease the car back from the trust.

Caution: *We always recommend that you use a trust whenever you use the gift and leaseback technique. It's unwise to give away property that would produce a tax loss if sold. You will lose the tax deduction for the loss.*[27]

Selling Assets and Leasing Them Back

You can give away your assets and then lease them back, but you can also sell them and lease them back. This is the number one financial planning strategy that Hollywood stars are using today. It also happens to work really well for people with small businesses. Although the concept can be fairly complicated, you need to be aware of this classic technique not only for saving tax dollars, but for putting Money Mastery Principle 10 to work for you. Selling assets and then leasing them back is a great way to get your money to do more than one thing for you at a time. Assets that are doing certain things for you can be used to do another whole set of tasks, thus setting your money in motion.

Here's a very simplified example of how it works:

This example assumes that one or both of your parents are alive and residing in a house that's paid off.

Step #1: Set up a joint bank account between you and all your siblings. (You don't have to include your siblings on this deal, but if you don't they'll hate you forever because it is so lucrative!). Each of you contributes to the account enough money to equal about $1,200.

Step #2: Offer to buy your parents' house. Get an appraisal to be sure of the value of the house and get a mortgage to pay the full value for it. Let's say their house is worth $250,000 — your parents will get top dollar for the house and there will be no commission involved. Since you are giving your parents a good deal, you are going to ask them to give you a good deal in return. Put $1,000 down on the house (from the money you collected from your siblings) and ask your parents to be your banker. They are going to finance you to the tune of $249,000 at 7 percent interest (or whatever the minimum IRS rate is for mortgages at the time) for 30 years. You have now become the new landlord.

Step #3: Immediately lease the house back to your parents at fair market value rent. Fair market value is whatever the going rate is in your area. Contact a realtor in your community for information. Now every month you will receive a rent check from your parents out of the money you paid them for the house. Take that rent check and pay a portion of the mortgage off each month. You will want to set the rent a little more or a little less than the mortgage payment to offset the cost of the interest on the mortgage.[28]

The following illustration is a visual image of the above example.

Purchasing Parents' Home and Leasing It Back

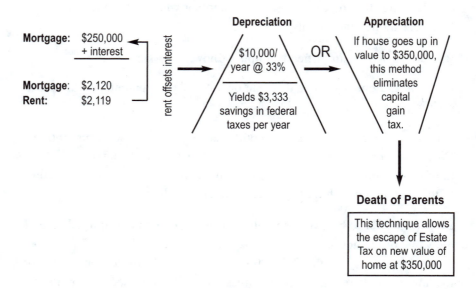

You can see from this illustration the tax advantages this technique affords you. Remember, you are the landlord — if your parents' house ever needs repair work, you can deduct those repair costs. You and your siblings may now depreciate your parents' house and take a portion on your tax returns. You and your siblings may each visit your parents as a tax-deductible caretaking expense. Upon the death of your parents, there will be no probate necessary for the house or furnishings because it is already in the children's estate. Finally, if the house appreciates, say $100,000 in value, you will have this appreciation amount locked into the children's estate and will not have to pay estate tax on the house.

Keep in mind that this technique does require that you dot your i's and cross your t's because there are a number of ways you can go wrong. Your lawyer should provide a letter stating your intent to sell and lease back the house.[29] Be sure to consult an attorney before attempting this method of income shifting.

Tip: Even more effective than a mortgage note from a lawyer, have him or her draw up a private annuity. This will allow you to pay your parents for the rest of their lives, based on their life expectancy. Upon the death of your parents, there will be no estate tax on this annuity, and no income tax recaptured or recognized.

✓ CHALLENGE #17:
Examine Methods for Shifting Income to Family Members

This week, we challenge you to examine each of the ways you could shift income to family members in order to obtain the most tax savings. Review the following checklist to determine which techniques will work best for you:

✓ Hire your spouse.

✓ Pay your spouse's medical expenses.

✓ Set up a "Medical Reimbursement Plan" to pay for all other expenses not covered by medical insurance premiums.

✓ Establish a "Supper Money" allowance for hard-working family "employees."

✓ Set up a SIMPLE IRA pension plan.

✓ Hire your dependent children age seven to 17.

✓ Determine what property you may have that could be given away to lower tax-bracket family members.

✓ Determine what property you can give away to lower-tax-bracket family members that can then be leased back.

✓ Determine if you are in a situation that would allow you to sell a family asset (such as a parents' home) and then lease it back.

In Conclusion...

We have discussed the power of change at length in the pages of this book. Our purpose in sharing the Money Mastery Principles and Tax-saving Strategies taught herein is to help you see that changing the way you look at money can totally change your life. Our personal convictions about the power of these principles and strategies are fueled by years and years of teaching them and seeing firsthand how they can totally transform people's lives. These concepts are true!

That's what this book is all about...getting you to look at yourself and how you think about money. We have, in many ways, asked you to shift your thinking away from what others teach about applying quick fixes and partial solutions to help solve financial problems. Instead, we have asked you to adopt a more grounded and principled approach that can help you build a solid foundation upon which you can stand, regardless of how your circumstances or the world may change. When you are principled, then you are empowered to make better financial decisions, regardless of the situation in which you may find yourself. A principled approach helps you make sense of every aspect of your financial life — from the way you spend and borrow, to the way you save for retirement, to the way you pay taxes. A principled approach helps you understand that it's not about the amount of money you make, but rather how wisely you use the money you already have. Only principle-based thinking enables the maximization of your financial power and the best use of your time and resources so that you can live your life the way you want to and not as a slave to others.

The Money Mastery Principles we have taught in this book have been understood and utilized for millennia. Timeless and unchanging, they have been practiced by the great financial masters throughout the ages. While new perhaps in the way that we have presented them, these principles will always be true and unchanging, whether you make them a part of your life or not. Steven R. Covey noted in his book, *The Seven Habits of Highly Effective People*, "Principles are like lighthouses. They are natural laws that cannot be broken. As Cecil B. deMille observed of the principles contained in his monumental movie, 'The Ten Commandments,' 'It is impossible for us to break the law. We can only break ourselves against the law.'...The degree to which people in a society recognize and live in harmony with [principles] moves them toward either survival and stability or disintegration and destruction."

We must agree. The degree to which you apply the principles of this book will determine whether you thrive financially or not. The choice is yours.

In conclusion, we challenge you to memorize all 10 Money Mastery Principles and all 7 Tax Strategies. Upon each decision to spend money we encourage you to ask yourself which principles or strategies apply. We invite you to make the Money Mastery Principles and Tax Strategies a regular topic of discussion at home and work.

In all matters of money, stick to the principles. In all matters of financial principles, make them a lens through which you can see clearly to make wise financial decisions today that will bring you lasting happiness tomorrow.

> *"Whatever you can do, or dream you can, begin.*
> *Boldness has genius, power, and magic in it."*
> — Goethe

The 10 Money Mastery Principles

Principle 1:   Spending is Emotional
Principle 2:   When You Track Your Money, You Control It
Principle 3:   Savings is Actually "Delayed" Spending
Principle 4:   Power Down Your Debt and Power Up Your Fortune
Principle 5:   Know the Rules
Principle 6:   The Rules Are Always Changing
Principle 7:   Always Look at the Big Picture
Principle 8:   Organizing Your Finances Enables the Creation of Additional Wealth
Principle 9:   Understanding Taxation Enables You to Retain More of Your Money
Principle 10: Money in Motion Creates More Money

The 7 Tax-saving Strategies

Strategy 1:   If You Don't Have a Home-Based Business, Start One!
Strategy 2:   Consider How to Best Legally Structure Your New Business Venture
Strategy 3:   Run Your Business Like a Business, and Not Like a Hobby
Strategy 4:   If Eligible for a Home Office Tax Deduction, Take It!
Strategy 5:   Properly Deduct Meals, Entertainment, and Auto Expenses
Strategy 6:   Mix Business with Pleasure by Making All Travel Tax-deductible
Strategy 7:   Shift Part of Your Income to Family Members

Appendices

Appendix A:

Money Mastery Tools, Products and Services

Spending Planner Worksheet/Report: Available at no charge through the Money Mastery Web site, http://www.moneymastery.com/Spending.aspx, or by calling Money Mastery customer support toll-free: (888) 292-1099.

Financial Assessment & Worksheet: Available at no charge through the Money Mastery Web site: www.moneymastery.com or by calling customer support: (888) 292-1099.

Retirement Worksheet: This tool is available on the Money Mastery Web site free of charge at http://www.moneymastery.com/Savings.aspx or by calling (888) 292-1099.

Money Mastery Enhanced: Powerful audio CD program teaches you how to further apply the concepts taught in *MONEY: What Financial "Experts" Will Never Tell You*. The package includes three audio CDs that explore the entire Money Mastery system; a guidebook to the 10 Money Mastery Principles; the Money Mastery How-to Manual; six Spending Master Tracking Registers; and the Master Plan Software. Order by calling (888) 292-1099 or online at www.moneymastery.com.

Spending Master Tracking Registers: Easy-to-use booklets contain a complete spending system, including a check register, a spending tracker, and a tax diary. Quantity of 12 can be purchased through Money Mastery by visiting www.moneymastery.com or calling (888) 292-1099.

Master Plan Software: Designed as a comprehensive tracking and forecasting tool, this software includes a spending planner and tracking system, debt management tools, and powerful financial calculators. The Spending Planner, Real Debt Report, Get Out of Debt Report, and Retirement Worksheet featured in various chapters throughout this book were created using the Master Plan software. These reports help track how money is being spent on a monthly basis; how to track its spending in the future; how much interest will be paid on current debt; how quickly debt can be eliminated by applying Power Down principles; how to plan for retirement by forecasting the value of investments over a long-term period; and how to predict how much of that retirement income will be subject to tax. Available at www.moneymastery.com or by calling Money Mastery Customer Support: (888) 292-1099.

Master Planner Comprehensive Organizational System: This comprehensive organizer includes everything necessary to master plan every area of your life and get all your financial affairs in order. From birth certificates to stock certificates, and from financial checklists to estate settlement checklists, the Master Planner is the most complete guide to total financial organization on the market today and includes five powerful organizational features: 1) mental organization, 2) personal and family organization, 3) financial document organization, 4) estate organization, and 5) business organization. Includes checklists for systematically applying each of the 10 Money Mastery Principles; valuable personal, family and estate resources; estate settlement and distribution forms; a complete section on how to properly structure and organize a small business; information on wills and trusts; and much more. Available online at www.moneymastery.com or through Money Mastery Coaching Services: (888) 292-1099.

Money Mastery's Comprehensive Listing of the Most Common Tax Deductions Businesses Can Take: This proprietary FREE report contains crucial information gathered from accountants over a period of many years who have dealt directly with the IRS. It includes common items that can be deducted from taxable income, many of which have been mistakenly overlooked by thousands of business owners. To order call (888) 292-1099.

Coaching Services: Mentoring services provide a personal, one-on-one relationship with a professional Money Mastery mentor through a one-year consulting contract. The Coaching package includes all the tools and techniques needed to maximize savings, control spending, eliminate debt, and reduce taxes. To order coaching services, please call: (888) 292-1099.

Tax Reduction Institute (TRI) Products, Tools, and Services

Tax Diary System: Includes everything needed to record all substantiating requirements for entertainment, travel, auto, and home office. Available through the TRI Web site, www.taxreductioninstitute.com, or by calling (800) TRI-0TAX (800-874-0829).

"Tax Strategies For Business Professionals" and "Tax Strategies for Home-Based Businesses": Audio tapes and workbook from Sandy Botkin's popular national tax reduction seminars. Includes everything you need to bulletproof your tax return and save the greatest amount of tax dollars. Call (800) TRI-0TAX or order online, www.taxreductioninstitute.com.

"Wealth Building Tax Secrets for Real Estate" by Sandy Botkin: Explains real estate tax planning for real estate professionals, investors, accountants, and financial advisors who want to make buyers and sellers more motivated. Order by calling TRI, (800) TRI-0TAX or online at www.taxreductioninstitute.com.

Tax Audit Defense: Includes unlimited consulting for one year; audit protection plus 100 percent coverage (accuracy guaranteed or TRI pays taxes and penalties); also includes retroactive service for three prior tax years. Call TRI: (800) TRI-0TAX or order online at www.taxreductioninstitute.com.

Tax Survival Kit: Includes "Tax Strategies for Business Professionals," the Tax Reduction Diary, CPA review of past two years filed tax returns; tax audit protection for federal and state tax returns plus one other business entity; one year of toll-free unlimited tax consulting; *Lower Your Taxes: Big Time* by Sandy Botkin; and TRI's quarterly tax planning newsletter. Call (800) TRI-0TAX or order online, www.taxreductioninstitute.com.

Tax Reduction Institute Seminars: Contact TRI if you would like to attend or sponsor a TRI Tax Reduction Seminar event, (800) TRI-0TAX.

Medical Plans and Self-employed Medical Reimbursement Plan Kits: Includes properly drawn-up independent contractor and employment contracts, and a legal self-insured medical reimbursement plan. Available upon request after purchasing "Tax Strategies" audio seminar and workbook, (800) TRI-0TAX.

Appendix B:

W-4 Withholding Calculator

Type the following URL address into your Internet browser:

http://www.irs.gov/individuals/article/0,,id=96196,00.html

This will send you to the Internal Revenue Service's Web site and its W-4 Calculation page. Using the IRS calculator is an easy way to properly determine exactly how much income tax to have withheld from your paycheck each month.

Appendix C:

Floor Plan Maximization Calculations for a Home Office Deduction

Using the floor plan below as an example, following are three ways you can determine the amount of space your home office occupies and the ways that space can be maximized:

1. Number of rooms the office occupies, divided by the total number of rooms in the house. This is a simple way if your home office occupies an entire room in your house:

Divide the number of rooms the office occupies   = 1
By the total number of rooms in the house   = 8
**The percentage of the house that can be deducted
using this method**   **= 12.5%**

2. **Total square footage the office occupies as a percentage of the total square footage of the house.** This method allows you to maximize your square footage by getting a bit more detailed:

Divide the total square footage of the home office   = 221
By the total square footage of the house   = 1,675
   (minus 75 for deck)
**The percentage of the house that can be deducted
using this method**   **= 13.19%**

3. **Net square footage applicable to office use.** This method allows the most amount of square footage for your home office. To calculate net square footage, deduct common areas:

First floor entry and stairway   = 128
Second floor stairway and landing   = 128
Second floor common area   = 24
Deduct deck (not a common area)   = 75
Your net square footage base   = 1,395
Divide the square footage of the home office   = 221
By this net square footage base number   = 1,395
**The percentage of the house that can be deducted
using this method**   **= 15.84%**

Appendix D:

Checklist for Properly Structuring and Launching a Business

Following is a checklist of most of the required information for starting up a business and structuring it properly. *Note: This list may not be comprehensive since each state has its own requirements.*

1. **Certificate of Occupancy:** If you are planning on occupying a building, you may have to apply to get this from your local city or county zoning department, especially if the building is new or you will conduct substantial improvements to the premises.

2. **Business License:** Many states require licensing of a business. Sometimes the license must be obtained from the state, and other times the city or county will issue it. Many home-based businesses and network marketing ventures do not ordinarily need a license. Check with your state or city government.

3. **Fictitious Business Name:** If you use a name for your business or sole pro-prietorship other than that of your own name, you must generally register the company name with the county.

4. **Trade Name and Trade Mark Protection:** If you want to protect your trade name and any special trade marks that you want developed to brand your busi-ness, you will need to file a "Registration of Trademark or Service Mark" with the U.S. Department of Commerce. For further information or to reach the Commissioner of Trademark and Patents, call (800) 786-9199.

5. **Copyrights and Patents:** If you have developed some special invention or have some written material that you don't want people to copy, you must file for a patent for invention or a copyright for written materials. This can be done by contacting the Commissioner of Trademarks, and the Patent and Copyright Applications office. Patent registration forms and questions: (800) 786-9199. To obtain copyright forms call (202) 707-9100. If you have a copyright ques-tion, call (202) 707-3000.

6. **Business Insurance:** All businesses should have some form of insurance to cover them from theft of equipment and for liability issues. Most homeowner policies exempt business equipment from their coverage. Check with your prop-

erty and casualty agent to see how extensively you are covered and what insurance you may need to obtain.

7. **Sales Tax Number:** In many states, you may be required to collect and remit sales tax. Thus, you should get a sales tax number in the states in which you will be conducting business, especially your home state. Many network marketing companies take care of this for you with the state in which you will be working. If you are joining a multilevel marketing company, check with them about this number.

8. **Unemployment Insurance:** If you have any employees or if you incorporate (incorporation assumes you are the "employee"), you will be required to pay both federal and state unemployment insurance. Contact your state unemployment insurance office for the forms and instructions. Also, you will need to get a Federal ID Number from the IRS by filing form SS-4 with the IRS. This will set up withholding and federal unemployment tax for any employees.

Tip: Use a payroll service to file all necessary employee forms such as W-2s, form 940 and 941 for unemployment and Social Security, etc. These services are fairly inexpensive to use and if you have employees, will save you lots of trouble. A good payroll service will charge about $40 per month for all these services. You can also get access to payroll services and employee forms by contacting the Tax Reduction Institute. (See Appendix A for more information.)

9. **Immigration Act:** If you have employees, you will need to verify employment eligibility by filing form I-9 for each new employee other than yourself or immediate family. Failure to do so could result in sizeable penalties. For additional information, call (800) 755-0777.

10. **Health and Safety:** Be aware that there are many health and safety laws which apply to employees. The Federal Occupational Safety and Health Administration (OSHA) has some standards and brochures of which you should be aware. Call them for information. If you plan to open a restaurant or a manufacturing facility and you will employ people, you will need to comply to their standards. In many cases, complying means posting some rules somewhere in your facility.

11. **Workers' Compensation:** If your business employs three or more people, Workers' Compensation Insurance must be carried to cover injured employees. The owner may usually exempt himself or herself from this if they wish.

12. **Minimum Wage Laws:** Be aware that there are minimum wage require-ments for employees that must be honored. If you have employees, find out what these requirements are and stay abreast of any changes.

13. **Form W-4 for Each Employee:** Each employee must fill out IRS Form W-4 for withholding and for claiming exemptions. If withholding or exemptions change within a year, a new form must be filed for each year change takes place. See IRS publication 505. Generally, for every $2,800 in new deductions that you expect, such as housing interest, expected losses from business, or for each dependent, you may claim an exemption.

Appendix E:

Calculating the Average Cost of a Meal at Home or Fast Food Restaurant

1. Count the number of people living in your household.
2. Determine what your overall grocery bill for one month is by consulting your Spending Planner.
3. Using the 50-30-20 rule which deems 50 percent of a grocery bill for dinners, 30 percent for lunches, and 20 percent for breakfast, figure how much of that grocery bill equals the meal you are eating Dutch treat. For example, suppose you spend $150 a week on groceries for a two-person household. What per-cent of that $150 equals dinner expense? Fifty percent or $70.
4. Divide seven nights of the week into $70 and the cost of eating dinner at home each night is $10.
5. Divide the number of people in the house into $10 and that gives you $5 per person. This $5 is the average cost to eat dinner at home. Now when you go Dutch treat at a business dinner, anything over $5 is deductible at 50 percent.

Appendix F:

Deducting the Cost of Expensive Cars

There are two basic depreciation methods for business automobiles: straight line and accelerated. Today's tax law places luxury car limits on depreciation. The accelerated rate (MACRS), straight line rate, and luxury limits for passenger cars for 2006 are:

Year	MARCS (or Accelerated)	Straight Line	Luxury Limit (Used Cars)	Luxury Limit (New Cars)
1	20.00%	10.00%	$2,960	$2,960
2	31.00%	20.00%	$4,700	$4,700
3	19.20%	20.00%	$2,850	$2,850
4	11.52%	20.00%	$1,675	$1,675
5	11.52%	20.00%	$1,675	$1,675
6	5.67%	10.00%	$1,675	$1,675

Calculation Examples: Say you purchase a new $40,000 car and use it 75 percent for business. How much can you depreciate your car in the first year?

Accelerated (or MACRS) Method:
$40,000 (cost of car) x 20% (MACRS) x 75% (business use) = $6,000

Straight Line Method:
$40,000 (cost of car) x 10% (S-Line) x 75% (business use)   = $3,000

Luxury Limit:
$2,960 (luxury limit) x 75% (business use)   = $2,220

You can see from this chart that although the depreciation limit for a luxury car in the first year is ordinarily $2,960, when you multiply that figure by the percentage of the car you used for business (which remember is 75 percent), then the most you can depreciate this luxury car in the first year is $2,220. If there were no luxury limit, you could have depreciated the car at the MACRS (modified accelerated cost recovery system) rate for $6,000. With this luxury limit law in force, how long will it take you to write off a car that costs say, $55,000? Roughly 25 years. — hopefully you and the car will both live long enough to do it!

Appendix G:

Home Office Deduction Savings Calculations

Example: Mr. Snyder files a joint tax return with his wife. The Snyders earn $150,000 in taxable income. That puts them in the 31 percent federal and 10 percent state tax bracket. Mrs. Snyder earns $78,000 from her job as an employee in town. Mr. Snyder works out of his home and earns net taxable income of $72,000, which is reported on Schedule C of their Form 1040.

	Total	Home Office Percentage	Tax Benefit Rate	Tax Refund
Mortgage interest	$10,401	$1,648	13.02%	$215
Real estate taxes	$947	$150	13.02%[1]	$20
Utilities	$1,704	$270	54.02%[2]	$146
Homeowners' insurance	$310	$49	54.02%	$26
General repairs	$600	$95	54.02%	$51
Pest control	$400	$63	54.02%	$34
Repairs to office	$200	$200	54.02%	$108
Depreciation: furniture	$1,886	$1,886	54.02%	$1,019
Depreciation: home	$2,545	$403	54.02%	$218
Cash in-pocket from deduction				**$1,837**

Economic Results:

Cash from home office deduction	$1,837
Cash from extra business mileage	$582[3]
Total first-year tax cash	$2,419
6% annuity due factor for 5 years	x 5.9753
Net cash after 5 years	**$14,454**

[1] Self-employment tax rate.

[2] 13.02 self-employment tax rate plus 31% federal tax rate plus 10% state tax rate.

[3] Snyder's home business allows him to reduce his personal mileage and increase his business auto expense by $1,077. Thus, $582 is refunded by the tax collectors ($1,077 x 54.02%).

Appendix H:

What Is the Best Way to Keep Accurate Records?

1. **Build a documentation system.** No matter what form of business entity you have (S Corp, C Corp, LLC, or Sole Proprietorship) you need to maintain the following as part of your documentation system:

- An accounting system
- Permanent files
- Business files
- Daily tax diary

Accounting System: An accounting system is the basic element of any business that evidences your business intent. It includes a balance sheet and a profit and loss statement. Your accountant or financial coach can help you set up a good accounting system.

Permanent Files: These include your prior year's tax returns, stock purchases and sales, equipment purchases, sales, and similar entries. Generally, you want to keep any record that relates to more than one tax year in your permanent file. If you purchase property, your permanent files should include the purchase documents, closing statement, deeds, and other expense related to the purchase.

Business Files: These include time sheets for part-time help, receipts, invoices, canceled checks and other evidence that you do business on a regular basis.

Daily Tax Diary: Your daily diary is the focal point of your documentation system. The smaller your business, the more important this diary becomes.

Your daily tax diary should include:

- All of your appointments
- Where and when you travel
- Where you go by automobile
- Where and when you entertain business contacts

While documentation is important, some people resist it because they assume it will be too time-consuming. But this stubborn resistance is just as shortsighted as refusing to track spending. The amount of time it takes to record necessary daily activities in your tax diary will be well worth the extra 10 or 12 seconds it takes to do so. Not only that, tracking your daily activities in this way will be just as emotionally revealing as tracking your money has been. Doing so will make you very aware of your daily habits, how you spend your time, and what you value. A good system can help you document your daily activities. Don't cheat yourself out of these deductions or the peace of mind that comes from good documentation. Record your activities every day using a tax diary!

2. **Use three-part checks.** Keep a separate business checkbook and use three-part checks. Regardless of how you have structured your business, the three-part check is necessary to build good, easy-to-use records for your regular files.

a) Send part one, the original, to the vendor.
b) Staple supporting evidence such as receipts or invoices to part two of the check and file it alphabetically in the vendor file.
c) Put part three in a numerical file for later viewing by the IRS (should you ever be audited) and for your own reference.

3. **Keep Form 1099 information separate.** Negligence penalties are automatic if you fail to report all the income that's reported to the IRS on Form 1099. The negligence penalty applies to your total underpayment of tax, not just the portion due to the negligence. Any deposit that would not normally be included in 1099 or W-2 should be copied. Thus, if you get a large gift (or give a large gift), insurance reimbursement, or transfer money from one account to another, make copies of the checks and keep transaction receipts. Failure to do so may result in the IRS treating the deposit as income.

4. **Become a packrat.** Because it's virtually impossible for you to know all of the receipts you are required to keep in case of an audit, gather every receipt and post every receipt to your accounting system, whether personal or business, for all money spent. Since you don't know what will be important and what's not, it's safest to save everything for at least three years. Remember, you carry the burden of proof.

5. **Use a business credit card.** To keep your record-keeping burden to a minimum, use a separate charge card for all your business expenses. The charge card copy acts as a receipt for your travel, entertainment, and gas and oil purchases. It also eliminates the need to make an audit trail for the deductible interest. By using one or more credit cards solely for business, you can deduct the finance charges on the business cards as well as the annual fees on all cards used solely for business.

Notes

Introduction

1   Paul Bannister, "Twenty-five Fascinating Facts About Personal Debt," bankrate.com, (April 2005).

2   Ibid.

3   2000 U.S. Census.

4   Bureau of Economic Analysis, http://www.bea.gov/briefrm/saving.htm, (January 2006).

5   "Our Hidden Savings," *Business Week Online*, (January 2005).

6   U.S. Economic Development Committee statistics as quoted by Ron Pierre, Department Head of Salt Lake County Aging Services, (April 2000).

7   Diane Stafford, "American Workforce Going Gray at an Exponential Pace," *The Salt Lake Tribune*, (April 19, 2005).

8   BillSaver University, "Household Spending Facts and Figures," billsaver.com, (April 2005).

9   Bureau of Economic Analysis statistics as quoted by Federal Reserve Board Governor Susan Schmidt Bies, www.federalreserve.gov, (April 2005).

10   Paul Bannister, "Twenty-five Fascinating Facts About Personal Debt," bankrate.com, (April 2005).

11   Diane Hales, "Smart Ways to Get Yourself Out of Debt," *Parade*, (February 13, 1994), p. 20.

12   Walter Williams, "The Legitimate Role of Government in a Free Society," *Imprimis*, (August 2000), p. 3.

13   Drew Miles, "Business Entity Strategies and Mentoring," www.pfbs.com, (January 20, 2005).

14   Walter Williams, "The Legitimate Role of Government in a Free Society," *Imprimis*, (August 2000), p. 3

Chapter 1

1   Interview with Richard A. Feinberg, Purdue University, (2006).
2   American Bankruptcy Association Meeting, (November 1998), Boston, Massachusetts.
3   Interview with Jim Christensen, author of *Rich on Any Income* and chairman of the board, Christensen & Combs, (2006).

Chapter 2

1   Tony Cook, "Secrets from the Millionaire Next Door," *Reader's Digest*, (November, 1997), p. 132.
2   "NBA Labor War," *Associated Press*, (October 20, 1998).
3   Douglas LaBier, *Modern Madness*, (New York: Simon and Schuster, 1989).
4   Jane Bryant Quinn, "How To Live On One Salary," *Woman's Day*, (November 1, 1994), p. 13.
5   Tony Pugh, "Americans Tap Credit Cards, Are Ill-prepared for Retirement," *Mercury News*, (April 25, 2001).

Chapter 3

1   Jonathan Clements, "Why It's Good to Be Rich," *Wall Street Journal* (*Deseret News* Sunday Edition), (January 16, 2005).
2   Tony Cook, "Secrets From the Millionaire Next Door," *Reader's Digest*, (November, 1997), p. 132.
3   Arden Dale, "Economics of Retirement Confuse Americans, Vanguard Study Finds," *Wall Street Journal*, (December 2004).
4   Diane Stafford, "American Work Force Going Gray at an Exponential Pace," *The Salt Lake Tribune*, (April 18, 2005).
5   U.S. Economic Development Committee statistics as quoted by Ron Pierre, Department Head of Salt Lake County Aging Services, (April 2000).
6   Owen Ullmann, "Billionaire and Activist Give Kids Same Advice: Avoid Credit Cards", *USA Today*, (October 12, 1999), p. 5A.

Chapter 4

1   U.S. Bureau of the Census, Statistical Abstract of the United States, (2005).
2   The Federal Reserve Board as quoted by BillSaver University, billsaver.com, (2004).
3   U.S. Bureau of the Census, Statistical Abstract of the United States, (2005).
4   U.S. Commerce Department's Bureau of Economic Analysis, (2004).

5   James L. Clayton, *Global Debt Bomb*, (New York: M.E. Sharpe, 2000), p. 11.

6   Ibid, p. 50

7   Ibid, p. ix

8   Paul Bannister, "Twenty-five Fascinating Facts About Personal Debt," bankrate.com, (April 2005).

9   BillSaver University, "Household Spending Facts and Figures," billsaver.com, (April 2005).

10   Paul Bannister, "Twenty-five Fascinating Facts About Personal Debt," bankrate.com, (April 2005).

11   Dennis Lythgoe, "Compelling 'Global Debt Bomb' Carries a Most Urgent Message," *Deseret News*, (December 19, 1999).

12   BillSaver University, "Household Spending Facts and Figures," billsaver.com, (April 2005).

13   "The Best Deals In the Cards," *Consumer Reports*, (January 1996), p. 34.

14   Dennis Lythgoe, "Compelling 'Global Debt Bomb' Carries a Most Urgent Message," *Deseret News*, (December 19, 1999).

Chapter 5

1   Lynn Brenner, "What We Don't Know About Money Will Hurt Us," *Parade*, (April 18, 1999).

2   Ibid.

3   Carma Wadley, "Living Resourcefully," *Deseret News*, (August 11, 1997).

4   "The New Rules of Borrowing," *Consumer Reports*, (July 1999), p. 14.

5   Ibid, p. 16.

6   Ibid, p. 14-15, (italics added).

7   Ibid, p. 15

8   The Associated Press, "Americans Ignorant About Credit, Survey Shows," msnbc.com, (September 21, 2004).

Chapter 6

1   Walter Williams, "The Legitimate Role of Government in a Free Society," *Imprimis*, (August 2000), p. 3.

2   Ibid, p. 3

3   U.S. House of Representatives Republican Study Committee, "Tax Facts," (April 15, 2004), p. 1.

Chapter 7

1   Denise M. Topolnicki, "The Five Threats To Your Retirement," *Money*, (November, 1993), p. 66.

2   Social Security Administration, Office of Policy, "Income of the Population 55 and Older," SSA Publication #: 13-11871, (March 2005).
3   Ibid.
4   John Pierson, "Thirty Years of Retirement," *Fortune*, (1993).
5   Social Security Administration, "Going Broke" chart, *USA Today*, (June 6, 1996), p. 1.
6   Ibid, p. 1.
7   Anne Willette, "For Boomers, Social Security Is Near Bust," *USA Today*, (June 6, 1996), p. 2B
8   Kenneth S. Apfel, "A Message From the Commissioner," Your Personal Earnings and Benefits Statement From the Social Security Administration, (1998).
9   John Pierson, "Thirty Years of Retirement," *Fortune*, (1993).
10   "U.S. Facing Aging Population as 77 Million Boomers Near Retirement Age," TodaysSeniorsNetwork.com, (2005).
11   John Pierson, "Thirty Years of Retirement," *Fortune*, (1993).
12   Charles E. Gerrard, "Long-term Care – Act Now," *Deseret News*, (April 18, 1999).
13   MarketWatch, "Illness and Injury as Contributors to Bankruptcy," (February 2005), p. W5-72.
14   Jonathan Clements, "Ten Problems That Often Hit Investors If They Lose Track of the Big Picture," *Wall Street Journal*, (March 10, 1998).

Chapter 8

1   Thomas J. Stanley, "Why You're Not As Wealthy As You Should Be," *Medical Economics*, (July 20, 1992), p. 107.
2   Ibid, p. 107.
3   Ibid, p. 108.
4   Loveridge & Associates, as quoted by Michael R. Loveridge, attorney at law, Salt Lake City, Utah, (2006).
5   Norman Vincent Peale, *A Guide to Confident Living* (New York: Simon & Schuster, 1976).
6   Ibid.
7   American Institute for Economic Research, "How to Avoid Financial Tangles," *Economic Education Bulletin*, (Great Barrington, Mass.), p. 147.

Chapter 9

1   The Tax Advisor quoting the National Taxpayer Foundation, (May 2000), p. 43.
2   Bart S. Croxford, "Using Life Insurance To Fund Retirement Has Many

Benefits," *Salt Lake Tribune*, (November 20, 1996).

3   Loveridge & Associates, as quoted by Michael R. Loveridge, attorney at law, Salt Lake City, Utah, (2002).

4   "Wills of the Famous," Chief Justice Warren Burger, courttv.com, (2005).

Chapter 11

1   Drew Miles, "Business Entity Strategies and Mentoring," www.pfbs.com, (January 20, 2005).

2   Jane Bryant Quinn, "How To Live On One Salary," *Woman's Day*, (November 1, 1994), p. 13.

3   David Darcangelo, *Wealth and Home*, (New York: McGraw-Hill, 1997), p. 13.

4   Section 172 of the Internal Revenue Code.

5   Ibid.

6   Section 172(b)(1)(A) of the Internal Revenue Code and the Income Tax Regulations.

7   Small Business Administration, Small Business Research Summary, No. 194, (March, 2000).

Chapter 12

1   Section 172 of the Income Tax Code (IRC).

2   Section 172(B)(1)(A) of the Internal Revenue Code.

Chapter 13

1   Section 183 of the Internal Revenue Code and the IRS Publication 535, p. 5.

2   Ibid, p. 5.

3   Section 183(d) of the Internal Revenue Code.

4   Section 183 of the Internal Revenue Code.

5   Section 1.183-2 of the Income Tax Regulations. See also Floyd Fisher, TC Memo, 1980-183 (1980), Moiruice Dreicer, 28 TC 642, AFFd, 702 F.2d 745 (CA Dist. Col. 1983).

6   Frank Suiter, TC Memo 1990-447 (1990); Charles Givens, TC Memo, 1989-529 (1989); Joseph Ransom, TC Memo 1990-381 (199) (Amway Distributor); Frank Harris, TC Memo 1992-638 (1992) (Mary Kay Distributor).

7   Rugel v. Commissioner, 127, F.2d 393 (8th Cir. 1942).

8   Frank Suiter, TC Memo 1990-447 (1990); Charles Givens, TC Memo, 1989-529 (1989); Joseph Ransom, TC Memo 1990-381 (199) (Amway Distributor); Frank Harris, TC Memo 1992-638 (1992) (Mary Kay Distributor).

9   Section 183-2(a) of the Income Tax Regulations. See also Jonas Brayand vs. Comm., 928 F.2d 745 (6th Cir. 1991).

10   Harry Van Scoyoc, TC Memo 1988-520 (1988).

11   Section 1.183-2(b)(I) of the Income Tax Regulations.

12   C. Frank Fisher, 50 TC 164. Acq.

13   Section 1.183-2(b) of the Income Tax Regulations. See also Joseph Ransom, supra; Abdolvahab Pirnia, TC Memo 1992-137 (1992).

14   Wenzel Tirbelmen, TC Memo 1992-137 (1992).

15   Sheldon Barr, TC Memo 1989-69 (1989).

16   Sherman Sampson, TC Memo 1982-276 (1982).

17   Percy Winfield, TC Memo 1966-53 (1966).

18   Sections 165 and 183 of the Internal Revenue Code. See also section 1.183-2(b)(6) of the Income Tax Regulations.

19   Section 1.183-2(b)(6) & (7) of the Income Tax Regulations.

20   Joseph Ransom, supra., TC Memo 1990-381 (1990) (Amway Distributor).

21   Section 1.183-2(b)(8) of the Income Tax Regulations.

22   Section 1.183-2(b)(9) of the Income Tax Regulations.

Chapter 14

1   Section 280A(C)(1) of the Internal Revenue Code.

2   Section 280A(C) of the Internal Revenue Code.

3   IRS vs. Solomon, No. 91-998. Supreme Court of the U.S., Jan. 12, 1993.

4   Section 932 of the Taxpayer Relief Act, which amended section 280(C)(1) of the Internal Revenue Code.

5   Section 280A(C)1A of the Internal Revenue Code and section 1.280A-2(C) of the Income Tax Regulations (ITR).

6   Section 280A-2(C) of the Income Tax Regulations.

7   Green vs. Commissioner, 707 F2d. 404 (9th Cir. 1983). See also Frankel vs. Commissioner, 82 TC 318 (9184) and section 280A-2(C) of the Income Tax Regulations.

8   Section 280A-s(C) of the Income Tax Regulations and Frankel vs. Commissioner cited above.

9   Section 280A(C)(1)(C) of the Internal Revenue Code.

10   Section 280A of the Internal Revenue Code and Jackson vs. Commissioner, cited above.

11   Gomex vs. Commissioner, 41 TCM 585 (9180); section 1.280A-2(g) of the Income Tax Regulations.

12   Huuer vs. Commissioner, 32 TC 947 (1959); see also Jackson vs. Commissioner cited above.

13   Section 280F of the Internal Revenue Code. See also Sherri A. Mulne TC Memo 1996-320.

14   Section 280A(C)(5) of the Internal Revenue Code.
15   Section 280F of the Internal Revenue Code. See also Sherri A. Mulne as cited above.
16   Section 179 of the Internal Revenue Code.
17   Section 1016(a)(2) of the Internal Revenue Code; and section 1.1016(a)(1) of the regulations.
18   Section 280A(C)(5) of the Internal Revenue Code.
19   Ibid.

Chapter 15

1   Section 274(d) of the Internal Revenue Code and Section 1.274-5(C)(2) of the Income Tax Regulations (ITR).
2   Section 1.274-5(C) of the Income Tax Regulations; see also, IR 95-56; Pntice 95-50, 1995-42 IRB.
3   Section 274(a) of the Internal Revenue Code; P.L. 99-514, Section 142 (a)(2)(A) amending Internal Revenue Code 274.
4   Section 274(b)(2)(B) of the Internal Revenue Code.
5   Section 274(n) of the Internal Revenue Code.
6   Sections 1.274-2(f)(2)(I)(a) and 1.274-2(c)(7) of the Income Tax Regulations.
7   Ibid.
8   Section 1.274-2(d)(4) of the Income Tax Regulations.
9   Ibid.
10   Sutter vs. Commissioner, 21 TC 170 (1953), acq. 1954-1 C.B. 6.
11   Section 274(k)(1)(B) and Section 274(k)(2) of the Internal Revenue Code.
12   Ibid.
13   Sections 1.274-2(b)(1)(i); 1.274-2(b)(1)(iii)(b) of the Income Tax Regulations.
14   Ibid.
15   Sections 274(a)(2)(C) and 162(a) of the Internal Revenue Code.
16   Section 1.274-2(e)(3)(ii) of the Income Tax Regulations.
17   Sections 1.274-2(e)(3)(ii) and 1.274-2(f)(2)(i) of the Income Tax Regulations.
18   Sections 274(a)(3), 274(a)(1)(B), and 274(a)(2)(A) of the Internal Revenue Code.
19   Robert Matlock vs. Commissioner, TC Memo 1992-324.
20   Sections 1.274-2(C)(7)(ii) and 1.274-2(d) of the Income Tax Regulations.
21   Ibid.
22   Section 1.274-2(d)(1)(ii) of the Income Tax Regulations.
23   Revenue Ruling 63-144, 1963-2 C.B. 129, Q&A 50.
24   Section 274(L)(1)(A) of the Internal Revenue Code.

25   Section 274(b)(1) and Section 274(j)(3)(A) of the Internal Revenue Code.
26   Section 274(b)(2)(B) of the Internal Revenue Code.
27   Section 1.274-3(e)(2) of the Internal Revenue Code.
28   Section 1.274-2(C)(4) of the Income Tax Regulations; Steel vs.
     Commissioner, 28 T.C.M. 1301 (1969).
29   Rev. Proc. 2005-78, 2005-51 I.R.B. 1177.
30   "Your Driving Costs," American Automobile Association, (2000).
31   Revenue Ruling 90-23, I.R.B. 1990-11, modified and superseded by
     Revenue Ruling 99-7, IRB 99-5.
32   Ibid.
33   Ibid.
34   Ibid.
35   Ibid.
36   Section 1.274-5(C) of the Income Tax Regulations (ITR).
37   Section 1.274-5T(C)(3)(ii)(C) of the Income Tax Regulations (ITR).
38   Ibid.
39   Sections 1.162-1(a) and 1.162-2 of the Income Tax Regulations (ITR).
     See also Commissioner vs. Griner, 71-2 U.S.T.C. Par. 9714.
40   Section 280F(a)(2)(A) of the Internal Revenue Code and Rev. Proc 99-
     14, 1999-5 IRB 56.
41   IRS Publication 535 and Section 280F-5T(e) of the Temporary Income
     Tax Regulations.
42   Rev. Proc. 2000-48, IR 2000-8. See also IRS Publication 535.
43   Sections 162 and 280F(d)(2) of the Internal Revenue Code. See also
     Section 1.280F-2T of the Income Tax Regulations and IRS Publication
     17 and 535.
44   Sandy Botkin, *Tax Strategies for Business Professionals*, (2001) p. 87.

Chapter 16

1   U.S. vs. Correll, 389 U.S. 209 (1967); Revenue Ruling 54-497, 1954-2
    C.B. 75, superseded in part by Revenue Ruling 75-432, 1975-2 C.B. 60;
    Revenue Ruling 75-170, 1975-1 C.B. 60.
2   Sections 1.162-2a and section 1.162-2b of the Income Tax Regulations.
    See also IRS publication 463.
3   Internal Revenue Code 162(a)(2); 62(2)(B); 1.162-2(a), (b) of the Income
    Tax Regulations.
4   Ibid.
5   Ibid.
6   Ibid.
7   See U.S. vs. Correll above.
8   Section 1.274-5(C) of the Income Tax Regulations.

9   IRS Manual Handbook HB 1763 314(4).
10   Section 274(m) of the Internal Revenue Code; see also Giodano vs. Commissioner, 36 T.C.M 430 (1977); Revenue Ruling 55-57, 1955-1 C.B. 315.
11   Section 1.162-1(a) and 1.162-2 of the Income Tax Regulations; Revenue Ruling 56-168, 1956-1 C.B. 93.
12   Endnote 5; also Revenue Ruling 63-145, 1963-2 C.B. 86; T.R.-493, 7/24/63; conference, 3/29/63.
13   Ibid.
14   Section 1.274-4(d)(2)(ii) of the Income Tax Regulations.
15   Sections 1.274-4(d)(2)(iii) and 1.162-2(b)(1) of the Income Tax Regulations.
16   Section 1.274-4(d)(2)(i) of the Income Tax Regulations.
17   Internal Revenue Code 274 (C)(2)(B); 274 (c)(1); 1.274-4(d)(1); 1.162-2(b)(1) of the Income Tax Regulations.
18   Section 1.162-2(a)(b)(1) of the Income Tax Regulations.
19   Section 1.274-4(d)(2) of the Income Tax Regulations.
20   Conference Report, p. II-27.

Chapter 17

1   Sections 3121(b)(3)(A) and Sections 3306(c)(5) of the Internal Revenue Code (IRC). See also IRS Pub. Circular E.
2   Section 1.162-7(a) of the Internal Revenue Code.
3   Section 105(h)(5) of the Internal Revenue Code; Section 1.105-11(b)(1) of the Income Tax Regulations; IRS Technical Advice Memorandum IRS Letter Ruling 9409006. See also footnote 4 noted in Chapter 16 and Revenue Ruling 71-588.
4   Sections 1.119-1 of the Income Tax Regulations. See also Revenue Ruling 71-411, 1971-2 C.B. 103; Revenue Ruling 71-267, 1971-1 C.B. 37 and IRS Pub 535.
5   Sections 408(k)(2)(A) and 408(k)(2)(B) of the Internal Revenue Code. See also IRS Pub. No 560, p. 4.
6   Section 219(g)(3)(B) of the Internal Revenue Code.
7   Ibid.
8   Ibid.
9   Section 162 of the IRC and Regulations thereunder.
10   Ibid.
11   Section 3121(b)(3) of the Internal Revenue Code.
12   Eller vs. Commissioner, 77 TC 934, Acq., 1982-2 C.B.
13   Revenue Proc. 2001-13, 2001-3 I.R.B. 337.
14   Section 3121(b)(3) of the Internal Revenue Code and Section 31.3402(n)-

1 of the Income Tax Regulations. See also IRS instructions in preparing Form 941 and Form 940.

15   Section 1.162-7(b)(3) of the Income Tax Regulations.

16   Rev. Proc. 2005-70, 2005-47, I.R.B. 279 (2006 figures).

17   Section 1.162-7(a) of the Income Tax Regulations.

18   Section 1.162-7(a) of the IRS Regulations.

19   See IRS Instructions for Preparing Form 940.

20   Section 31.3402(n)-1 of the Income Tax Regulations and IRS Instructions for Preparing Form 941.

21   Section 6109(e) of the Internal Revenue Code.

22   Sections 2503(b), 274(b)(1), and 102(a) of the Internal Revenue Code.

23   Section 2503(b) and section 2513(o) of the Internal Revenue Code.

24   Sections 2513(a), 6019, and 2503(b) of the Internal Revenue Code. See also section 25.2513-1(c) of the Income Tax Regulations.

25   Section 1001 and Section 1012 of the IRC. Section 1015(a) of the Internal Revenue Code.

26   Section 1(g) of the Internal Revenue Code and Rev. Proc 2001-13, I.R.B. 2001-3 (December 2000).

27   Rev. Proc. 2005-70, 2005-47, I.R.B. 279 (2006 figures).

28   Rev. Proc. 2005-70, 2005-47, I.R.B. 279 (2006 figures).

29   Matthews vs. Commissioner, 61 TC 39 (1973), rev'd 75-2 U.S.T.C. Par 967 (5th Cir. 1975); Frank Lyons Co. vs. Commissioner, 435 U.S. 561 (S.Ct 1978).

Index

About the Authors

Peter R. Jeppson

Powerfully impacted at age 19 by a serious car accident, Peter Jeppson knows first-hand the crushing burden of the financial problems facing most people today. After Peter was terribly burned in the accident, he incurred hundreds of thousands of dollars in medical expenses as he struggled to recover. Using the principles he now teaches through the Money Mastery® program, Peter was able to get out from underneath that financial burden in just five years. Today, he is a nationally recognized speaker, author, and financial mentor. He co-founded Time & Money, LLC, a Utah-based service company specializing in principle-based money management and financial literacy, and is the co-owner and co-author of Money Mastery®, a financial literacy and coaching program designed to help individuals and families get in total control of their finances.

Peter has been inspiring people as a motivational speaker for 29 years. He has lectured to just over 1 million people in over 4,800 seminars and speaking engagements on various subjects including personal finance, financial planning, self-improvement and fire and burn education.

He is the co-author of *Money Mastery: 10 Principles That Will Change Your Financial Life Forever,* and author of the four-book series *How to Spend Your Way to Financial Success,* and *The Peter Jeppson Story* motivational audio program.

Alan M. Williams

Few experts today understand how to solve the financial problems facing most people like Alan Williams, a nationally published author, speaker, and personal financial mentor with a 38-year background in corporate management and finance. In 1994, he combined his financial experience with that of Peter Jeppson, to form Time Time & Money, LLC, a Utah-based service company specializing in financial literacy and principle-based money management. Along with Peter, Alan is known as the "Betty Crocker" of the financial literacy industry, using his extensive knowledge in debt restructuring, insurance, tax law, and estate organization to provide unique inter-related training between all areas of personal finance. Alan is a principal author and developer of Money Mastery®, a financial literacy and coaching program that helps individuals and families get in total control of their finances, and the co-author of *Money Mastery:10 Principles That Will Change Your Financial Life Forever.*

Sanford C. Botkin

Sandy Botkin is an attorney and certified public accountant who currently serves as CEO and principal lecturer of the Maryland-based Tax Reduction Institute (TRI).

Over the past 10 years, Sandy has taught more than 50,000 taxpayers how to legally and ethically cut their annual tax burden by up to half through his popular Tax Strategies seminars. Prior to joining TRI, Sandy spent five years as a legal specialist in the Office of Chief counsel for the IRS and was one of eight attorneys selected to train all new attorneys in the Internal Revenue Service's tax division.

Sandy is the author of numerous technical articles for national publications, is an adjunct professor of accounting and law at the University of Maryland and Columbia Union College, and is listed in "Who's Who in Business." He is the co-author of *Money Mastery: 10 Principles That Will Change Your Financial Life Forever,* and the author of *Lower Your Taxes: BIG TIME!*